"Churches that don't minister holisti[...] die. Randy Stinson and Timothy Pau[...] and they cast a compelling picture of how to move toward a gospel-focused mission to see families conformed to the image of Christ. This book will prompt you to think, to scribble notes, and probably even to call together some key leaders of your church to do a new thing together."

—Russell D. Moore, Dean of the School of Theology,
The Southern Baptist Theological Seminary

"I thank God for Randy Stinson and Timothy Paul Jones, who have served us well by bringing together some of the best minds and hearts in family ministry, and in doing so, they have provided the church with an excellent resource for pursuing the joy of the next generations."

—David Michael, Pastor for Parenting and Family Discipleship,
Bethlehem Baptist Church

"From time to time, a new book surfaces that clearly, convincingly, and boldly shouts truth that every evangelical needs to know. *Trained in the Fear of God*, a resource for Christian leaders and households, represents one of the latest publications to hold that esteemed honor. . . . By balancing a biblical foundation with extremely practical ideas, it successfully deals with the monumental challenges that face both home and church. It specifically structures a framework for a congregational culture that coordinates every ministry to champion the role of parents as primary faith-trainers in their children's lives. Most importantly, *Trained in the Fear of God* adopts the proper view of itself, in its focus and content; even though family ministry is quite valuable, it is not the church's ultimate objective. That prominent purpose is always reserved for glorifying God through his gracious gospel. Bravo!"

—Ronald T. Habermas, Professor of Discipleship and Christian Education,
Midwestern Baptist Theological Seminary

"Many pastors and lay leaders are embracing the importance of ministry to and through the family today. *Trained in the Fear of God* provides a strong theological and historical foundation for why this is important and how it has happened in the past. This then leads to ideas and reflections on how family ministry can be developed and strengthened in the church today. I appreciate both the foundational nature of the text and the practical ideas for those who want to develop it but aren't sure where to start. This is a great text for a foundational family ministry course and for pastoral and lay leaders to read and discuss together as they assess their church's ministries and move toward a stronger family-equipping emphasis."

—Kevin E. Lawson,
Director, PhD and EdD programs in Educational Studies,
Talbot School of Theology, Biola University

TRAINED
IN THE
FEAR OF GOD

Family Ministry in Theological, Historical, and Practical Perspective

RANDY STINSON

TIMOTHY PAUL JONES

EDITORS

Trained in the Fear of God: Family Ministry in Theological, Historical, and Practical Perspective

© 2011 Randy Stinson and Timothy Paul Jones

Published by Kregel Publications, a division of Kregel Inc., 2450 Oak Industrial Dr. NE, Grand Rapids, MI 49505.

Library of Congress Cataloging-in-Publication Data
Trained in the fear of God: family ministry in theological, historical, and practical perspective / Randy Stinson, Timothy Paul Jones, editors.
    p. cm.
    Includes indexes.
    1. Church work with families. 2. Families—Pastoral counseling of. 3. Families—Religious life. I. Stinson, Randy, 1967- II. Jones, Timothy P. (Timothy Paul)
    BV4438.T73 2011
    259'.1—dc23
                                                                    2011024221

ISBN 978-0-8254-3907-0
ISBN 978-0-8254-8903-7 (epub)

⊠

To the rising generation of ministers
who have embraced anew the vision of churches
where the hearts of the generations are turned toward one another,
for the sake of the gospel.

CONTENTS

ACKNOWLEDGMENTS

The purpose of *Trained in the Fear of God* is to provide biblical and theological foundations for the practice of family ministry in evangelical Protestant churches. The perspective of this text is primarily Western with more focus on North America than on Europe or Australia—although my work with Australian churches and with pastors from the United Kingdom has suggested that, when it comes to family ministry, they are facing many of the same struggles as their American counterparts.

Even with a chapter on family ministry in African American churches, there is much research yet to be done that relates to family ministry in ethnic-minority contexts, particularly in Asian and Latino communities. Having spent nearly two decades of ministry in two rural communities and then in a low-income suburban neighborhood, I have worked to make certain that this text is applicable in a variety of contexts. At the same time, it is difficult to sidestep the fact that much of the conversation about family ministry is currently unfolding in suburban communities that are far whiter and far wealthier than the cities they encircle. I hope to see this conversation shift in the next decade, even as I pray for a time when every congregation—including my own—more thoroughly reflects the divine vision of a blood-redeemed multitude from every tribe and tongue, every nation and people, standing shoulder to shoulder as they sing praises to their common Savior.

By design, *Trained in the Fear of God* includes no chapters that relate specifically to age-organized programs in the church—no step-by-step guides for how to do "family-equipping children's ministry" or "family-based youth ministry" will be found here. Another of my books addresses those issues,[1] but the focus of this text is to provide theological and historical foundations for the church's ministry to families and for the mission of Christian families in the church and to the world. *Trained in the Fear of God* is not an endpoint but a launching pad, not a capstone but a foundation

---

1. Timothy Paul Jones, *The Family Ministry Field Guide: How Your Church Can Equip Parents to Make Disciples* (Indianapolis: Wesleyan Publishing House, 2011).

9

stone, not the final word but a substratal framework for future conversations about family ministry.

In most of life's journeys, one's companions on the journey are no less important than the journey itself or, in some cases, even the intended destination. Dorothy would never have made it back to Kansas without Toto and her three needy companions; if it hadn't been for Han Solo and his Wookiee sidekick, Luke Skywalker could have never destroyed the Death Star; and, without Samwise Gamgee, Frodo would never have completed his mission to save Middle Earth.

So it is with a mission of the magnitude that this book represents.

The baristas at Starbucks Coffee on Shelbyville Road in St. Matthews and at Quill's Coffee on Bardstown Road in Louisville fueled this project with copious quantities of caffeine. Apart from a fortuitous meeting with editor Jim Weaver, this book would never have been published at all. Without editorial assistance from Kimberly Davidson, you would find footnotes in a dozen different styles and paragraphs that run on for pages. Apart from the many ways in which the leadership of The Southern Baptist Theological Seminary values us not only as teachers and mentors but also as researchers and scholars, neither Randy Stinson nor I would ever have found the time to complete this book. The doctoral students in my course Models of Student and Family Ministry critiqued and refined my thinking in ways that are reflected throughout this book. Casey Harpe indexed the manuscript. My valued Garrett Fellows—Lilly Park and W. Ryan Steenburg—worked far beyond the call of duty, even when facing comprehensive examinations, to provide me with flexibility and feedback that I needed to complete editorial tasks.

My most valued partners in this project have been my wife, Rayann, and our daughters Hannah and Skylar—not because they have contributed any words to the pages that succeed this one but because they have modeled what is described in these pages. This is not to claim, even for a moment, that our household somehow transcends struggles and sins, missed family devotions and mismanaged frustrations. It is to say instead that we work with one another to embrace the gospel anew day by day, and I am grateful for the ways that they rehearse the gospel with me.

TIMOTHY PAUL JONES,
Associate Professor of Leadership and Church Ministry,
Editor of *The Journal of Family Ministry*,
The Southern Baptist Theological Seminary

FOREWORD

When leaders wake up to discover the church needs a major course correction, they tend to move forward in two companies. One group is driven forward by the question, what works? The other—usually smaller—group is driven forward by the question, what is true?

Leaders by the thousands are waking up to the fact that churches have, for the most part, missed it in relating to families and parents. Today, as those leaders gather around white boards and tear sheets, they are choosing one of those two ways of moving forward.

Randy Stinson and Timothy Paul Jones are inviting leaders to move forward courageously toward what is true, rather than simply considering what might work. *Trained in the Fear of God* is a clear presentation of biblical truth related to families, illuminated by Christian writings from the centuries since the canon was closed.

But here is the best news of all: Because of God's brilliance, that which is *true* is also that which ultimately *works*—because what is true brings glory to the triune God and brings Christ's kingdom on earth in and through families.

RICHARD ROSS,
Professor of Student Ministry,
Southwestern Baptist Theological Seminary

INTRODUCTION

The Problem
with Family Ministry

Bryan Nelson with Timothy Paul Jones

Your family lives in a war zone. With every exploding shell, the house shakes. Your physical body may never feel the shell shocks, and the plaster on your walls may remain intact—but the impacts are present all around you. Long after your children fall asleep and the chaos of the day fades into the quietness of evening, the shelling continues.

To be sure, when you look out your window and survey a suburban backyard, a busy city block, or the rolling hills of a rural landscape, what you see probably doesn't *look* like a war zone. But don't let such serene scenery fool you! Beyond the doors of your household and mine, a battle rages. The battle is about glory, and who will receive it. The battle is about authority, and who will exercise it.

> This is war because the same serpentine dragon who—in that celestial conflict that John glimpsed on Patmos—longed to consume the fruit of Mary's womb also wants to devour our children (Rev. 12:1–9). His weapons in this conflict are, however, neither the priests of Molech nor the soldiers of Herod (Jer. 32:35–36; Matt. 2:16). The Enemy's weapons in our children's lives are slickly-promoted celebrities and clothing and commercials that subtly but surely corrode their souls.[1]

What we wrestle against in this battle is not "flesh and blood, but against the rulers, against the authorities, against the cosmic powers over this present darkness, against the spiritual forces of evil in the heavenly

---

1. Timothy Paul Jones, *The Family Ministry Field Guide: How Your Church Can Equip Parents to Make Disciples* (Indianapolis: Wesleyan Publishing House, 2011).

places" (Eph. 6:12). Faced with the recognition that our households are targets in a cosmic conflict, it is tempting for Christian families to seek some sort of bunker to escape the battle—hunkering down in well-fortified homes or churches, dreaming about a heavenly kingdom and hoping for the rapid return of Jesus. But that is not our calling: In God's design, Christian households and churches are not shelters *from* the conflict; they are gospel-empowered training bases *for* the conflict.

God has graciously gifted my wife and me with two precious daughters. Surrounded by play kitchens, plastic dolls, and princess dresses, it would be easy to lose sight of our vast responsibility for these two creatures of God. It is only the Word of God that keeps us grounded in the reality that we are training our children for a conflict that transcends empirical observation. When my wife and I look at our girls, we see two beautiful gifts that God has placed in our household—but we also recall how the first family fell in the garden of Eden and how deeply the prince of darkness despises the gospel that was proclaimed even there (Gen. 3:15). We are reminded that, because this gospel is transforming our lives and the lives of our children, our household is a target for the enemy. We know our calling to train our children in the fear of God. To neglect this training would be to send our daughters into battle unprepared, unprotected, unaware.

> What you do for God beyond your home will typically never be greater than what you practice with God within your home.
>
> ✛✛
>
> Timothy Paul Jones

Tonight, audible reminders of war ring in my ears—literally. Above my daughters' playful laughter, I hear tanks at Fort Knox running maneuvers. Only a few miles from my home, troops are training. Thunderous cannon peals are very real reminders to me of physical conflicts in which these soldiers could soon be engaged. In this moment, the thunder also reminds me of another conflict—one that swirls unseen around my family, even here and even now. This book has been written with a desire for the development of church ministries that partner with families to train children to enter into battle against the darkness.

COORDINATION OF COMMAND

But how do we prepare our children for this battle? Are my wife and I alone in this overwhelming task? If so, who are *we* to stand against all the powers of darkness? Scripturally speaking, the primary responsibility for the spiritual formation of children *does* rest squarely in the hands of parents. Yet, as followers of Jesus, we are not only parents of children but also the adopted children of God (Rom. 8:15–23; Gal. 4:5; Eph. 1:5; 1 John 3:2). Our adoption as God's children makes us part of a larger family (Matt. 12:48–50; Mark 3:32–35). That larger family is the church, the household of God (Gal. 6:10; Eph. 2:19; 1 Tim. 3:15). The same Spirit that caused us to trust in Jesus in the first place also fills this family of God and draws us into partnership with one another (Eph. 4:1–6; Phil. 1:27–2:4).

And so, my wife and I are not alone in this task. God has adopted a community of sisters and brothers to partner with us as we train our children in the fear of God. That partnership of families within the larger community of faith is, in its simplest form, what the contributors to this text mean by *family ministry*. Family ministry describes *how* a church partners with parents so that the Christian formation of children occurs not only at church but also in the household. Building on this observation, Timothy Paul Jones has defined the term "family ministry" as *the process of intentionally and persistently coordinating a congregation's proclamation and practices so that parents are acknowledged, trained, and held accountable as primary disciple-makers in their children's lives.*[2]

> ## A Definition for Family Ministry
> ⤞⤝
> Family ministry is the process of intentionally and persistently coordinating a congregation's proclamation and practices so that parents are acknowledged, trained, and held accountable as primary disciple-makers in their children's lives.

The problem is, many contemporary Christian parents do not see their households as training grounds for cosmic combat. Even among parents who *do* glimpse this calling, far too many fathers and mothers have never been equipped to function as active partners in the training of their children. Some have even assumed that their children's spiritual preparation is something that occurs mostly or even completely within the confines of their local church.

That's why family ministry matters so deeply today. God intended the household to serve as a primary training ground for cosmic conflict. Yet an overwhelming number of parents have surrendered this God-ordained

---

2. Adapted from Timothy Paul Jones, "Models for Family Ministry" in *A Theology for Family Ministry*, ed. Michael and Michelle Anthony (Nashville: B&H, 2011, forthcoming).

role. As a result, the most difficult battles may be far closer to home than we think.

TRAINED IN THE FEAR OF GOD

The emphasis on parents discipling their children is far from new. Even among first-century followers of Jesus, the necessity of training children in the fear of God was not a novel idea. The apostles echoed assumptions in their epistles (Eph. 5:21–6:4) that Spirit-inspired authors had already woven throughout the Old Testament (Exod. 20:20; Deut. 4:10; 31:13; Ps. 34:11). In synagogues and Christian communities alike, this was not an optional focus for particularly ambitious parents. Training children in the fear of God represented a nonnegotiable responsibility.

In the generations that followed the apostles, several variations of the same clause appear in documents penned by different authors in a variety of places, suggesting a well-known expectation among early Christians: "Train your children in the fear of God." Clement, the leading pastor in Rome near the end of the first century, declared, "Let our children receive the instruction that is in Christ. Let them learn . . . how the fear of God is good and great and saves all those who live in this fear in holiness with a pure mind."[3] In a letter to Christians in Philippi, second-century church leader Polycarp of Smyrna held husbands responsible to partner with their wives "to train their children in the fear of God."[4] The *Didache* and the letter of *Barnabas* provide summaries of Christian practices that date to the first and second centuries AD. Both writings include the same command to Christian parents: "You shall not remove your hand from your son or your daughter. You shall train them in the fear of God from their youth up."[5]

So what did these authors means when they called parents to train their children in the fear of God? To be trained in the fear of God was,

---

3. Translated from 1 *Clement* 21.8, in *The Apostolic Fathers*, vol. 1, ed. and trans. Bart D. Ehrman, Loeb Classical Library (Cambridge: Harvard University Press, 2003).

4. Translated from Polycarp of Smyrna, **Pros Philippesious Epistolē** (*Epistle to the Philippians*), 4:2, based on the text in *Apostolic Fathers*, vol. 1, trans. Kirsopp Lake; Loeb Classical Library (New York: Macmillan, 1913; repr. 1997; Christian Classics Ethereal Library, http://www.ccel.org/l/lake/fathers/polycarp-philippians.htm.

5. Translated from *Didache* 4.9, in *Apostolic Fathers*, vol. 1 (ed. and trans. Ehrman); *Barnabas* 19.5, in *The Apostolic Fathers*, vol. 2, ed. and trans. Bart D. Ehrman, Loeb Classical Library (Cambridge: Harvard University Press, 2003).

at least in part, to be disciplined to live with reverence for an order that transcends immediate experience or comprehension. This is not the cultivation of a "spirit of fear" that would cause God's children to shrink back in terror at the thought of their heavenly Father (Rom. 8:15; 2 Tim. 1:7; 1 John 2:28; 4:18). Training in the fear of God is disciplined guidance that calls persons to seek the unseen workings of God in ways that lead to lives of growing contentment, holiness, and centeredness in the gospel (2 Cor. 5:6–11; 7:1).

THE PROBLEM WITH FAMILY MINISTRY

Although the concepts behind family ministry are far from new, church-based family ministry _has_ turned trendy in some circles over the past few years. After decades on the back burner of congregational life, family ministry has suddenly become a hot topic. Type "family ministry" into a good search engine, and your computer will crank out nearly fifty million results in less than a second. Conference after conference claims to provide congregations with the missing key that will enable the church's staff to launch a lasting family ministry.

As a pastor and as a father this renewed focus on family ministry is at once encouraging and frightening. It's encouraging because many Christians seem to be regaining a biblical perspective on God's vision for the role of parents. For too many years, churches and parents have encouraged paid professionals to take the primary role in the discipleship of children.[6] This, even as research continues to reveal that—although other significant adults are also important—parents remain the most influential people in children's spiritual, social, and behavioral development.[7]

Why then does this new emphasis on family ministry also concern me?

---

6. For discussions, see the Barna Group, "Parents Accept Responsibility for Their Child's Spiritual Development but Struggle with Effectiveness," Barna Update, May 6, 2003, http://www.barna.org/barna-update/article/5–barna-update/120–parents-accept-responsibility-for-their-childs-spiritual-development-but-struggle-with-effectiveness; Dennis Rainey, _Ministering to Twenty-First Century Families_ (Nashville: Thomas Nelson, 2001), 57–58; Brian Haynes, _Shift: What It Takes to Finally Reach Families Today_ (Loveland, CO: Group, 2009), 37; and Steve Wright, _ApParent Privilege_ (Raleigh, NC: InQuest, 2009), 17–18.

7. Regarding spiritual development in particular, see Christian Smith and Melinda Lundquist Denton, _Soul Searching: The Religious and Spiritual Lives of American Teenagers_ (New York: Oxford University Press, 2005), 261. For the perspective of a family-equipping practitioner, see Wright, _ApParent Privilege_, 17.

Simply this: in many cases, churches are focusing on family ministry as a reaction to dismal retention statistics. It has been repeatedly reported over the past few years that somewhere between 65 percent and 94 percent of churched youth drop out of church before their sophomore year of college.[8] As a result, many congregations are shifting their ministry models *not* because of convictions that have grown from a seedbed of sustained scriptural and theological reflection. Instead, what motivates them is the supposed crisis of abysmal retention rates—a crisis that they plan to solve by launching a series of family ministry programs. Their focus on family ministry is a pragmatic reaction rooted in a desire for numbers with no standard by which to judge the results other than an increasing number of warm bodies.[9]

In contrast, the goal of this book is to call congregations to develop a theologically grounded, scripturally compelled perspective on family ministry and then to make Spirit-guided transitions in every ministry to move wisely toward this ministry model. Such shifts may increase the numbers that appear in the spreadsheet columns that summarize your congregation's buildings, budgets, and bodies. Then again, these changes could have a negligible or even a negative effect on those numbers! But the spreadsheet numbers aren't the point. From the perspective of the contributors to this text, biblical faithfulness in ministry to families is the goal.

Even if numeric gains *were* the goal, there is every reason to question the infamous statistics that point to overwhelming numbers of youth dropping out of church. For example, the highest of these percentages was drawn from an informal averaging of youth ministers' "gut feelings" about retention rates in their ministries—not exactly reliable research methodology! Even the most robust survey mixed participants in ways that may have polluted the research results.[10] Perhaps most significant of all is the simple fact that, even at their best, statistical outcomes are subject to change as new information comes to light. As a result, such numbers cannot provide sufficiently stable foundations or motivations for widespread change among the churches of God.

---

8. Kara Powell and Krista Kubiak, "When the Pomp and Circumstance Fades: A Profile of Youth Group Kids Post-Youth-Group," *Youthworker Journal* (September/October 2005): 51, http://www.youthspecialties.com/articles/when-the-pomp-and-circumstance-fades-a-profile-of-youth-group-kids-post-you/.

9. David F. Wells, *God in the Wasteland: The Reality of Truth in a World of Fading Dreams* (Grand Rapids: Eerdmans, 1994), 221. See also Haynes, *Shift*, 37–38.

10. Brandon Shields, "Family-Based Ministry: Separated Contexts, Shared Focus," in *Perspectives on Family Ministry: 3 Views*, ed. Timothy Paul Jones (Nashville: B&H, 2009), 103–5.

WHERE FAMILY MINISTRY HAS BEEN

Before examining where family ministry may be headed, it will be helpful to take a look at where family ministry has been. Over the past couple of centuries, three distinct trends have characterized church-based ministries to families in the industrialized Western world. Timothy Paul Jones has traced the historical development of these three strands and identified them as *comprehensive-coordinative, segmented-programmatic,* and *educational-programmatic*.[11]

Comprehensive-Coordinative Family Ministry

Comprehensive-coordinative ministry seeks to coordinate the church's ministries so each ministry actively and comprehensively partners with parents in the Christian formation of their children. One historical example of comprehensive-coordinative ministry can be found in the work of a nineteenth-century pastor named Samuel W. Dike. Seeing how Christian parents in his Vermont congregation had disengaged from their children's spiritual growth, Dike developed a plan that he dubbed "the Home Department."[12]

Samuel W. Dike's Home Department equipped parents with needed materials and training to imprint biblical truths in their children's lives. Even when Dike launched the Home Department in the 1880s, he did not intend to supplant efforts such as young people's societies or Sunday schools. Dike's purpose was for the congregation to partner with parents so that the faith training of children occurred both in classes at church and in the day-by-day contexts of their households.

Despite early initial acceptance in thousands of churches, the Home Department met a rapid demise, largely due to misapprehension about the original purpose. By 1907, Dike's original design had been nearly forgotten, and the Home Department had degenerated into little more than a program for the distribution of study booklets to shut-ins.[13] Throughout the twentieth century, a more segmented approach to ministry rose to dominance, especially in American churches.

---

11. Timothy Paul Jones, "Models for Family Ministry" in *A Theology for Family Ministry*, ed. Michael Anthony and Michelle Anthony (Nashville: B&H, 2011, forthcoming).
12. Edmund Morris Fergusson, *Church-School Administration* (New York: Fleming H. Revell, 1922), 124–25.
13. Flora V. Stebbins, *The Home Department of To-day* (Philadelphia: The Sunday School Times Company, 1907), 3.

Segmented-Programmatic Ministry to Family Members

In a segmented-programmatic congregation, every church ministry is segmented by age with little interaction or continuity between them. Ministry to families means having a separate ministry for each member of the family. Segmented-programmatic ministry developed out of the church-based young people's societies that had emerged in the nineteenth century. In some sense, the segmented-programmatic approach in the churches mirrored what was happening in the larger American culture as a growing public education system clustered youth in tightly graded classes. In the economic boom that succeeded the Second World War, churches solidified segmented-programmatic practices as they increasingly called ministers who focused on particular age groupings.

Whether or not such an approach ought to be called "family ministry" at all is debatable. What is beyond debate is the dominance of this ministry paradigm, particularly in American churches. Segmented-programmatic ministry so thoroughly dominated church administration in the twentieth century that, even in the opening decades of the twenty-first century, many church members know no other approach. In less than two centuries, the segmented-programmatic paradigm became, at least in people's perceptions, "traditional." It would be a flagrant overgeneralization to blame parental abdication on segmented church programming. At the same time, the growth of professional, age-focused ministers may have made it easier for parents to perceive that the training of their children in the fear of God must be someone else's responsibility.

Educational-Programmatic Family Ministry

In the late nineteenth and early twentieth centuries, the informal family improvement societies of earlier generations gave way to formal "Family Life Education" programs. By the mid-twentieth century, not only universities but also many states and counties featured Family Life Education departments.[14] Soon, denominations and congregations were establishing Family Life Education departments too. One advantage of this educational-

---

14. Margaret E. Arcus, Jay D. Schvanefeldt, and J. Joel Moss, "The Nature of Family Life Education," in *Handbook of Family Life Education: Foundations of Family Life Education*, vol. 1, ed. Margaret E. Arcus, Jay D. Schvanefeldt, and J. Joel Moss (Thousand Oaks, CA: SAGE, 1993); Stephen F. Duncan and H. Wallace Goddard, *Family Life Education: Principles and Practices for Effective Outreach* (Thousand Oaks, CA: SAGE, 2005), 3.

programmatic approach was that it could coexist with segmented-programmatic ministry. Family Life Education could be added quite easily to the existing array of programs in age-segmented churches.

Educational-programmatic ministry was the perspective promoted in some of the most popular twentieth-century textbooks for church-based family ministries. In 1957, Oscar Feucht edited a text entitled *Helping Families through the Church: A Symposium on Family Life Education.*[15] Feucht's approach provided practical helps for developing programs to educate families for healthier relationships and to equip parents to train their children. In the 1960s and 1970s, many churches expanded their Family Life Education programs to provide counseling and support groups for troubled family members. Textbooks from Charles Sell and Diana Garland provided foundations for educational-programmatic family ministry that incorporated therapeutic components.[16] While not disregarding parents' responsibility to disciple their children, Family Life Education focused primarily on developing healthy family relationships.

Figure 1.1: Modern and Contemporary Approaches to Family Ministry

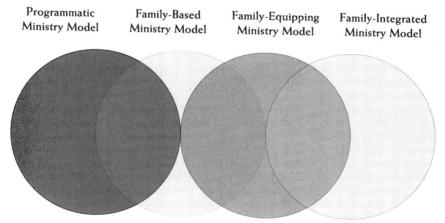

| Programmatic Ministry Model | Family-Based Ministry Model | Family-Equipping Ministry Model | Family-Integrated Ministry Model |

Envisioning the Relationship Between the Models of Ministry

15. Oscar Feucht, ed., *Helping Families through the Church: A Symposium on Family Life Education* (St. Louis: Concordia, 1957).
16. Diana R. Garland, *Family Ministry: A Comprehensive Guide* (Downers Grove, IL: InterVarsity Press, 1999); Charles M. Sell, *Family Ministry*, 2nd ed. (Grand Rapids: Zondervan, 1995). Sell's book was originally published in 1981 as *Family Ministry: The Enrichment of Family Life through the Church.*

COMING FULL CIRCLE

As the twentieth century faded into the twenty-first, a renewed recognition of the need for biblically motivated parental engagement in children's discipleship began to emerge among many evangelical pastors and scholars. Now a rising generation of family ministry practitioners is proclaiming anew the ancient biblical truths that call parents to function as primary faith-trainers in their children's lives. Within this larger movement, three identifiable family ministry models have emerged: *family-based*, *family-integrated*, and *family-equipping*.[17] Each of these models recognizes that the family is a fundamental context for the discipleship of children. Yet none of them ignores the crucial role of the larger faith community in children's Christian formation. Perhaps most important, significant proponents of each of these models have made it clear that what they are pursuing is not a programmatic panacea to improve retention rates but a biblically grounded partnership between churches and families.

None of these three family ministry models is absolutely exclusive of the others. The worship celebration in a family-integrated congregation, for example, might look a lot like the intergenerational worship in a family-equipping church. Much of the programming in a family-based congregation will likely look like the segmented-programmatic models of previous decades, though family-based churches will involve parents in as many events as possible. Still, each model of family ministry represents a distinct and identifiable approach to the challenge of drawing the household and the church into a life-transforming partnership.

---

17. In the new edition of *God, Marriage, and Family*, these three distinct models are presented as three variants of family integration, with the family-integrated model—which is criticized sharply—identified as "more purist" in the "conviction and application of family integration." Andreas J. Köstenberger with David W. Jones, *God, Marriage, and Family: Rebuilding the Biblical Foundation*, 2nd ed. (Wheaton, IL: Crossway, 2010) 259–60; see also 372–73n20. Family-based ministry, however, emerged in the 1980s and 1990s, not as a modification of family integration but as a course correction that assumed the continued existence of age-organized ministries to youth and children (see, e.g., the first edition of Mark DeVries, *Family-Based Youth Ministry: Reaching the Been-There, Done-That Generation* [Downers Grove, IL: InterVarsity Press, 1994]). The practice of family equipping, on the other hand, grew largely out of a conviction that family-based ministry was well-intentioned but insufficient (see Jay Strother, "Responses," in *Perspectives on Family Ministry: 3 Views*, ed. Timothy Paul Jones [Nashville: B&H, 2009], 127). Throughout this time, family integration in its contemporary form was developing independently from family-based and family-equipping models.

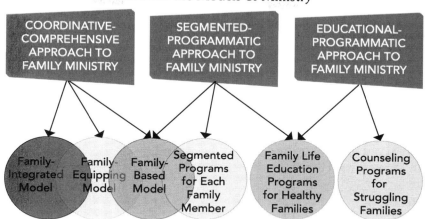

Figure 1.2: Envisioning the Relationship
Between the Models of Ministry

The Family-Integrated Model for Church Ministry: A Complete Break from Age-Segmented Structures

The family-integrated approach represents a complete break from the "neo-traditional" segmented-programmatic church. Proponents of family integration contend that the modern American practice of age segregation goes beyond the biblical mandate—and may even obstruct parents' obedience in discipling their children. As a result, in a family-integrated church, all or nearly all age-organized classes and events are eliminated, including youth group, children's church, and even age-graded Sunday school classes. The generations learn and worship together, and the entire community of faith calls parents—and particularly fathers—to embrace a primary responsibility for the evangelism and discipleship of their children.

Proponents of family-integrated ministry have sometimes described the local church "as a family of families."[18] In this, family-integrated churches are *not*, however, redefining the essential nature of the church.[19]

---

18. For this quotation as well as a fuller description of family-integrated ministry, see Voddie Baucham Jr., *Family Driven Faith: Doing What It Takes to Raise Sons and Daughters Who Walk with God* (Wheaton, IL: Crossway, 2007), 191–95.

19. This point has been repeatedly clarified by proponents of family-integrated ministry; see, e.g., Paul Renfro, "Why Family Integration Still Works," in *Perspectives on Family Ministry: 3 Views*, ed. Timothy Paul Jones (Nashville: B&H, 2009), 89–90. Despite these

When it comes to the nature of the church, family-integrated churches stand with other models of church ministry, affirming the orthodox confessions of faith. "Family of families" is a functional description of how family-integrated churches structure their processes of evangelism and discipleship.

In the latter decades of the twentieth century, church planter Henry Reyenga as well as Reb Bradley at Hope Chapel in California were promoting family integration in American churches. Voddie Baucham and Paul Renfro, from Grace Family Baptist Church in Texas, have been some of the most articulate recent defenders of family integration. Other promoters and practitioners of family-integrated ministry include Doug Phillips at Vision Forum and Scott Brown from the National Center for Family Integrated Churches.

Family-Integrated Model for Church Ministry
><

Proponents of family-integrated churches believe that "there is no scriptural pattern for comprehensive age-segregated discipleship, and that age-segregated practices are based on unbiblical, evolutionary and secular thinking which have invaded the church" ("A Biblical Confession for Uniting Church and Family," National Center for Family-Integrated Churches, http://www.ncfic.org/confession). As a result, family-integrated congregations "reject the emphasis on family-fragmenting, facility-based programs which disregard the Church as a people in community and which displace family outreach." From a family-integrated perspective, "the church's relationships are nurtured primarily through daily discipleship in everyday life, especially fathers and mothers training their families to fulfill the great commission, living out the gospel in ministry to the saints and witness to the lost."

Families in family-integrated congregations view their households as contexts for mutual discipleship as well as evangelism of unbelievers. As a result, they are likely to invite unbelievers into their homes for meals on a regular basis. Through intentional hospitality, unbelieving families observe the dynamics of a Christ-centered family, providing opportunities for the

---

clarifications, the charge that "family of families" entails ecclesiological revision continues to be repeated, most recently in the second edition of Köstenberger with Jones, *God, Marriage, and Family*, 259.

believing family to share the gospel. Small group Bible studies bring entire families together—including singles, single-parent households, and children of nonbelieving parents who have been enfolded into believing families.

The Family-Based Model for Church Ministry: Activities and Emphases to Empower Parents within Age-Segmented Structures

The family-based model seeks to merge a comprehensive-coordinative vision for parents with the segmented-programmatic perspective that remains prevalent in many contemporary churches. Mark DeVries pioneered this approach in his book *Family-Based Youth Ministry* after recognizing that "the real power for faith formation was not in the youth program but in the families and the extended family of the church. . . . Our isolated youth programs cannot compete with the formative power of the family."[20] DeVries identified two key priorities in creating and maintaining a family-based model. First, churches must empower the parents to participate in the discipleship of their children. The second priority is to equip the extended family of the church so that the generations build relationships with one another. In this model, age-segmented ministries continue with minimal change, but the congregation constantly creates opportunities to involve parents and other adults. The model that Reggie Joiner has dubbed "sup-

> **Family-Based Model for Church Ministry**
> ⇥⇤
> Family-based churches retain separate, age-segmented ministry structures. The difference between family-based models and typical segmented-programmatic models is that family-based churches intentionally include intergenerational activities in each ministry and consistently train parents to function as disciple-makers in their children's lives.

---

20. Mark DeVries, *Family-Based Youth Ministry*, 2nd ed. (Downers Grove, IL: InterVarsity Press, 2004), 61, 67. A new chapter in the second edition of *God, Marriage, and Family* incorrectly states that "family-based ministry" is not widely known or widely pursued, overlooking the fact that family-based ministry first made an appearance in the early 1990s, in the first edition of Mark DeVries, *Family-Based Youth Ministry* (1994), and has remained widespread both as a practice and as terminology ever since. See Köstenberger with Jones, *God, Marriage, and Family*, 2nd ed., 372–73n20.

plemental family ministry" would probably describe the more program-matic side of family-based ministry.[21]

Proponents of the model are quick to assert that the segmented-programmatic paradigm is neither faulty nor broken. The segmented per-spective simply needs to be rebalanced so parents are empowered and intergenerational relationships are emphasized. "There are," Brandon Shields asserts,

> "no pressing reasons for radical reorganization or restructuring of pres-ent ministry models. There is certainly no need for complete integra-tion of age groups. What churches need to do is simply refocus existing age-appropriate groupings to partner intentionally with families in the discipleship process."[22]

Family-based congregations add new activities and expand existing oppor-tunities so that the generations grow in their appreciation for one another. In the process, the church's leadership calls parents to engage actively in Christian formation within their household.

The Family-Equipping Model for Family Ministry: Transforming Age-Organized Ministries to Co-champion the Family and the Community of Faith

Timothy Paul Jones coined the term *family-equipping ministry* to describe the family ministry paradigm that he and Randy Stinson developed for the School of Church Ministries at The Southern Baptist Theological Seminary. Soon afterward, Randy Stinson located and brought together an informal coalition of ministers who were doing in practice precisely what he and Jones had sketched out in theory. Leading early practitioners of the family-equipping model included Jay Strother at Brentwood Baptist Church in Tennessee, Brian Haynes at Kingsland Baptist Church in Texas, and Steve Wright at Providence Baptist Church in North Carolina.[23]

---

21. Reggie Joiner, *Think Orange: Imagine the Impact When Church and Family Collide* (Colorado Springs: David C. Cook, 2009), Concentrate 6.2.
22. Shields, "Family-Based Ministry," 98–99.
23. For the model as practiced by these ministers, see Jay Strother, "Family-Equipping Ministry: Co-champions with a Single Goal," in *Perspectives on Family Ministry: 3 Views*, ed. Timothy Paul Jones (Nashville: B&H, 2009); Haynes, *Shift*; Steve Wright with Chris Graves, *reThink: Decide for Yourself, Is Student Ministry Working?* (Wake Forest, NC: InQuest Publishing, 2007).

In many ways the family-equipping model represents a middle route between the family-integrated and family-based models.[24] Semblances of age-organized ministry remain intact in family-equipping contexts. Many family-equipping churches even retain youth ministers and children's ministers. Yet every practice at every level of ministry is reworked to champion the place of parents as primary disciple-makers in their children's lives. Because parents are primary disciple-makers and vital partners in family-equipping ministry, every activity for children or youth must resource, train, or directly involve parents.[25]

Whereas family-based churches develop intergenerational activities within existing segmented-programmatic structures and add family activities to current calendars, family-equipping churches redevelop the congregation's structure to cultivate a renewed culture wherein parents are acknowledged, trained, and held accountable as the primary faith trainers in their children's lives. As in family-integrated churches, children whose parents are unbelievers are connected with mature believers in the types of relationships that Paul described in his letter to Titus (2:1–8). Every level of the congregation's life is consciously recultured to "co-champion" the church's ministry *and* the parent's responsibility.

> **Family-Equipping Model for Church Ministry**
> ↠↞
> Family-equipping churches cultivate a congregational culture that coordinates every ministry to champion the role of the parents as primary faith-trainers in their children's lives.

To envision the family-equipping model in action, imagine a river with large stones jutting through the surface of the water. The river represents the Christian growth and development of children in the church. One riverbank signifies the church, and the other riverbank connotes the family. Both banks are necessary for the river to flow forward with focus and power. Unless both riverbanks support the child's development, you are likely to

---

24. Much that is found in Joiner, *Think Orange*, fits in the overlap between the family-based and family-equipping paradigms, at least from an organizational and programmatic perspective; many of the associated publications may be helpful in resourcing the development of family-based and family-equipping ministries. The content and approach of materials from the reThink Group, however, seem in many cases to be driven more by ecclesial pragmatism than by substantive theological or biblical considerations.

25. For the "resource, train, involve" principle as well as the term "co-champion," see Wright with Graves, *reThink*.

end up with the destructive power of a deluge instead of the constructive possibilities of a river. The stones that guide and redirect the river currents represent milestones or rites of passage that mark the passing of key points of development that the church and families celebrate together.

Most of the authors whose contributions appear on these pages view family-equipping ministry as the ideal. At the same time, the principles that they present will be useful far beyond family-equipping churches, particularly in family-integrated and family-based contexts. Even segmented-programmatic and educational-programmatic ministries may find this text helpful as their leaders seek to develop theological foundations for their ministries to families.

FAMILY MINISTRY IS NOT THE ANSWER

Before you begin reading this book, a few words of warning about family ministry are in order—words that may seem to work against the success of this very book! Our words of warning are simply these: family ministry is *not* the answer; family ministry will *not* fix your church's problems; and, family ministry will *not* transform people's lives.

The gospel is what changes people—not programs or practices; not models or methods; but solely and only the gospel of Jesus Christ. Every local church should be concerned first about how the gospel is portrayed, presented, and practiced in the congregation. This *includes* considering how local congregations teach on the subjects of marriage and parenting and how they encourage and minister to families. Healthy families are not, however, the goal. To place anything as the church's goal besides the glory of God experienced through the gospel is to create an idol, and the idol of family ministry is no less loathsome to God than the orgiastic shrines of Canaan or the pantheon of ancient Rome.

> "In the midst of our various responsibilities and many possible areas of service in the kingdom of God, one overarching truth should motivate all our work and affect every part of who we are: Christ died for our sins."
>
> ✜
>
> C. J. Mahaney, *Living the Cross-Centered Life*

The believing household *is* a target for the enemy, but Christian families are not the answer to humanity's problems. The gospel is the answer. Our households are not targeted because Christian families are flawless families. Our households are targeted because they are God-ordained contexts where cross-centered, gospel-empowered living can be constantly rehearsed and practiced. Through these day-by-day rehearsals of the gospel, children and parents alike are trained in the fear of God.

PART 1

THE CHARACTER OF GOD AND THE CREATED ORDER

A Biblical and Theological Framework for Considering Family Relationships

Past family ministry texts have tended to begin with such topics as "The Family of Family Ministry" or "Families Today," interpreting the family first from the perspective of the latest social-scientific research. One text defends this decision by identifying such data as "the primary means for understanding" families and as "the foundation for intervening in and changing family and church life."[1]

The editors of this text respectfully disagree.

While recognizing the value of comprehending contemporary contexts, it is our conviction that current social trends can never provide satisfactory starting points, means, or goals for family ministry. The foundation and goal for intervention and transformation is not found in social-scientific research but in the gospel of Jesus Christ. Of course, the perceptions and functions of the family have changed over time, and families in every era have faced struggles that were particular to their place in history. Yet the primary framework for understanding families is to consider families within the context of God's creation, humanity's fall, a crucified and risen Redeemer, and God's guarantee that he will someday turn the groaning of the cosmos into glory divine.

The divine design for families is rooted not in fleeting social conventions but in the eternal character of God. It is only through God the Father

---

1. Diana R. Garland, *Family Ministry: A Comprehensive Guide* (Downers Grove, IL: InterVarsity Press, 1999), 20.

that any family "in heaven [or] on earth" will be able to discover the character and identity that God intended (Eph. 3:14–15).

That's why this book begins not with reflections on our present contexts but with an examination of the Word of God. James M. Hamilton Jr. explores God's design for families in the Old Testament, while Robert L. Plummer takes a look at the witness of the New Testament and the early church fathers. These chapters are followed by reflections from Bruce A. Ware on how the doctrine of God must shape family relationships. In contrast to the blurring of gender roles within many families and the widespread acceptance of homosexual relationships in contemporary culture, Scripture spells out distinct roles for each sex and celebrates the lifelong covenantal coupling of one man with one woman. Randy Stinson and R. Albert Mohler Jr. demonstrate how God's primeval patterning of human beings as *male* and *female* is essential to understanding God's intention for families.

1

THAT THE COMING GENERATION MIGHT PRAISE THE LORD

Family Discipleship in the Old Testament

James M. Hamilton Jr.

God gave to Adam the task of ruling and subduing the earth (Gen. 1:28). This apparently meant that Adam's vocation entailed expanding the borders of Eden until the whole earth became a place where, as in Eden, God was known, served, worshipped, and uniquely present. Adam sinned and experienced expulsion from Eden. Yet God did not give up his plan to cover the dry lands with his glory. God promised to raise a seed from the woman who would crush the head of the serpent, defeating evil (Gen. 3:15). Later, God made promises to Abraham that would overcome the curses resulting from sin. These promises were passed through Isaac to Jacob and then to the tribes of Israel.[1]

Having brought Israel out of Egypt, God brought them into a new Eden, the land of promise. Adam's task then became Israel's task: to expand

---

1. For further explorations of these themes, see James M. Hamilton Jr., *God's Glory in Salvation through Judgment: A Biblical Theology* (Wheaton: Crossway, 2010); James M. Hamilton Jr., "The Skull Crushing Seed of the Woman: Inner-Biblical Interpretation of Genesis 3:15," *The Southern Baptist Journal of Theology* 10, no. 2 (2006): 30–54; James M. Hamilton Jr., "The Seed of the Woman and the Blessing of Abraham," *Tyndale Bulletin* 58, no. 2 (2007): 253–73; and T. Desmond Alexander, "Genealogies, Seed, and the Compositional Unity of Genesis," *Tyndale Bulletin* 44, no. 2 (1993): 255–70.

the borders of the realm wherein the Lord was present, known, served, and worshipped (see, e.g., Num. 14:21; Ps. 72:19). But Israel sinned just as Adam had, and Israel was exiled from the land just as Adam was exiled from Eden.[2] Through the prophets, God promised that he would restore Israel and accomplish his purpose of covering the lands with his glory as the waters cover the sea (Isa. 6:3; 11:9; Hab. 2:14).

In the fullness of time, God the Father sent God the Son. Jesus withstood temptation, conquered the land, overcame death by dying and rising from the dead, and commissioned his followers to make disciples of all nations.[3] When the full number of the nations have come in, all Israel will be saved (Rom. 11:25–27), and Jesus will cover the dry lands with the glory of the Lord.

The purpose of this chapter is to explore what the Old Testament tells us about how the family factors into God's purpose of covering the dry lands with his glory. Examining the family does not shift our focus either from God's purpose or from the promised seed of the woman through whom it would be accomplished. To the contrary, the seed of the woman came from a divinely designed line of descent—a *family*. God's instruction indicated that the royal family was to be a model for all other families in Israel. And, though that family failed, God kept his word and raised Jesus through this line of descent. This is clear from God's commands to fathers and kings in Deuteronomy as well as in the ways that King Solomon expressed these instructions in the book of Proverbs.

INSTRUCTIONS FOR FATHERS AND KINGS IN DEUTERONOMY

Even before the instructions given in Deuteronomy 6, God had been preparing fathers in Israel to teach their children. Exodus 12:26–27 and 13:14 instructed fathers to celebrate the Lord's power and mercy to Israel whenever their children asked the meaning of Passover. These particular instances

---

2. Stephen G. Dempster, *Dominion and Dynasty: A Biblical Theology of the Hebrew Bible*, New Studies in Biblical Theology, vol. 15 (Downers Grove, IL: InterVarsity Press, 2003), 67.
3. G. K. Beale, *The Temple and the Church's Mission: A Biblical Theology of the Dwelling Place of God*, New Studies in Biblical Theology, vol. 17 (Downers Grove, IL: InterVarsity Press, 2004); and James M. Hamilton Jr., *God's Indwelling Presence: The Holy Spirit in the Old and New Testaments*, NAC Studies in Bible and Theology (Nashville: B&H, 2006).

were generalized and made comprehensive as Moses prepared the people for life in the Promised Land. In the first eleven chapters of Deuteronomy, Moses motivated Israel to keep "the Torah," the life-giving instruction of God. The Ten Commandments (Deut. 5:6–22) summarize God's instruction, while the commands, statutes, and judgments in Deuteronomy 12–28 exposit the Ten Commandments.[4] The book of Deuteronomy closes with a last will and testament from Moses in Deuteronomy 29–34.

The instructions that Moses directed to *fathers* can be found in the section of Deuteronomy that is mainly focused on urging Israel to maintain God's instruction when they enter the land (Deut. 1–11). The instructions for *kings* come in a section of the book (Deut. 16–18) that exposits the fifth commandment, "Honor your father and your mother" (Deut. 5:16). In some sense, this fifth commandment is an umbrella instruction that covers the way that Israel was to embrace the God-ordained authority not only of parents but also of kings, judges, prophets, and priests.

Instructions for Fathers in Deuteronomy 6

God called Israel to enter the land and to live according to God's instruction for God's glory. If Israel lived the way God instructed them to live, their lives would be blessed and their enemies defeated. Their inheritance would include not only be the plot of ground allotted to them in the Land of Promise but also all the nations (Ps. 2:8). God's glory would cover the dry lands as the waters cover the seas (see Deut. 4:6; 6:25; Num. 14:21; Isa. 6:3; 11:9; Hab. 2:14; Ps. 72:19). For Israel to accomplish this purpose, they had to maintain the divine instruction. As we soon shall see, Moses made clear in Deuteronomy—particularly in Deuteronomy 6:4–9—that *fathers of households* were responsible to see that this happens.

It would be difficult to overstate the significance of the declaration in Deuteronomy 6:4 that there is one and only one God. This text is known as the Shema, because *shema* is the imperative form of the word "Hear!" that opens verse 4. Israel is summoned to hear and heed this truth, that "the LORD our God, the LORD is one." The emblematic declaration that the Lord—the one whose holy name "Yahweh" points back to his revelation of himself to Moses at the burning bush (Exod. 3:14)—is Israel's one God is exposited in Deuteronomy 6:5–9.

---

4. See table 2.16, "Deuteronomy's Exposition of the Ten Commandments," in Hamilton, *God's Glory in Salvation through Judgment*, 128.

Because Yahweh, the Lord, is the sole deity, he is to be loved (Deut 6:5), obeyed (v. 6), and considered constantly in every household (v. 7). He is the subject of reminders on the hand (6:8), he is the criterion for understanding life (v. 8), and he is the one memorialized on doorposts and gates (v. 9). These items in Deuteronomy 6:6–9 are not simply about *laws* but about *the one who gives the laws.*

The call to recognize the Lord alone as God in Deuteronomy 6:4 is followed by what Jesus identified as the first and greatest commandment: to love the Lord with all that one is and has (see Matt. 22:37–38). Heart, soul, and strength are to be exerted to exhaustion in love for the Lord. Emotions, life, and physical body powered by loving the Lord. This can mean nothing less than that everything one thinks, does, and feels is to be focused on loving God. The connection between loving Yahweh and having his commands on the heart in Deuteronomy 6:5–6 anticipates words that Jesus says in John 14:15, "If you love me, you will keep my commandments."

Pause here and consider the profound significance of

> Hear, O Israel: the LORD our God, the LORD is one.
> You shall love the LORD your God with all your heart
> and with all your soul and with all your might.
> And these words that I command you today shall be on your heart.
> You shall teach them diligently to your children, and shall talk of them
> when you sit in your house,
> and when you walk by the way,
> and when you lie down,
> and when you rise.
> You shall bind them as a sign on your hand,
> and they shall be as frontlets between your eyes.
> You shall write them on the doorposts of your house and on your gates.
>
> → Deuteronomy 6:4–9

what Moses announces in Deuteronomy 6:4–6: Yahweh alone is God; Israel is to love him; his commands are to be on the heart. What comes next in this text was intended to be of great significance. The hearer might wonder, "What will Moses say next? Something about kings or armies or economics? Or is there something more fundamental than those things? Something that will produce righteous kings? Something that will teach soldiers that there are things worth more than peace, more than life? Something that will ensure economic stability? But what could possibly be significant enough to accomplish all of that?"

And indeed, the high and beautiful truth that the Lord *is* the only true and living God who is to be loved and obeyed *is* followed by something very significant! What follows this text is an explanation of the *means* for passing on the knowledge of this one God to generations yet to come. If Yahweh alone is God, he deserves to be worshipped, loved, and obeyed even after the current generation dies. To ensure the ongoing worship of the Lord, Moses declared, "You shall teach [these words] diligently to your children, and shall talk of them when you sit in your house, and when you walk by the way, and when you lie down, and when you rise" (Deut. 6:7).

The first phrase of Deuteronomy 6:7 could be translated very directly as follows: "And you shall repeat them[5] to your sons and you shall talk about them." (Although many translations change the word for "sons" to the more generic "children," the use of the Hebrew term for "sons" in this text is intentional and significant.) There is nothing complicated here. The Hebrew verbs rendered "you shall repeat" and "you shall talk" are second person masculine singular forms. Unlike English, which does not distinguish between masculine and feminine forms of the second person pronoun "you," Hebrew has a masculine form for "you" and a feminine form for "you." The fact that these forms are masculine singular means that, as Moses addressed the nation of Israel, he directed the responsibility to teach the "sons" toward the fathers. The fact that the form is singular urges the conclusion that Moses did not give this responsibility to some abstract group of fathers in the community but to each individual father. It doesn't take a village; it takes a father.

Every father with a son was commanded to repeat to his son the "words" that Moses commanded. The words Moses commanded were to be on their hearts (Deut 6:6), and they were to repeat those commands to their sons (v. 7). Fathers in Israel were commanded to embrace the theological confession that the Lord alone is God (v. 4). They were to love him (v. 5), know his Word so they could obey (v. 6), and they were to repeat God's words to their sons.

Notice that Deuteronomy 6:7 not only calls each individual father to repeat the words to his sons, but it also calls him to "talk about them." At the very least this would seem to imply that, once the words were restated, the father told his sons what these words meant. Explaining what the words meant seems to have been designed to open up discussions of *why* the words said what they did. Because the Lord alone is God (v. 4), one would also expect discussions of how to overcome obstacles to keeping

---

5. Ludwig Koehler and Walter Baumgartner, *The Hebrew and Aramaic Lexicon of the Old Testament*, vol. 2 (Leiden; Boston: Brill, 2001), 1607.

God's words by loving God (v. 5) as well as discussions of how to avoid inadvertent transgressions by keeping God's words on one's heart (v. 6).

In the second half of Deuteronomy 6:7, Moses provided intensely practical instructions to Israelite fathers regarding *when* they were to repeat and to discuss these words: *all the time.* "When you sit in your house, and when you walk by the way, and when you lie down, and when you rise," Moses declared (v. 7). At the beginning of each day and at the end of each day, fathers were called to repeat and to discuss God's words. In between rising in the morning and lying down at night, as fathers went from place to place with their sons, they were to repeat and discuss God's words. When fathers sat in their homes with their sons, they were to repeat and discuss God's words.

The point of Deuteronomy 6:8–9 is not to bring about some perfunctory practice of attaching God's words to hands, foreheads, doorposts, and gates. In the Old Testament the "hand" is often a figurative reference to physical power, and the "eye" is the organ of perception. It may be that Moses was calling Israel to bind God's words to their strength, so to speak, and to make God's words the filter for their perception. Similarly, the writing of words on the doorposts of homes and the gates of cities (v. 9) accomplished nothing if Israelite fathers failed to recognize the Lord alone as God (v. 4), to love him (v. 5), to obey his commands (v. 6), and to teach God's words to their sons (v. 7). Every household was to be marked by the words of God as a reflection of the inward reality that Israel is devoted to Yahweh.

What about daughters and wives? Were they somehow excluded by these instructions to fathers and sons? Daughters and wives are not mentioned directly in the text—and yet they are *more* included and *more* protected, not less, when this was put into practice. Wives whose husbands obeyed these commands would constantly hear God's word repeated and discussed. Daughters of fathers who heeded these commands would scarcely be able to avoid the repetition and discussion of God's words. More importantly, when fathers repeated and discussed God's words with their sons, they ensured that future wives and daughters would be led by husbands and fathers who would do the same. The father was the key to the family, and a son was a future father.

Instructions for Kings in Deuteronomy 17

Obedience to the commands of Deuteronomy 6 does not occur easily or automatically for fathers and their families. How then could

Israel develop a culture where fathers would follow the commands of Deuteronomy 6?[6] Deuteronomy 17 answers that question: A royal ruler would be called to develop this culture. Deuteronomy 17:14–17 explains who the king must be and what he must not be: The king was to be an Israelite (vv. 14–15); he was not to return the people to Egypt so that he could acquire many horses (v. 16); he was not to multiply wives for himself (v. 17a); and he was not to obtain excessive silver and gold (v. 17b). All of these instructions are about trusting the Lord. Israel was to trust the Lord even if a foreigner looked like he might make a more impressive king; Israel's king was to trust the Lord to deliver in battle, not mighty horses (v. 16; cf. Ps 20:7); the king was to be like Abraham with Sarah and to trust in the Lord—not in a multitude of wives—to provide offspring (Deut. 17:17a); and the king was to believe that the Lord would provide his needs, not precious metals (v. 17b).

> And it shall be when he sits on the throne of his kingdom that he shall
>   write for himself a copy of this Torah on a scroll, from before the Levitical
>   priests.
> And it shall be with him,
> and he shall read in it all the days of his life,
> in order to learn to fear the Lᴏʀᴅ his God
> to keep all the words of this Torah
>   and these statutes to do;
> lest his heart be exalted over his brothers,
> and lest he turn from the commandment to the right or left;
> in order for his days to be made long over his kingdom, he and his sons in
>   the midst of Israel.
>
> → **Deuteronomy 17:18–20**
> *(author's translation)*

And how would the king learn to trust the Lord for his position, protection, posterity, and provision(Deut. 17:15–17)? According to Deuteronomy 17:18–20, the king was to undertake three tasks with a single purpose: (1) the king was to write his personal copy of the Torah scroll; (2) he was to keep this scroll with him; and (3) he was to read it all his days. And what was

---

6. See the definition of "culture" provided by David Wells: "The set of shared values that are held to prescribe what is normal in a society." David F. Wells, *God in the Wasteland: The Reality of Truth in a World of Fading Dreams* (Grand Rapids: Eerdmans, 1994), 200.

the purpose of this process? "That he may learn to fear the LORD his God" (v. 19). The study of God's instruction would develop a king who feared the Lord. The king who feared Yahweh would reign long in the land, ensuring future generations of God-fearing kings (Prov. 20:28; 25:5; 29:14).

There are several significant points of contact between Deuteronomy 6:4–9 and 17:18–20: The verb used to describe the fathers' "repeating" of the words in Deuteronomy 6:7 is from the same root as the noun used to describe the "copy" of the Torah that the king is to make according to Deuteronomy 17:18. Fathers were to "repeat" the words to their sons, and the king was to make a "repeat" of God's instruction. Obviously, the content of what fathers would repeat in oral form and what the kings would repeat in written form was the same: the words of God.

Moses instructed fathers to repeat the words to their sons at the bookends of each day and at every opportunity between morning and evening (Deut. 6:7). This kind of constant reference to God's instruction is also in view in Deuteronomy 17:19: the king was to keep his own copy of the Torah "with him" to read "all the days of his life." The goal of Deuteronomy 17:18–20 is precisely what 6:6 described: the word of God was to be on the king's heart. Immediately before the commands in Deuteronomy 6:4–9, Moses exhorted fathers to fear the Lord with their sons and grandsons so that they would keep the law and lengthen their days in the land (v. 2). This material from Deuteronomy 6:2 is repeated in 17:19. Kings were to fear the Lord so that they would keep the Torah and lengthen their days and the days of their sons (see also 5:16).

Deuteronomy 6 and 17 clearly have the same goal: to create a people on whose heart is the instruction of the Lord. Israel as a nation takes up Adam's role to cover the dry lands with God's glory, justice, mercy, goodness, truth, and righteousness. The king of Israel would be the primary agent and exemplar that the Lord would use to accomplish this program.[7] Every father in Israel was to follow the king's example as a man who knew the Lord, on whose heart was the instruction of the Lord, and who was conveying these instructions to those in his care. The king was like the father to the nation. He led his family to love the Lord by obeying his instruction, and every father in Israel was to follow his example.

---

7. See Jamie A. Grant, *The King as Exemplar: The Function of Deuteronomy's Kingship Law in the Shaping of the Book of Psalms*, Academia Biblica, vol. 17 (Atlanta: Society of Biblical Literature, 2004).

THE EXAMPLE OF SOLOMON

In the book of Proverbs, Solomon functions as an example of the obedience in Deuteronomy 6:7 and 17:18–20. Proverbs opens with an ascription that identifies Solomon as both _son_ and _king_ (Prov. 1:1; cf. 10:1; 25:1). Throughout Proverbs, Solomon constantly addressed his son or sons (see, e.g., 4:1). In the third chapter of Proverbs, he twice addressed his words to "my son" (vv. 1, 21). The addresses to "my son" in Proverbs 3:1 and 3:21 each open sections that very clearly connect with Deuteronomy 6:1–12 and 6:21–35. Between these two sections on God's life-giving instruction are two sections that focus on wisdom: Proverbs 3:13–18 and 3:19–20.

Connections between Proverbs 3 and Deuteronomy 6 and 17 are abundant—too plentiful, in fact, to be explored completely here (see table on next page). But it is clear that Proverbs 3 represents a concrete expression, in the life of King Solomon, of the commands expressed through Moses to fathers and to kings in Deuteronomy (see table 1.1). King Solomon modeled for the nation the pattern of all good teachers in the book of Proverbs: He obeyed the words of God; he reformulated the teaching of these words in new and memorable ways; he advocated the joys and blessings of obedience; and, he illustrated the anguish that inevitably results from disobedience.

"SO THAT A PEOPLE YET TO BE CREATED MAY PRAISE THE LORD"

Moses did not summon Israel to obey because he was teaching a law-based religion. As in the New Testament, love for God is demonstrated by means of obedience. Neither were the laws of Moses a stepladder to earn one's way into heaven. Many of these laws would not make sense to any worldly-minded person. Release debts in the seventh year? That doesn't seem like sound economic policy! Yet it is what Moses commanded in Deuteronomy 15:1. In Proverbs 3:5–6, Solomon urged his son and all Israel to trust the Lord with all their hearts, including when they were confronted with such commands. Deuteronomy 15:9–10 even warned Israel not to anticipate the seventh year and stop making loans. In Proverbs 3, Solomon urged his son and all Israel not to shrink from helping neighbors until a more advantageous time (vv. 9, 28). Solomon was obeying Moses by teaching God's instruction in pursuit of a righteous society that would shine with the very glory of God.

Table 1.1: The Influence of Deuteronomy 6 and 17 on Proverbs 3					
Proverbs 3		**Deuteronomy 6**		**Deuteronomy 17**	
3:1	"My son"	6:2	"your son"	17:20	"his sons"
		6:7	"your sons"		
3:1	"let your heart keep my commands	6:6	"these words which I command you … on your heart"	17:19	"it shall be with him"
3:2	"length of days and years of life"	6:2	"lengthen your days"	17:20	"continue long"
3:16	"length of days"				
3:3	"bind them [love and truth] on your neck"	6:8	"bind them [these words] as a sign on your hand"		
3:5	"trust in the LORD with all your heart	6:5	"love the LORD your God with all your heart"		
3:6	"in all your ways know him"	6:7	"talk about them … when you walk in the way"	17:19	"he shall read in it all the days of his life"
3:17	wisdom's "ways" are pleasant				
3:23	"then you will walk safely in your way"				
3:7	"Do not be wise in your own eyes"			17:19	"lest his heart be exalted over his brothers"
3:14	wisdom better profit than "silver" or "gold"			17:17	"silver and gold he shall not multiply for himself in excess"
3:21	"My son, do not let them [wisdom and discretion] depart from your eyes"	6:8	"they shall be as frontlets between your eyes"		
3:23–24	"walk … in your way … when you lie down "	6:7	"talk about them … when you walk in the way, and when you lie down"		
*Biblical text adapted by author from ESV.					

Supreme concern for Yahweh prompts fathers to teach their sons; this relationship cannot rightly be reversed. Exalting sons over the Lord would break the first commandment, with the result that teaching sons this very commandment to sons would expose the father's hypocrisy. Whole-life love for Yahweh results in his commandments being on the heart; this relationship cannot rightly be reversed either. Devotion to commandments divorced from love for the Lord would also break the primary commandment, leading only to an onerous and condemning sense of duty.

These laws could only be fulfilled by those whose lives were dominated by the reality that the Lord alone is God. Love for God was to find expression in a consuming desire to please him, in a commitment to obey him, and in a constant preoccupation of mind, heart, and imagination with his wonders. Only those who lived to worship Yahweh as an expression of such love, only those who trusted him more than what they could see with their eyes, would be able to convey his laws to their children. If these commands were rightly obeyed and conveyed in Israel, the rising generation would be told the glorious deeds of the Lord (Ps. 78:4), so that they would sing his praises to their children (v. 6) such that "a people yet to be created may praise the LORD" (Ps. 102:18).

2

BRING THEM UP IN THE DISCIPLINE AND INSTRUCTION OF THE LORD

Family Discipleship among the First Christians

Robert L. Plummer

I t's Sunday schools!" he told me. "They've destroyed the faith of children!" Such was the assertion made to me by a father in San Antonio. Over a plate of Italian food, this man proceeded to offer a brief historical sketch of what he saw as the systematic removal of parental responsibility for the discipleship of children. This happened, he believed, because churches have institutionalized children's programming.

To be sure, this well-meaning man *did* make some good points about the impotence of many men in the spiritual leadership of their households. At the same time, is church-based children's programming really to blame for this impotency? And is the abolition of Sunday school really the answer? The man's analysis seemed, at best, like an extreme and reactionary response to a problem that is much broader than a congregation's Sunday school or children's programs.

Since that conversation several years ago, I have been pleased to see the publication of many more resources devoted to a thoughtful discussion of the role of families and churches in the Christian nurture of children. This chapter is part of that ongoing conversation. My purpose is to investigate the New Testament and other writings from the first three centuries of Christian faith, asking the question, How, during this time period, did discipleship occur in the context of Christian families—or did it? What were the expectations for Christian training in the household? And how did the community of faith partner with believing households?

FAMILY RELATIONS IN THE BIBLICAL METANARRATIVE

The inspired authors of the New Testament wrote within the framework of a foundational story—a "metanarrative"—that they assumed on the basis of the Old Testament and the teachings of Jesus. It is possible to summarize the major movements of this metanarrative under four headings: creation, fall, redemption, and consummation. To understand the perspective of the earliest Christians on parent-child relations, let's first look together at what early Christians—not only the New Testament authors but also the ante-Nicene church fathers from the first three centuries of Christianity—assumed about families in light of the four movements of this divine metanarrative.

Creation

Early Christian writers consistently assumed that God created the entire world good and that family relationships are intrinsic to that creational order (see, e.g., 1 Tim. 2:13–15).[1] Unless they possess the rare supernatural gift of singleness, men and women are expected to marry (Matt. 19:12; 1 Cor. 7:2–7). Except for the believer's loyalty to God, the marriage relationship is to be unrivaled in intimacy and mutual commitment (Gen. 2:24; Matt. 19:5–6; Eph. 5:31). Fundamental to this expectation within the created order is the responsibility of parents to bear and to care for children—feeding them, clothing them, disciplining them, instructing them, and ultimately blessing them as they leave to form their own families (Isa. 49:15; Matt. 7:9–11; Gal. 4:1–2; 2 Cor. 12:14; 1 Tim. 5:8–14). Adult children live with an obligation to care for ill or aging parents (1 Tim. 5:4).

So prevalent were these assumptions in early Christianity that Christian writers repeatedly appealed to these tangible realities as analogies for spiritual matters (see, e.g., Matt. 7:11; 1 Thess. 2:7, 11–12; 1 Tim.

---

1. See also Ignatius of Antioch, *To the Philadelphians*, 4.3–5. Unless otherwise indicated, quotations from church fathers in this chapter are from Michael Holmes, *The Apostolic Fathers: Greek Texts and English Translations*, rev. ed. (Grand Rapids, Mich.: Baker Academic, 1999).

1:2; Philem. 1:10). In his teachings, Jesus assumed this creation-based reality of family. For example, in Matthew 7:11, Jesus declared, "If you
then, who are evil, know how to give good gifts to your children, how
much more will your Father who is in heaven give good things to those
who ask him!" Notice how, even in a world stained by sin, Jesus assumed
a benevolent parental attitude toward children—an attitude that seems
to be rooted in creational structures. Similarly, early Christian writers assumed the universal obligation of children to obey even while admitting
the undisputed reality of their disobedience (see, e.g., Heb. 12:5–11).

Fall

Early Christian writers also consistently affirmed the brokenness of the
present world order. Due to the rebellion of our first parents, all creation
groans beneath the weight of sin (Gen. 3:1–24; Rom. 8:20–22). Sometimes,
people talk about coming from dysfunctional families. The reality is that,
because of sin, we are all "dysfunctional" at the deepest level. Disharmony
in family relationships is a sign of our fallenness. Children are exasperating
and disobedient (Mark 13:12; 1 Tim. 1:9; 2 Tim. 3:2). Parents are harsh,
neglectful, even evil (Isa. 49:15; Col. 3:21; 1 Tim. 5:8)—all because our
world is broken.

Because of the brokenness of our world, family members do not do
naturally what they ought to do. Members of Christian families must be
instructed and trained in their obligations to one another. Husbands and
wives must be reminded to love their spouses and children in Christ-
honoring ways (Eph. 5:22–33; Titus 2:4). In a world untainted by sin,
such obligations would have been natural and spontaneous; now, however, such God-honoring behavior is impossible apart from the regenerative work of the Holy Spirit. Even born-again believers must be renewed
daily through the application of God's Word to their hearts by the Holy
Spirit. A sixteenth-century pastor named Martin Luther had this to say
about the selfish tendency of a fallen man when he considers his familial
duties:

> [O]ur natural reason . . . takes a look at married life . . . and says, "Alas,
> must I rock the baby, wash its diapers, make its bed, smell its stench,
> stay up nights with it, take care of it when it cries, heal its rashes and
> sores, and on top of that care for my wife, provide for her, labor at my
> trade, take care of this and take care of that, do this and do that, endure

this and endure that, and whatever else of bitterness and drudgery married life involves? What, should I make such a prisoner of myself? O you poor, wretched fellow, have you taken a wife? [Woe, woe] upon such wretchedness and bitterness! It is better to remain free and lead a peaceful, carefree life; I will become a priest or a nun and compel my children to do likewise."

Luther then showed how a Christian might look at the same mundane tasks of family life through the eyes of faith:

What then does Christian faith say to this? It opens its eyes, looks upon all these insignificant, distasteful, and despised duties in the Spirit, and is aware that they are all adorned with divine approval as with the costliest gold and jewels. It says, "O God, because I am certain that you have created me as a man and have from my body begotten this child, I also know for a certainty that it meets with your perfect pleasure. I confess to [you] that I am not worthy to rock the little baby or to wash its diapers, or to be entrusted with the care of the child and its mother. How is it that I, without any merit, have come to this distinction of being certain that I am serving [your] creature and [your] most precious will? O how gladly will I do so, though the duties should be even more insignificant and despised! Neither frost not heat, neither drudgery nor labor, will distress or dissuade me, for I am certain that it is thus pleasing in [your] sight."[2]

Family life exposes our own sinful tendencies as well as forcing us to deal with the sins of people around us. As a result, family life can result not only in great joy but also in great frustration (see 1 Cor. 7:28).

Yes, children *are* a wonderful blessing from the Lord (Ps. 127:3–5). Yet anyone who has spent any time with children must also agree that these blessings can sometimes be quite exasperating. "Every child is sometimes infuriating," C. S. Lewis observed, "[and] most children are not infrequently odious."[3] Sociological studies report that many men find the addition of small children to the household to be a disheartening relational and emotional challenge. One researcher discovered that some of the

---

2. Martin Luther, "The Estate of Marriage" (1522) in *Martin Luther's Basic Theological Writings*, 2nd ed., ed. Timothy F. Lull (Minneapolis: Fortress Press, 2005), 159.
3. C. S. Lewis, *The Four Loves*, in *The Inspirational Writings of C. S. Lewis* (Edison, NJ: Inspiration Press, 1994), 286.

angriest people in society were parents with small children.[4] It is helpful to acknowledge openly these effects of the fall, particularly in the context of the community of faith. Otherwise, Christian parents may find themselves struggling silently in daily failure and frustration, unwilling to seek help and unable to see their struggles in light of God's grace and the ultimate promise of a new creation.

Redemption

The inspired authors of the New Testament present the gospel of Jesus as the fulfillment of God's promise to establish a new covenant with his people, to write his truth on their hearts, and to place his Spirit within them (Jer. 31:31; Ezek. 36:24–27; Luke 22:20). On the cross, Jesus endured God's judgment for the sins of humanity; through his resurrection, Jesus initiated God's new creation. Part of his ongoing restoration of the created order includes the restoration of proper relationships between parents and children. Regarding John the Baptist, Luke reported that the herald of the new covenant would "go before [the Messiah] in the spirit and power of Elijah, to turn the hearts of the fathers to their children, and the disobedient to the wisdom of the just, to make ready for the Lord a people prepared" (Luke 1:17).

By faith, all redeemed persons—Jews and Gentiles alike—become members of God's family and heirs of the promises made to Abraham (Gal. 3:29). As children of Abraham through faith early Christians embraced the Old Testament Scriptures as their Bible (1 Tim. 4:13; 2 Tim. 3:16). They viewed passages in the Old Testament about the importance of parents passing on spiritual truth to their children (Gen. 18:19; Deut. 6:4–9; 32:46) as authoritative divine instruction. The "newness" of the new covenant was found in the Messiah's consummated work of salvation and in the regenerative work in the Spirit—not in any radical alterations in parent-child relationships.

---

4. "Angriest Americans: Young People, Parents," LiveScience.com, posted December 3, 2009, http://www.msnbc.msn.com/id/34264093/ns/health-behavior/ (accessed December 14, 2009). The full details of the study reported in this article are to be found in Scott Schieman, "The Sociological Study of Anger: Basic Social Patterns and Contexts" in *International Handbook of Anger: Constituent and Concomitant Biological, Psychological, and Social Processes*, ed. Michael Potegal, Gerhard Stemmler, and, Charles Spielberger (New York: Springer, 2010), 329–48; and Neil Chethik, *VoiceMale: What Husbands Really Think about Their Marriages, Their Wives, Sex, Housework, and Commitment* (New York: Simon & Schuster, 2006).

Consummation

Biological and adoptive family relations, while vitally important in this life, are not eternal. Jesus made it clear that, in the new heavens and earth, marriages will no longer mark our existence; all believers will be "like [the] angels in heaven" (Matt. 22:30). If our children stand beside us in eternity, it will not be as our children but as our blood-redeemed brothers and sisters (Rev. 7:9–12). Even as parents rightly pour out their lives in caring for their children, they must realize that what matters eternally is that their children know and love the Lord. The category of biological lineage or legal progeny will fade into insignificance at the dawning of eternity (Matt. 3:9).

> "While Jesus affirmed marriage and blessed children, he conceived of the community of believers in familial terms transcending those of people's natural relations."
>
> ❖❖
>
> Andreas Köstenberger
> *God, Marriage and Family*

Even in this life, foundational family loyalties must pale in comparison with our ultimate loyalty to the triune God. Jesus said, "If anyone comes to me and does not hate his own father and mother and wife and children and brothers and sisters, yes, and even his own life, he cannot be my disciple" (Luke 14:26).[5] This does not absolve believing parents of their responsibility to train their children in the fear of God; it does mean that every aspect of parenting is to be undertaken in light of a greater allegiance to the glory of God.

INSTRUCTIONS FOR FAMILIES IN THE NEW TESTAMENT

Beyond the overarching contours of the divine metanarrative, what explicit New Testament instructions do we find addressed to parents? The New Testament authors regularly remind parents of their basic creational

---

5. On Luke 14:26, Robert Stein comments, "From Matt 10:37 we know that this means to 'love [one's family] less.' This is evident from Gen 29:30–31, where Jacob's greater love for Rachel (29:30) is phrased as hating Leah (29:31, RSV). . . . A person who commits himself or herself to Christ will develop a greater love for both neighbor and family, although at times loving and following Christ may be seen as renunciation, rejection, or hate if the family does not share the same commitment to Christ." Robert H. Stein, *Luke*, New American Commentary, vol. 24 (Nashville: Broadman & Holman, 1992), 397.

obligation to nurture and to love their children (Col. 3:21; 1 Tim. 2:15; 5:8). This included an apparent assumption that Christian fathers should discipline their children for wrongdoings (Heb. 12:9).

"He Must Manage His Household Well"

One of the New Testament qualifications for men to be elders or deacons in the church is the capacity to manage a household well (1 Tim. 3:4–5, 12; Titus 1:6). This does not mean that fathers can somehow force their children to become believers.[6] It does mean that, as long as their children are living in their households, elders and deacons must discipline and love their children so that their families maintain orderly and respectful household environments. This is not merely a suggestion for elders and deacons; it is an essential expectation for their role.

"In the Discipline and Instruction of the Lord"

Throughout the New Testament, the inspired authors consistently assumed that believers would be eager and able to spread the good news of Jesus (Matt. 28:18–20; Eph. 6:15–17; Phil. 2:16; Col. 4:6; 1 Thess. 4:12; 1 Peter 2:9–12).[7] At one point, Paul spoke of the loving concern that he expected a believing spouse to have for the salvation of a nonbelieving husband or wife (1 Cor 7:12–16). Though it is rarely mentioned in any explicit way, part of the deep love that parents have for children includes a desire for them to know and to respond to the gospel—a concern that a Christian is always to have for all persons (1 Cor. 10:33–11:1). The New Testament passage that speaks most clearly about this spiritual concern of a parent for child is Ephesians 6:4: "Fathers, do not provoke your children to anger, but bring them up in the discipline and instruction of the Lord."

In looking at this text, one must first note that Paul singled out *the father* as primarily responsible for his children's moral and spiritual care.

---

6. The adjective *pistos* in Titus 1:6 refers to the children's faithfulness—that is to say, in this context, submission or respectful obedience. See George W. Knight III, *The Pastoral Epistles: A Commentary on the Greek Text*, New International Greek Testament Commentary (Grand Rapids: Eerdmans; Carlisle, UK: Paternoster, 1992), 289–90.
7. Robert L. Plummer, *Paul's Understanding of the Church's Mission: Did the Apostle Paul Expect the Early Christian Communities to Evangelize?* Paternoster Biblical Monographs (Milton Keynes, UK: Authentic, Paternoster, 2006).

This focus on fathers does not exclude mothers; it does, however, highlight the biblical headship of the husband—a theme reiterated throughout
Scripture (Eph. 5:22–23). A father is uniquely responsible to God for his
children.

Early Christians did possess some practical parental instructions in
Proverbs and other Old Testament texts (see, e.g., Deut. 6:4–9; Prov.
13:24; 19:18; 22:15). Particularly in the New Testament, however, the instructions for parents tend to be more general.[8] As a result these inspired
instructions are equally applicable in oral and written cultures—in environments with a wealth of Christian resources as well as those with almost none. In one setting, a father might fulfill Ephesians 6:4 by sharing
the stories about Jesus that he himself has learned orally while he and his
son work side by side in a field. In another setting, a father might warn or
encourage his daughter via a timely text message sent to her cell phone.
In yet another time or place, a father might employ puppets or songs or a
family project to present the truths of the Bible in a creative and winsome
manner. The biblical principle of Ephesians 6:4 allows a broad range of
possible expressions. What remains the same, regardless of context or culture, is that God has called parents—and particularly fathers—to function
as primary faith trainers in their children's lives.

In the narrative of Acts, the reports of household conversions highlight the importance of parents passing on the faith to their children. In
three separate instances, a father's initial interest in the Christian faith resulted in his entire family responding to the gospel (Acts 10:1–2; 16:31–
33; 18:8). The biblical descriptions of what the persons in the household
did—they heard, received, and believed the proclaimed message—suggest that infants were not included among the baptized members of the
household.[9] What is clear in Acts is the foundational role of a father in
guiding his family toward Christian faithfulness. In one instance where
no father is mentioned, the mother takes on this foundational role (Acts
16:1–3, 15). Other texts that identify households by husband or wife—
perhaps indicating which person was the initial believer—further highlight the foundational spiritual role of parents (1 Cor. 1:11, 16; 16:15–16;
2 Tim. 1:5).

---

8. William Barclay, *Train Up a Child; Educational Ideals in the Ancient World* (Philadelphia:
Westminster, 1959), 235–36.

9. Everett Ferguson, *Baptism in the Early Church: History, Theology, and Liturgy in the First Five
Centuries* (Grand Rapids: Eerdmans, 2009), 178.

"Do Not Provoke Your Children to Anger"

Paul was realistic about the challenge of sinful fathers raising sinful children. One natural reaction to the demands of raising a child is frustration or anger, which may in turn provoke a similar response in the child (Col. 3:21). Apart from the renewing work of God's Spirit, sinful fathers are likely to leave a legacy of emotionally abused and resentful children. Empowered by God's Spirit, however, not only can Christian fathers _not_ provoke their children, but they can even "bring them up in the discipline and instruction of the Lord" (Eph. 6:4).[10] Paul did not provide step-by-step details for bringing up children "in the discipline and instruction of the Lord." The text does clearly indicate that Christian fathers should train their children in gospel-centered spiritual truths ("instruction"), as well as providing discipline that is shaped by the character of Jesus ("of the Lord").

"Children, Obey Your Parents"

The primary explicit instruction given to children in the New Testament is that children must obey their parents (Eph. 6:1). In Colossians 3:20–21, Paul even declared, "Children, obey your parents in everything, for this pleases the Lord." (In telling children to obey their parents in "everything," Paul was, of course, using hyperbole. The apostle was not commanding children to obey instructions that were iniquitous or ridiculous.)[11] Similarly, in Ephesians 6:1–3, Paul wrote: "Children, obey your parents in the Lord for this is right. 'Honor your father and mother' (this is the first commandment with a promise), 'that it may go well with you and that you may live long in the land.'" Paul qualified this exhortation with the prepositional phrase, "in the Lord." What Paul seems to have been saying was that obedience to parents is always informed by the lordship of the Messiah and that bowing one's will to parents is ultimately an expression of bowing one's knee to the Lord. Paul left no room for ambiguity. Obeying one's parents "is right."

By quoting Exodus 20:12, Paul reminded his readers that this obedience stands in continuity with expectations for families in the Old Testament.

---

10. In reference to Ephesians 6:4, Ernest Best writes, "[Fathers] are not to irritate their children but to provide the conditions under which Christian maturity can develop." Ernest Best, _Ephesians_, New Testament Guides (Sheffield, UK: JSOT, 1993), 57.

11. See further discussion on detecting and interpreting hyperbole, see Robert L. Plummer, _40 Questions about Interpreting the Bible_ (Grand Rapids: Kregel, 2010), 219–26.

But there is this difference: empowered by God's Spirit, New Testament believers can fulfill what was previously impossible. Believing children can honor their parents and experience both eternal and temporal blessings.

Later in the New Testament, Paul reminded Timothy, a young man who came from a household with a believing mother, to treasure the spiritual legacy that he had received through his mother and grandmother (2 Tim. 1:5–6). Paul's conversation with Timothy reminds Christian parents today what a privilege they have in setting the spiritual course for their children's lives.

PARTNERSHIP BETWEEN CHURCH AND HOUSEHOLD IN THE NEW TESTAMENT

New Testament instructions to parents and children were first communicated orally to an assembled body of believers. The presence of direct commands to children in the texts (Eph. 6:1; Col. 3:20–21) suggests that children of various ages and varying commitments were present with their parents. Both parents and children received instructions in the presence of one another and in the presence of the community of faith.

But how did early Christians cooperate and share in the training of one another's children? The text of the New Testament does not explicitly provide this information. Believers did, however, regularly meet for fellowship and worship in one another's homes as well as sacrificially sharing material resources (Acts 2:44–47). Such habits would, at the very least, provide a winsome context for the children in attendance. If pagan guests could visit a Christian gathering and exclaim, "God is really among you," (1 Cor 14:25), certainly children in regular attendance could be expected to do the same. If the nonbelieving outsider could look at the followers of Jesus and say, "See how they love one another"[12] (cf. John 13:35), certainly the child of Christian parents could be expected to reach the same judgment.

While the New Testament clearly assigns parents the primary role of managing and instructing their households, biblical authors also recognized that God gifts specific people within the local community of faith to instruct and to shepherd the congregation (Eph. 4:11; 1 Tim. 3:2). Every man is called to shepherd his family (Eph. 5:25–29; 6:4), but not every

---

12. Tertullian, *Apology* 39.7. For texts from Tertullian, see http://www.tertullian.org/Latin/Latin.htm.

man is gifted in quite the same way to function in the role of a teacher. In some cases, persons other than elders are gifted to teach within in the community of faith (Col. 3:16; cf. Heb. 5:12; James 3:1). The recognition of such gifting within the broader community suggests that children might benefit from gathering to receive teaching from God-gifted instructors other than their parents. In some cases, these gatherings might occur in age-organized contexts.

EXAMPLES AND INSTRUCTIONS FOR FAMILIES AMONG EARLY CHRISTIAN WRITERS

In the Christian writings that followed the New Testament era, the instructions for parents are similar to the ones found in the New Testament. Early Christian leaders reminded husbands and wives of their obligation to love one another, to live in orderly households, and to love their children.[13]

"I Received from My Parents This Good Confession"

Over and over, parents were called to train their children in the Christian faith:

> You shall not withhold your hand from your son or your daughter, but from their youth you shall teach them the fear of God. (*Didache* 4.9, first or second century AD)

> Let our children receive the instruction that is in Christ: let them learn how strong humility is before God, what pure love is able to accomplish before God, how the fear of him is good and great and saves all those who live in it in holiness with a pure mind. (*1 Clement* 21.8, late first or early second century)[14]

> Fathers, "bring up your children in the nurture and admonition of the Lord" and teach them the Holy Scriptures, and also trades, that they

---

13. See, e.g., *1 Clement* 21.6, 8; Ignatius of Antioch, *To the Philadelphians* 4.3, 5; *Epistle of Barnabas* 19.5.
14. English translations of these texts from the *Didache* and *1 Clement* are from Michael W. Holmes, ed. and trans., *The Apostolic Fathers: Greek Texts and English Translations*, 3rd ed. (Grand Rapids: Baker, 2007).

may not indulge in idleness. Now the Scripture says, "A righteous father educates his children well; his heart shall rejoice in a wise son." (Ignatius, *To the Philadelphians* 4.5, late first or early second century)[15]

You shall not abort a child nor, again, commit infanticide. You must not withhold your hand from your son or daughter, but from their youth you shall teach them the fear of God (*Epistle of Barnabas* 19.5, late first or early second century)

[Christians] marry just like everyone else, and they have children, but they do not cast out their offspring. (*Epistle to Diognetus* 5.6, second century)

Then instruct your wives to continue in the faith delivered to them and in love and purity, cherishing their own husbands in all fidelity and loving all others equally in all chastity, and to teach their children with instruction that leads to the fear of God. (Polycarp, *To the Philippians* 4.2, second century)

As in Ephesians 6:4, these texts do not provide step-by-step instructions for the parental discipleship of children. Yet parents are presented with a fundamental obligation to function as primary faith-trainers in their children's lives.

This second-century account of martyrdom makes it clear that early Christian parents *did* impress vital theological truths on their children:

A man called Paeon stood up and said, "I also am a Christian."
The prefect Rusticus said: "Who taught you?"
Paeon said, "I received from my parents this good confession."
Euelpistus said, "I listened indeed gladly to the words of Justin, but I too received Christianity from my parents."
The prefect Rusticus said, "Where are your parents?"
Euelpistus said: "In Cappadocia."
Rusticus said to Hierax: "Where are your parents?"
He answered, saying, "Our true father is Christ, and our mother our faith in him. My earthly parents are dead, and I was dragged away from Iconium in Phrygia before coming hither."[16]

---

15. This longer version of Ignatius's letter is found in the *Ante-Nicene Fathers*, ed. Alexander Roberts and James Donaldson. English translations of the letter are by these editors.
16. *Martyrdom of Justin and His Companions* 4 (ca. 165), quoted by James Riley Estep Jr., "The Christian Nurture of Children in the Second and Third Centuries," in *Nurturing*

As in Paul's letter to Ephesus early Christian writers do not provide specific examples of how children must be instructed. Yet the basic obligation remains clear. Just as the earliest Christians in the post–New Testament period found different ways to convey the faith to their children, so today, believers in varying cultures and with diverse educational backgrounds will find different ways to convey the gospel to their children in winsome and faithful ways.

> → "I received from my parents this good confession," Paeon said to Rusticus in the second century. Could the children in your church make such a statement? In family-equipping congregations, parents are trained to convey Christian doctrines to the children in their homes. How does your church train parents to equip their children to articulate the "good confession" of Christian faith? ←

"God Is Angry with You"

When parents failed to heed their obligation to pass on the "good confession" of a living faith to their children, the results could be disastrous. The unknown author of a second-century text known as Shepherd of Hermas recognized the tragedy of such failures. Throughout this document, a divine messenger upbraids Hermas—the Christian man addressed in the text—for his failure to provide spiritual leadership for his family:

> God is angry with you . . . in order that you may convert your family, which has sinned against the Lord and against you, their parents. But you are so fond of your children that you have not corrected your family, but have allowed it to become terribly corrupt. This is why the Lord is angry with you. But he will heal all your past deeds that have been done by your family, for because of their sins and transgressions you have been corrupted by the cares of this life. (Shepherd of Hermas, *Vision* 1.3.1)[17]

Children's Spirituality: Christian Perspectives and Best Practices, ed. Holly Catterton Allen (Eugene, OR: Wipf and Stock, Cascade Books, 2008), 71. See also Justin Martyr, *First Apology* 15.

17. Also see Shepherd of Hermas, *Vision* 2.3.1, 3.9.1; *Mandate* 12.3.6; and *Similitude* 5.3.9, 7.1.6.

When children failed to obey their parents, such failure was viewed concurrently as disobedience to God, with temporal and eternal consequences.[18]

PARTNERSHIP BETWEEN CHURCH AND HOUSEHOLD IN THE FIRST THREE CENTURIES OF CHRISTIAN FAITH

In writings from the first three centuries of Christianity, children were addressed alongside their parents, reminding us that children were part of Christian gatherings.[19] In a few texts, Christian leaders gave general exhortations about the importance of training the next generation. The most natural way to read these passages is as proclamations addressed primarily to parents. These passages do not, however, preclude the broader community's involvement in children's discipleship. "Let us fear the Lord Jesus Christ, whose blood was given for us," Clement of Rome urged his entire congregation in the late first century. "Let us respect our leaders; let us honor the older men; let us instruct the young with instruction that leads to the fear of God."[20] From Clement's commands to the believers in Rome, it appears that the community of faith bore a corporate responsibility to train the young (*neoi*, that is to say, persons who were no longer children but also not yet fully mature).

Pastors in ancient churches were quite willing to engage personally in the spiritual development of young people. According to Eusebius of Caesarea (AD 260–340), the apostle John once entrusted a child to the care of a local elder. The young boy was baptized—but then, as a young adult, turned astray and joined a gang of thieves. Hearing this, the apostle John mounted a horse and personally pursued the young man into the mountains to call him to repentance,[21] crying out, "Why, my son, do you flee from me, your own father, unarmed, aged? Pity me, my son; fear not; you have still hope of life. I will give account to Christ for you. If need be, I will willingly endure your death as the Lord suffered death for us. For you, I would give up my life. Stand and believe! Christ has sent me!"

By the second and third centuries, the practice of infant baptism seems to have been widespread in many areas, with baptized children partaking

---

18. Ignatius of Antioch, *To the Philadelphians* 4.3 (long version); Shepherd of Hermas, *Similitude* 7.1.6.
19. Ignatius, *To the Smyrnaeans* 13.1 (long version); Ignatius, *To Polycarp* 8.2 (long version)
20. *1 Clement* 21.6.
21. Eusebius of Caesarea, *Historia ecclesiastica* 3.23. Thanks to Jared Kennedy for pointing out this story to us.

of the Lord's Supper.[22] Even if such practices represent well-intended mis-apprehensions of the apostolic understanding of baptism, they also demonstrate the early church's passion to pass along the Christian faith to the next generation. In the third century, Cyprian mentioned a boy of unspecified age who served as a lector—a reader of the Scriptures—in the church.[23]

> Parents in ancient Rome often "exposed" unwanted infants, abandoning them to die or to be gathered by slave-traders or purveyors of prostitution. Even among the earliest Christians, this practice was forbidden—but Christians apparently went beyond merely forbidding such abandonment. Believers in Jesus rescued, nurtured, and raised these infants in their own homes. At least as early as the early fifth century, churches were establishing clear procedures to make certain that members were rescuing children rather than kidnapping them.[24]

AN AGE-OLD STRUGGLE

"It's Sunday schools!" he assured me in that Italian restaurant in San Antonio. "They've destroyed the faith of children!"—and he blamed church-based children's programs for the failure of parents to disciple their progeny. And yet, it is clear from the New Testament and other early Christian texts that, centuries before Sunday schools even existed, Christian parents struggled at times to fulfill their calling to disciple their children. Then, as now, it was not a church program that caused the problem or provided the solution. What was needed was—and is—to call parents back to the gospel of Jesus Christ. As parents live genuine lives of repentance and faith together in community with other believers, their faith will be both "caught by" and "taught to" each generation. Parents must embrace their roles not only as providers and disciplinarians but also as primary disciple-makers in their children's lives.

---

22. Estep cites Hippolytus, *Apostolike Paradosis* 21, 23 as well as Cyprian, *On the Lapsed* 25, in Estep, "Christian Nurture of Children in the Second and Third Centuries," 68–69.
23. Cyprian of Carthage, *Epistles* 32, cited in Estep, "Christian Nurture of Children in the Second and Third Centuries," 67.
24. The canons of the Council of Vaisons (AD 442) as well as a law from Emperor Honorius (AD 384–423) testify to these guidelines. It is very likely that children were being rescued at least as early as the second century. Andrew Cain and Noel Lenski, eds., *The Power of Religion in Late Antiquity* (Farnham, Surrey, UK; Burlington, VT: Ashgate, 2010), 123–26. For a child to be adopted in the Roman Empire, it was typically required that the biological father be known; therefore, these children could not be legally adopted.

3

THE FATHER, THE SON, AND THE HOLY SPIRIT

The Trinity as Theological Foundation for Family Ministry

Bruce A. Ware

T he title of this chapter may raise some immediate questions in the minds of readers: Is there really a connection between the doctrine of the Trinity and the design and practice of family ministry? To many persons, the Trinity seems to be nearly impossible to understand and quite removed from real-life issues. How could the Trinity truly be relevant to *anything* that takes place in our daily lives, including the issues related to church and family ministry?

It may come as something of a surprise to some readers that the doctrine of the Trinity is really and truly one of the most practical doctrines in the whole of what we believe in the Christian faith. Why? Because the Trinity helps us to understand how the persons of the Godhead—the Father, the Son, and the Holy Spirit—relate to one another and so work in this world as well as how the triune God has designed many relationships among us humans to take place. Wherever you have human relationships—which is about everywhere you look!—you have the opportunity to ask, How do relationships among the trinitarian persons help us understand how our relationships are to be lived out in ways that better reflect something of the triune God and better express God's designed purposes for us, his human creatures made in his image?

In order to see how the doctrine of the Trinity is foundational for family ministry, we will consider three areas. First, a brief summary of the doctrine of the Trinity will clarify what it is that Christians ought to believe. Second, we will consider some broad areas of trinitarian relationships in order to see how the doctrine of Trinity provides helpful example and instruction for how we should live in relationship with others. Finally, we will explore how truths about the Trinity, rightly understood, provide foundational underpinnings for family-equipping ministries in the church.[1]

The Nicene Creed
✛

I believe in one God, the Father Almighty, Maker of heaven and earth, and of all things visible and invisible.

I believe in one Lord Jesus Christ, the only-begotten Son of God, begotten of the Father before all worlds; God of God, Light of Light, very God of very God; begotten, not made, being of one substance with the Father, by whom all things were made; who, for us and for our salvation, came down from heaven, and was incarnate by the Holy Spirit of the virgin Mary, and was made man; and was crucified also for us under Pontius Pilate; he suffered and was buried; and the third day he rose again, according to the Scriptures; and ascended into heaven, and sits on the right hand of the Father; and he shall come again, with glory, to judge the living and the dead; his kingdom shall have no end.

I believe in the Holy Spirit, the Lord and Giver of Life; who proceeds from the Father; who with the Father and the Son together is worshipped and glorified; who spoke by the prophets.[2]

---

1. For further study of the doctrine of the Trinity, both as a central doctrine of the Christian faith and for the relevance and application it has for the Christian life, I recommend the following: Donald Fairbairn, *Life in the Trinity: An Introduction to Theology with the Help of the Church Fathers* (Downers Grove, IL: InterVarsity Press, 2009); Robert Letham, *The Holy Trinity: In Scripture, History, Theology, and Worship* (Phillipsburg, NJ: P&R, 2004); Bruce A. Ware, *Father, Son, and Holy Spirit: Relationships, Roles, and Relevance* (Wheaton, IL: Crossway, 2005); James R. White, *The Forgotten Trinity: Recovering the Heart of Christian Belief* (Minneapolis: Bethany House, 1998).
2. For more on the Council of Nicaea and this creed, which represents the understanding not only of the Council of Nicaea in 325 but also the Council of Constantinople in 381, see Ware, *Father, Son, and Holy Spirit*, 36–41.

WHAT DO CHRISTIANS BELIEVE ABOUT THE TRINITY?

The Christian faith affirms that there is one and only one God. Moses instructed the children of Israel, "To you it was shown that you might know that the LORD, He is God; there is no other besides Him" (Deut. 4:35 NASB). God himself boldly declares through the prophet Isaiah, "Besides Me there is no God. I will gird you, though you have not known Me; that men may know from the rising to the setting of the sun that there is no one besides Me. I am the LORD, and there is no other" (Isa. 45:5–6 NASB). James in the New Testament agrees. "You believe that God is one," he writes. "You do well; the demons also believe, and shudder" (James 2:19 NASB).

Christian faith also affirms that this one God eternally exists and is fully expressed in three persons: the Father, the Son, and the Holy Spirit. Each member of the Godhead is equally God, each is eternally God, and each is fully God—not three gods but three persons of the one eternal Godhead. Each person is equal in essence to the other divine persons. Each possesses fully and simultaneously the identically same, eternal divine nature. Yet each is also an eternal and distinct personal expression of that one and undivided divine nature.

The equality of essence among the members of the Trinity is greater than the equality that exists among human beings or among any other finite reality. For example, my wife, Jodi, and I are equally human, in that each of us possesses a human nature. Her nature is of the same kind as my nature—that is to say, *human nature*. Our equality is real and actual "equality of kind." Each of us has the same kind of nature as the other.

Equality of Identity in the Trinity

The equality of the three divine persons is even more firmly grounded than my equality with Jodi. The Father, the Son, and the Holy Spirit each possesses not merely the same kind of nature—that is to say, *divine nature*. The Father, the Son, and the Holy Spirit each also possesses fully and eternally the *identically same nature*. Their equality, then, is not merely an equality of kind but what might be called an "equality of identity."

There is no stronger grounding possible for the full equality of persons of the Godhead than this: the Son possesses eternally and fully the identically same nature as the nature that is possessed eternally and fully by the Father and by the Spirit; hence, their equality is not merely an equality of kind but is in fact an equality of identity. And so we affirm today what the church has explicitly affirmed as orthodox since the days of the Councils of Nicaea in AD 325 and Constantinople in AD 381: the oneness of God—and thus the full essential equality of the Father, the Son, and the Holy Spirit—is constituted precisely in a oneness of divine nature possessed fully, simultaneously, and eternally by each of the divine persons. There is one and only one God, precisely because there is one and only one eternal and infinite divine nature which is the common possession and full possession of the Father, and of the Son, and of the Holy Spirit. God is *one* in essence and *three* in persons.

Roles and Relationships within the Trinity

Now notice this carefully: since by nature or essence the Father, Son, and Spirit are identically the same, what distinguishes the Father from the Son and each of them from the Spirit *cannot* be their one and undivided divine essence. At the level of the divine essence, each is quite literally indistinguishable as each possesses eternally and fully the identically same divine nature.

What, then, distinguishes the Father from the Son and each of them from the Spirit? What distinguishes the persons of the Trinity are (1) the particular *roles* that each has within the Trinity and in the work each carries out in the world, and, (2) the respective *relationships* that each has with the other divine persons and within the creation that the triune God has made. Since the Father, Son, and Spirit must be distinct from each other as distinguishable persons, while they are in another sense identical to each other in their common essence, their distinction from one another must be in these areas of roles and relationships, since they cannot be distinct in regard to their divine essence. How, then, are the roles and relationships of the Father, the Son, and the Spirit, distinct from one another? And how do these distinctions help us in understanding better the ways in which the Trinity can provide a foundation for family-based ministry?

WHAT ARE THE DISTINCT ROLES AND RELATIONSHIPS OF THE TRINITARIAN PERSONS?

The Father, Son, and Holy Spirit are each fully God. They are each equally God. They each fully possess one undivided divine nature. Yet each person of the Godhead is different in role and relationship with respect to the others. To distinguish the roles and relationships that exist in among the triune persons, we might say this: the *Father* is supreme in authority among the persons of the Godhead, and he is responsible for devising the grand purposes and plans that take place through all of creation and redemption (see, e.g., Eph. 1:3–4, 9–11). The *Son* is under the Father's authority and seeks always to do the Father's will. Although the Son is fully God, he nonetheless takes his lead from the Father and seeks to glorify the Father in all that he does (see, e.g., John 8:28–29, 42). The *Spirit* is under both the Father and the Son. As the Son sought to glorify the Father in all he did, the Spirit seeks to glorify the Son, to the ultimate praise of the Father (see, e.g., John 16:14; 1 Cor. 12:3; Phil. 2:11).

To understand how these roles are expressed, consider some of the works that God accomplishes. Often we think of these as the works of "God," and rightly they are. Yet these are the works of the *triune God*, with the Father, Son, and Spirit each contributing to the whole of the work and together accomplishing all that God brings to pass.

Trinitarian Roles in God's Work of Redemption

Consider God's work of redemption: the Father purposed and planned that our redemption as sinners would be accomplished. The Father planned that it would take place through the work of his Son, such that his Son would have the highest place of exaltation in the end (Eph. 1:9–10). The Father is the one who chose us *in Jesus* before the world had yet been created (Eph. 1:3–4). The Father chose *the Son* to be the one who would come as our Savior and die for our sins (Acts 2:23; 1 Peter 1:20). When the Son came, he made it clear over and again that he came down from heaven to do his Father's will (John 6:38), even declaring in Gethsemane that his upcoming death on the cross was specifically the will of his Father (Matt. 26:39).

The Son, for his part, came in full obedience to the Father. His coming was not his own doing but occurred because of the Father's initiative (John 8:42). Of course the Son is in full agreement with this, his Father's will, but that it was the will of the Father is recognized and acknowledged by the Son over and over again. The Son had the distinct role of becoming incarnate in order to take on our sin and provide his life as a substitute sacrifice for us (Phil. 2:6–8; 1 Peter 2:24). While it is true that the Son bore our sin on the cross, it is also true that the Father is the one who put our sin upon his own Son, in order to save us through the death that he would bring about through his Son (Isa. 53:10; 2 Cor. 5:21).

The Spirit, for his part, came as the prophets foretold to anoint and empower the Son for the work that he was sent by the Father to accomplish (Isa. 11:2; 61:1–3; Luke 4:18–21). The Spirit so worked in the Son that he the Messiah was able to accomplish all of the good works and perform the miracles he did, as the Father directed him (John 5:19) and the Spirit empowered him (Acts 10:38). When the atoning work of the Son was complete, the Spirit raised Jesus from the dead (Rom 8:11) and empowered the disciples of Jesus on the day of Pentecost (Acts 2:1–21). As Peter makes clear in his sermon that day the Spirit's coming occurred because he was ultimately sent by the Father, though he was sent most directly upon these believers by the Son (John 15:26; Acts 2:33). The Spirit's coming upon believers was to empower the proclamation of the gospel (Acts 1:6–8), to regenerate unbelievers, to baptize them into the body of Christ (Titus 3:5; 1 Cor. 12:13), and to work in all who trust Jesus to make them fully like their Savior (2 Cor. 3:18).

Many more examples may be found throughout Scripture, but God's work in redemption is sufficient to illustrate this point: *God works as the Father, the Son, and the Spirit, with each person accomplishing the specific work that each one is responsible to do.* Within the carrying out of these roles, there seems to be a very clear relationship in which the Father is supreme in authority, the Son submits fully to the will of the Father, and the Spirit seeks to carry forward the work of the Son to the ultimate praise of the Father (Phil. 2:11).[3] The distinctions in their work, then, must be recognized if we are to understand rightly the outworking of God's purposes and plans.

Unity of Purpose and Harmony of Mission within the Trinity

One further truth is essential for us to understand this pattern: there is full harmony in the work of the triune God, with no jealousy or bitterness, only love and harmony. The Father never considers himself better than the Son or Spirit—even though he has authority over both and stands as the divine designer and grand architect of all that takes place! In fact, rather than putting himself forward, the Father designs all things so that his Son, not himself, is given the primary spotlight in the history of creation and redemption.

The Son never begrudges the fact that he is the Son under the authority of the Father. Just the opposite: the Son loves nothing more than

---

3. For further explication and clarification of submission structures within the Trinity, see Ware, *Father, Son, and Holy Spirit,* 46–66, 87–102.

to do the will of the Father (see, e.g., John 4:34). While always submitting completely and fully to the Father, the Son does so with joy and delight (Heb. 12:2). The Spirit, while being third in the Trinity and always under the ultimate authority of Father and Son, considers it his delight to honor and to glorify the Son (John 16:14; 1 Cor. 12:3).

Clearly, when we behold the Trinity for what it is, we should marvel! We should be amazed at the unity and harmony of this common work within authority and relationships that have marked their roles and responsibilities throughout all eternity. Unity of purpose and harmony of mission, yet with differentiation in lines of authority and submission within the Godhead! This truly is a marvel to consider.

TRINITARIAN FOUNDATIONS FOR FAMILY MINISTRY

How does this doctrine of the Trinity constitute the foundation for family ministry in the church? In short, the Trinity provides us with a model in which we understand the members of a family as fully equal in their value and dignity as human beings made in God's image. Yet each member has distinct roles and relationships within the family; these roles and relationships are worked out within an authority-submission structure that God designed as purposefully reflective of God himself.[4]

In other words, the Trinity presents us with the truth that the Father, the Son, and the Spirit are fully equal in their essence while also presenting the truth that the authority-submission structure of the Trinity is inviolable with the Father as supreme, the Son under the Father, and the Spirit under the Father and the Son. Each divine person is fully equal as God. Yet the Father and Son and Spirit each carries out a distinct role and does so within an eternal relational structure of authority and submission.

This trinitarian perspective helps us to understand the family. All the members of a family are equal in who they are as human beings. Each one is equal in value and dignity and worth; in this, they mirror the equality that we see among the three persons of the Trinity. Because of this equality

---

4. For interaction with alternative positions on this matter, see for example, Stephen D. Kovach and Peter R. Schemm, "A Defense of the Doctrine of the Eternal Subordination of the Son," _Journal of the Evangelical Theological Society_ 42 (1990): 461–76, and Benjamin B. Phillips, "Method Mistake: An Analysis of the Charge of Arianism in Complementarian Discussions of the Trinity," _Journal of Biblical Manhood and Womanhood_ (Spring 2008): 42–47.

of dignity and worth, each member of the family ought to be accorded respect and be treated as someone created in the image of God.

Also mirrored in the family are trinitarian distinctives that relate to roles and relationships. The husband and father has, under God, the highest place of authority in the household. His wife submits to him, and his children obey both him and his wife. The wife is under the authority of her husband, but is over the children in the household, partnering with their father to ensure that they learn godliness and obedience. The children are under the authority of both of their parents, understanding that they are to learn from their father and mother what is most important in life, all the while obeying their parents with joy and gladness. Both the equality and the distinctiveness that we see in the Trinity should be reflected in household relationships. The church's ministries must understand both this *equality* and this *differentiation* and seek to reinforce this in what the church encourages and teaches.

HOW CAN CHRISTIAN FAMILIES REFLECT TRINITARIAN ROLES AND RELATIONSHIPS?

Let's carefully consider some aspects of family relationships where the equality and differentiation of the members of a family can and should be seen as reflective of the equality and differentiation within the Trinity.

Implications for Husbands and Fathers

Married men and fathers must realize and embrace the truth that God has invested in them a special responsibility for the spiritual leadership that they should develop in relation both to their wives and children. In a real and vitally important sense, husbands and fathers bear responsibility for the Christian nurture of their households—a responsibility that differs from that of their wives and from other members of the household. The husband of the household is granted a privilege and a duty, before the Lord, to direct the discipleship and development that takes place with their wives and with their children.

This is abundantly clear as it relates both to the spiritual well-being of a husband's wife and of a father's children. No clearer or more forceful passage could be mentioned here than Paul's words to the church in Ephesus (Eph. 5:25–6:4). A husband is called to regard his relationship with his wife in a manner that is likened to Christ's relationship with the church. Jesus loved the church dearly and deeply and gave himself for her "that he might sanctify her, having cleansed her by the washing of water with the word, so that he might present the church to himself in splendor, without spot or wrinkle or any such thing, that she might be holy and without blemish" (vv. 26–27). Then Paul added these words: "In the same way husbands should love their wives as their own bodies" (v. 28). It simply is impossible to have given a more forceful or more compelling directive to husbands for how they must consider their responsibility as spiritual leaders and lovers for their wives. One phrase particularly captures the end goal that a husband must keep in his mind as the final purpose for Christ's love toward the church: "that she might be holy and without blemish" (v. 27). The headship of the husband must take to heart the sober and joyous responsibility to work, to serve, to love, to pray, and long for the continual spiritual growth of his wife.

According to Ephesians 6:1–2, children are to obey their parents and to honor their fathers and mothers, recognizing that this is the first commandment with a divine promise (cf. Exod. 20:12; Deut. 5:16). Notice that "parents"—that is, fathers *and* mothers—are in view in these first two verses of Ephesians 6. One might expect that, in the next verse, Paul would have continued to urge *both* parents—but he doesn't! Instead, Paul aimed his next direction specifically toward fathers of households: "Fathers, do not provoke your children to anger, but bring them up in the discipline and instruction of the Lord." The point is clear: *fathers* in particular bear special responsibility for the faith training of their children. As heads of their houses, some fathers might abuse their authority in ways that would provoke their children to anger—but that is not God's way. Instead, fathers are to create an atmosphere where they lead their children in the discipline of obedience to Jesus and in learning the wisdom of Jesus. Fathers have the God-given mandate and privilege of blessing their children by cultivating a household environment where children grow to respect, love, and follow Jesus, in obedience to their fathers and in honor of both their fathers and mothers.

Both headship relationships—the husband guiding his wife and the father directing his children—can be easily perverted into one of two sinful tendencies. One sinful response is for men to abuse their headship by being heavy-handed, mean-spirited, harsh, or demanding in unloving ways. God has *not* given husbands this authority for the purpose of gratifying their own pleasures or for exploiting opportunities for their own comfort! Godly authority is exercised out of benevolence, not out of selfishness. The husband's headship must be invested in constant healing, restoration, growth, and joy in family relationships.

The second sinful perversion of headship is far more sinister yet far less obvious. In this perversion, husbands and fathers abdicate their God-given responsibility. Such men are not necessarily mean-spirited; they are simply not there. When we abdicate our responsibilities as husbands and fathers, we become apathetic, distant, often absent, uninterested and uninvolved in the spiritual direction of our wives and children. The harm that we inflict on our families through apathy and uninvolvement can wound just as deeply as the harm that is inflicted through heavy-handed selfishness. The souls of our wives wilt before our eyes, and our children grow more distant and more attached to peers than parents as they seek the love and leadership that they lack from their fathers.

God has assigned husbands and fathers a sacred stewardship that involves responsibility for the spiritual growth and well-being of wives and children. The roles and relationships within the Trinity call us to realize that God intends households to reflect a reality that is true in the Godhead itself. And since this is true, church ministries must be designed in ways that acknowledge and equip husbands and fathers to carry out these responsibilities. In too many cases, well-intended church ministries have usurped the father's role in the discipleship of his children. How much better to train men so that they can lead their families to grow in love for God and in knowledge of God's Word! Family ministry must give focused attention to the training of men. In a very real sense, as the husbands and fathers go, so goes the family and, as households in a congregation go, so goes the congregation.

> → Does your congregation openly acknowledge husbands as spiritual leaders in their homes? How does your church equip fathers to lead times of family worship, to demonstrate love to their wives, to communicate effectively with their children, and to manage conflict in their households? In what ways does your congregation hold husbands accountable as godly and gracious leaders? If you cannot clearly articulate how your church equips husbands in these areas, consider how you will lay this crucial foundation for family-equipping ministry.

Implications for Wives and Mothers

Here is a simple yet revolutionary and countercultural observation: every New Testament passage offering instruction directly to wives includes one common element. In every instance, wives are commanded to submit to their husbands (Eph. 5:22–24; Col. 3:18; Titus 2:3–5; and 1 Peter 3:1–6). Today, however, it is rare, even at Christian weddings, for the bride's vows to include a promise to "submit to" her husband.

Our culture despises submission as much as it despises authority, but God calls us to a different mind and heart on this matter. And here, wives can benefit enormously from the doctrine of the Trinity in realizing that submission is itself reflective of the very submission eternally given by the Son to his Father, and by the Spirit to the Father and the Son. In this sense, God calls wives to be what he *is*, just as he has also called husbands to be what he also *is*. In obeying the biblical command to submit to their husbands, it is not enough to grit your teeth and submit, resenting this calling. Why is such begrudging submission insufficient? It is because such an attitude fails to understand the nature of submission as a reflection of the Son's submission to the Father, and the Spirit's submission to the Father and the Son. In the Trinity, just as the Father exercises his authority with impeccable wisdom and goodness, so the Son and Spirit give joyous and glad-hearted submission to the Father, always longing to do just what is asked or commanded of them.

In addition, just as the husband's thoughtful and loving headship should reflect Christ's relationship to the church (Eph. 5:25–27, 31–32), so the wife's glad-hearted and consistent submission should reflect the church's privilege of absolute submission before the lordship of the Messiah (vv. 24, 31–32). Therefore, the type of submission a wife is called to render to her husband is joyful and glad-hearted. A wife, then, should seek before God to render submission that seeks to help, longs to serve, and looks for opportunities to assist in any way that will be an encouragement and help to God's calling upon her husband's life. Just as God calls all of us to submit to authority with whole heart and willing spirit, so this special calling and privilege is given to wives as a reflection of the triune relations within the Godhead.

But let's be clear about this also: submission can be very difficult. Unlike the church's relationship to Jesus, in which the church can be confident that anything Jesus commands will be wise and good, husbands cannot be counted on to lead with flawless wisdom and goodness. In fact, sometimes husbands are pitifully unlike Christ, and submission can be very difficult. Wives are not commanded to "retrain" their husbands, though they might endeavor to do so through fervent and godly example. Wives nonetheless are commanded to submit to these imperfect husbands.

The most striking passage in the face of the difficulties of submitting is Peter's instruction to wives. Peter specifically addresses wives whose husbands are unbelieving. Presumably, these husbands may be the most difficult for a Christian wife to live with and under. An unbelieving husband might have far less in common with his wife's spiritual interests. Despite this, Peter instructs these wives to be subject to their own husbands, so that they may be guided toward the Messiah through the godly conduct of their wives (1 Peter 3:1–2).

I find it astonishing that it is in this text, of all New Testament passages that teach on husband-and-wife relations, that the strongest language is used to describe a wife's submission! Peter appealed to Sarah as an example and said that she "obeyed Abraham, calling him lord" (1 Peter 3:6a), indicating that they would be Sarah's "children" if they fearlessly followed this example (v. 6b).[5]

Make your relationship to your husband an issue of spiritual accountability before the Lord, and live before your husband in a way that honors Christ. God will honor you as you seek to honor him and his Word. He will bless you enormously as you seek to obey him by being faithful to fulfilling what he has called you to do.

> ✦ Divinely-designed differences between men and women were part of God's creation order before the fall of humanity. Redemption in Christ aims at removing sinful *distortions* of these distinctions, but the *distinctions* themselves remain as part of God's good plan. "In the family, husbands should forsake harsh or selfish leadership and grow in love and care for their wives; wives should forsake resistance to their husbands' authority and grow in willing, joyful submission to their husbands' leadership."
> **"The Danvers Statement on Biblical Manhood and Womanhood," CBMW**

Implications for Children

Children are given the role both of obeying their parents and of honoring their father and mother. Every parent understands that you can

---

5. A question may be raised here regarding how women should respond if their husbands engage in abusive behaviors. While this specific issue is beyond the scope of this chapter, the editors recommend reference to Ware, *Father, Son, and Spirit*, 146–48; David Powlison, Paul David Tripp, and Edward T. Welch, "Pastoral Responses to Domestic Violence," in *Pastoral Leadership for Manhood and Womanhood*, ed. Wayne Grudem and Dennis Rainey (Wheaton, IL: Crossway, 2003), 265–76; and the CBMW Council, "Statement on Abuse," Council on Biblical Manhood and Womanhood, http://www.cbmw.org/Resources/Articles/Statement-on-Abuse.

receive obedience—at least *outward* obedience—without receiving honor. Children must view honoring their parents as essential to their role in the household. To honor parents is to respect them as persons and to listen attentively to their instruction as persons older and wiser. Parents bear primary responsibility for how children are raised, but children bear responsibility for responding to parents in appropriate ways. Even now, learn to view your parents as God's gifts to you and to consider their words of advice, warning, encouragement, and instruction.

The equality that exists in the Trinity is reflected in the equality by which God has made every human being. Since each member of your family is made in the image of God, each should be treated in ways that are fitting to who they are. Insults, unhealthy sarcasm, lying, and hurting one another have no place in a family, because they dishonor both God and those made in his image. Parents and church ministries together must cultivate an atmosphere where children learn to speak to one another and act toward each other in ways that find approval in God's sight.

> → Consider carefully the activities and the events that occur in youth and children's ministries in your church. Do these activities encourage youth and children to be *more respectful* toward their parents' authority or *more resistant*? Do church-sponsored ministries help children to see their parents as God-ordained authorities and spiritual leaders? What attitudes will need to change to move these ministries toward a family-equipping approach?

THE TRINITY AND FAMILY-EQUIPPING MINISTRY

Family-equipping ministry seeks to partner with husbands, wives, parents, and children to assist them in learning what it means to be a family as God intends them to be. Men embracing biblical manhood, women embracing biblical womanhood, and children embracing their biblical roles under their dads and moms—this is what the family-equipping church seeks to foster and to advance. In each of these roles, the model of the Trinity provides invaluable guidance, for we see in the Trinity that the ones who submit are fully equal to the one who holds ultimate authority in their relationships. Equality and distinction, oneness and difference, unity and harmony, mark the Trinity. These same realities, in finite measure, ought to mark the family relationships we enjoy, as persons created in the very image of the triune God.

4

MALE AND FEMALE, HE CREATED THEM

Gender Roles and Relationships in Biblical Perspective

Randy Stinson

Most definitions and descriptions of Christian manhood and womanhood tend to major on the *Christian* and minor on *manhood* or *womanhood*. As a college student I recall gathering with a group of fellow students and attempting to list the characteristics of a Christian man. One by one we called out characteristics like love, joy, peace, and patience. Of course, all of these traits *should* characterize Christian men. The problem was that the young women were in the room next to us listing the precise same characteristics for a Christian woman.

But are there not specific differing ways in which men and women will live out the Christian life? Are there not certain ways in which I must instruct my sons that I will not with my daughters and vice versa? There are no generic people; there are men and there are women. Likewise, there are no generic Christians; there are Christian men and there are Christian women.

So why does biblical manhood and womanhood matter? A biblical understanding of manhood and womanhood matters because the structure of the home and church matters. A poorly structured edifice is weak, unstable, and will never stand the test of time. Many times it may look good on the outside, even giving the appearance of strength. Yet, faced with a storm or some other impact, such a structure will topple. On the other hand, if careful attention is given to the foundational and internal strength of the structure, the exterior may chip, a shingle or two may be blown away, but the structure is likely to withstand wind, rain, and storms.

This is true for church and family as well. God has given instructions regarding how these two institutions should be ordered. The effectiveness of generational discipleship hinges on our willingness to submit ourselves to Scripture and structure our households and churches according to the Bible.

The whole point of this book is that God has chosen a particular means to pass on the gospel to generation after generation as the church and home partner together. Special responsibility is given to parents and particularly fathers to serve as primary disciple-makers in their children's lives. The theological foundations of the household and church, then, are significant. After all, a poorly structured household or church will not be effective in this necessary task. Throughout the last generation or so, the culture has been dealing with significant confusion about manhood and womanhood. This confusion has crept into the church and has caused enormous debate and weakened many churches. The family-equipping model is not another program for your church. It is a way of life grounded in a Scripture-saturated order of the household that includes not only certain roles but also specific responsibilities connected to those roles.

> How might the fruit of the Spirit look the same in a man's life and in a woman's life? In what ways might the fruit of the Spirit be enacted differently among men and women?
> → Galatians 5:22–26 ←

FUNDAMENTAL EQUALITY OF MEN AND WOMEN

Revealed in Creation

It is important to begin where the Bible itself begins—in the garden of Eden, prior to the fall. It is here that we see a picture of manhood and womanhood before sin entered the world. Adam and Eve were created in God's image, equal before God as persons and distinct in their manhood and womanhood (Gen. 1:27). The equality of men and women, then, is the necessary foundation from which to deal with all gender-related issues. In the creation account, it is seen that men and women are, in their essence, equal in the sight of God. Neither has more or less value in their standing before their Creator. Even in assigning Eve as Adam's helper, God emphasizes her equality by designating her as *ezer kenegdo*, a helper perfectly suited for Adam (Gen. 2:18). In order for her to be perfectly suited for him, she must be equal to him. She is not his property or his doormat. She is his equal and his complement. This is further seen in Adam's expression of delight upon first seeing Eve. She is bone of his bones and flesh of his flesh (Gen. 2:23). She is from him, his same substance, his equal.

Marred But Maintained in the Fall

The results of the fall extend into every human relationship primarily because of a sinful disdain for the image of God in humanity. People murder one another, but God says this is prohibited because every person is created in the image of God (Gen. 9:6). Human beings oppress one another, but the order of creation is what establishes the sinfulness of oppressing the poor: "The rich and the poor have a common bond, the LORD is the maker of them all." (Prov. 22:2 NASB) Our speech toward one another can be demeaning or profane, and it is the fact of our equal creation "in the likeness of God" that reveals the depth of this iniquity (James 3:9).

With specific regard to the relationship between men and women, the apostle Paul declared that, in Christ, "there is neither Jew nor Greek, slave nor free, male nor female" (Gal. 3:28 NIV)—indicating *not* that ethnicity or gender is lost in Christ but that our inheritance before God is wholly equivalent. We are equal in our standing before God in Christ. In addition to this, Peter admonished the husband to deal with his wife "in an understanding way" and to treat her as an equal "heir" of the grace of life (1 Peter 3:7 NASB). Thus God's standard remains in place. Despite sinful denials and distortions of God's created order, human beings maintain their equality before God.

FUNDAMENTAL DISTINCTIONS BETWEEN MEN AND WOMEN

Revealed in Creation

In addition to their equality, Adam and Eve were distinct in their roles prior to the fall. This can be seen most clearly in Adam's headship in marriage in the opening chapters of Genesis. Adam was created first. The concepts of derivation and birth order come into play here, and Adam's headship is assumed as Eve is created subsequently. The fact that Adam was created first is clearly a very important part of the narrative. He had natural precedence by order of creation—no wonder, then, that Paul made much of this order in his letters to Timothy and to the Corinthian church (1 Cor. 11:1–9; 1 Tim. 2:11–13).

God designated Eve as Adam's helper, again suggesting the man's headship (Gen. 2:18). Woman was, out of all the creatures, uniquely suited for the man, created as his equal partner. Yet her designation as Adam's *helper* demonstrates a distinction in their roles. Not only is Adam formed first, but God also gives him land and an occupation. In all of this, God also provides a spouse, created as his helper (1 Cor. 11:7–9).

Adam's naming of all the creatures also suggests Adam's headship. The responsibility of naming each animal involved recognizing the nature of each creature and was a reminder to Adam that all were his responsibility but none was his equal (Gen. 2:19–20). This is why upon seeing the woman for the first time Adam declared her "flesh of my flesh" (Gen. 2:23). With this statement he acknowledged their equality yet immediately demonstrated his headship by naming the woman Eve.

The Creator's command to leave and cleave was addressed to the man (Gen. 2:24; cf. Matt. 19:4–5), demonstrating that the responsibility to establish the household and marriage rested on the man's shoulders. And, the man was designated as "Adam"—the same term that described the entire human race (Gen. 5:1–2). This designation, given to the man, implied his headship over the human race and, in particular, in relation to Eve (Gen. 1:26–28).

Since roles are a part of the original creation, then they are inherent in the lives of all men and women and thus should find an echo in every human heart. The idea that men and women are equal in their value yet distinct in their roles, though rejected by modern feminism and even many evangelicals, is a result of God's purposeful and beautiful design.

Marred by the Fall

The fall distorted the roles of men and women. When God told the woman, "Your desire will be for your husband, yet he will dominate you," (Gen. 3:16 HCSB) he was not introducing a new role; God was declaring that the previously existing roles would now be contorted with challenges and difficulties. The word "desire" in Genesis 3:16 appears again in Genesis 4:7, in God's description of how sin would destroy Cain. This desire of

Eve, then, was not intended to be positive; it represented the introduction of usurpation and competition that did not exist before the fall.

Even now, these difficulties can be found in families. If a wife seeks to usurp her husband's headship, the husband may abdicate his divinely ordained role. If the husband is harsh or domineering, the wife may shrink toward a servile attitude. The proper relationship of the Christian husband and wife involves the loving, humble headship of the husband and the intelligent, willing submission of the wife (1 Peter 3:1–7, Eph. 5:22–33).

In the church, the root problem is the same: resistance to biblically prescribed roles. In some cases, this resistance is willful and intentional. In many more instances, it results from well-intended yet misconstrued teachings of Scripture. The Bible teaches that the leadership positions of the church are to be held by men (1 Tim. 2:12) and yet also affirms that the example of Jesus and the fruit of the Spirit must govern this leadership (Eph. 5:22–33; Gal. 5:22–23). For men in the church, the practical outworking of resistance to biblical roles can manifest itself either in ungodly domination or in weakness and passivity. The Bible prohibits women from usurping this authority structure (1 Tim. 2:12) and yet also affirms the role of women in particular ministries, especially as they relate to other women (Titus 2:3–5).[1] For a woman in the church, perversions of biblical roles may lead to dissatisfaction with and rejection of these biblically ordained responsibilities.

Redeemed in Christ

The original creation involved male headship and female submission between Adam and Eve, and sin brought about a perversion of these roles. In the Christian household, redemption does not negate the distinct roles of men and women; instead, seen in light of God's redemption, these roles become a picture of the relationship between Christ and the church (Eph. 5:22–33, Col. 3:18–19).

Men should bear primary leadership responsibility not only in their households but also in the church. In the church as in the household, redemption does not blur gender roles. To the contrary, redemption empowers men and women to fulfill their roles in ways that acknowledge qualified men as teachers and leaders both of men and women. For those

---

1. See "The Danvers Statement on Biblical Manhood and Womanhood," Council on Biblical Manhood and Womanhood, http://www.cbmw.org/Resources/Articles/The-Danvers-Statement.

who claim that this limits the involvement of women, it must be noted that a vast range of needs and opportunities exist for women to teach and lead other women in faithful obedience to God's design and to God's Word (Titus 2:3–5).

THE IMPORTANCE OF BIBLICAL CONSISTENCY

Why should this matter? Why can't people just arrange their churches and marriages in ways that seem best to them? In other words, what is at stake here?

1. The authority of Scripture is at stake.

The Bible clearly teaches that men and women are equal in value and dignity and have distinct and complementary roles in the household and the church. If churches disregard these teachings and accommodate to the culture, then the members of those churches and subsequent generations will be less likely to submit to God's Word in other difficult matters as well. Caving in to cultural pressures will ultimately soften the theological underbelly of the church, and the church will be more susceptible to compromise when facing other challenges.

2. The health of the family is at stake.

If families do not structure their households according to God's design, they will lack a proper foundation from which to withstand the temptations of the devil and the onslaughts of the world. This in turn keeps the husband and wife from reflecting the gospel in their relationship (Eph. 5:22–33).

3. The health of the church is at stake.

If the church disregards a divinely designed structure, the church will be less effective in accomplishing its mission. Furthermore, whenever a church compromises the Word of God at one point, it becomes easier and easier to do it at other points where obedience may become difficult at some other point in the future. This affects not only this generation but also future generations (Deut. 6:1–9).

4. The advance of the gospel is at stake.

Paul, inspired by the Holy Spirit, called husbands and wives to relate to one another as a picture of Christ and the church (Eph 5:22–33). Husbands and wives who fail to model the relationship of Jesus to his bride provide a false and distorted picture of the gospel. When a husband is domineering, he promotes an inaccurate picture. When he is abdicates his role as the head of the household, he distorts the picture. The same is true of a wife who either usurps her husband's headship or becomes a doormat. If we care deeply about the gospel, we must care deeply about the authenticity of the picture we portray. This is much more than a discussion about who is taking out the garbage or who is mowing the lawn. A marriage that cares little about the roles of men and women ultimately cares less about the gospel.

THE IMPLICATIONS OF GOD'S CREATION OF HUMANITY AS MALE AND FEMALE

The Church

Churches should structure themselves so that the primary teaching roles of the church are held by men. This would not only mean the teaching and preaching to the gathered assembly of believers, but would also include Sunday school classes or household Bible studies where both men and women are present.

In the church, there are immeasurable opportunities for those who genuinely want to serve the Lord. We are all aware of the many afflictions of mankind, and we should be motivated to action by the fact that God has a place of service for all believers. The body of Christ is designed to include a diversity of gifts (1 Cor. 12:7–21). This diversity brings about a certain unity, since each member of the body is set there according to God's good pleasure (v. 18). The biblical position on gender roles is not preoccupied with restriction but concerns itself with every member's participation in the body of Christ. While authority over men in the church *is* a responsibility given to men alone (1 Tim. 2:12), there are many ministries that do not require this teaching or ruling function. So many genuine needs exist in the church and in the world that no man or woman should feel excluded from ministry based on whether one is qualified to serve as an elder or pastor.

The Household

Male headship does not mean that men are in any way more important, more intelligent, or inherently better than their female counterparts. Likewise, the submission of women to men in their households and in churches does not mean that their place in either institution is inferior. Headship and submission, equality and dignity, are not mutually exclusive; ideally, they coexist in marriage and the church structure.

Husbands should be particularly mindful of Peter's admonition to live with their wives in an understanding way and to treat them as full equals as joint heirs of the grace of life (1 Peter 3:7). Husbands who fail to treat their wives this way and "become bitter against them" (Col. 3:19 HCSB) will have their prayers hindered. Wives who joyfully and intelligently submit to the authority of their husbands are reflecting Jesus, who submitted himself to the will of God the Father (John 8:28). Wives are never, of course, required to submit to a husband who is leading them into sin. In all of life, God is our final authority and we must "obey God rather than men" (Acts 5:29).

It is the pattern of Scripture and life that most husbands and wives will also become fathers and mothers. In order to adequately pass down the gospel to the generations, the vehicle for doing so must be effectively reproduced as well. For this to take place, husbands and wives should, in front of their children, clearly model the gospel-picture of the roles that God has given them. This is the primary means by which children will understand their own gender identity, embrace their roles as men and women, and pursue these roles with Spirit-driven passion in their future households.

Just as the responsibility to subdue and exercise dominion over the earth is shared by husbands and wives, so is the responsibility of fathers and mothers to raise their children. Both fathers and mothers are to be equally obeyed and honored (Eph. 6:1–2). Just as the husband has a unique leadership role in marriage, so too he bears a unique responsibility in the parenting process. He is the person primarily responsible for the overall spiritual direction of the household; this includes the children. Many fathers today have physically abandoned their families, or they remain in the household but are emotionally distant.[2] Yet consider the many instructions in Proverbs for sons to listen to their fathers. Consider also the New

---

2. David Blankenhorn, *Fatherless America: Confronting Our Most Urgent Social Problem* (New York: Harper Collins, 1995).

Testament instructions to fathers: "Do not provoke your children to anger, but bring them up in the discipline and instruction of the Lord" (Eph. 6:4). The Bible does not minimize the role of mothers but clearly gives a heightened sense of accountability and responsibility to fathers.

WHAT WILL BE DONE DIFFERENTLY WHEN GOD'S DESIGN FOR MEN AND WOMEN BECOMES PART OF A CONGREGATION'S CULTURE?

Churches Will Rethink the Processes of Christian Formation for Men and Women

Much of what the church does by way of discipleship for men and women occurs in the form of Bible studies and fellowships. These activities are certainly biblical, but they often occur without the necessary work and service which should accompany Bible study and fellowship.

With regard to the spiritual formation of women, the Bible makes clear that there is a necessary function for older women in the church to carry out toward the younger women in the church. But over the last twenty years or so this function may have been neglected or minimized. I am personally grateful for technological advances such as the Internet and video resources that have allowed congregations to be exposed to great teaching they otherwise would not have had. However, there is some concern that these resources have inadvertently squelched the real function of Paul's teaching in Titus 2. Video and Internet resources can adequately deliver content, but it seems his emphasis is on relationship as the means of spiritual formation. Paul admonishes them,

> Older women likewise are to be reverent in behavior, not slanderers or slaves to much wine. They are to teach what is good, and so train the young women to love their husbands and children, to be self-controlled, pure, working at home, kind, and submissive to their own husbands, that the word of God may not be reviled (Titus 2:3–5).

Paul is saying that there are definitely some key skills, pursuits, and inclinations that need to be taught and trained, but he is indicating here that it will occur in relationship. This kind of "training" will happen as many hours of time are spent living life together.

Over the last decade, my wife has had multiple opportunities to be involved in the mentoring of young women, and we have noticed that while these women are very eager to learn, their questions have become more and more basic. They ask why is this? We believe this is because we are dealing with one of the first full generations of women whose mothers worked outside of the household. As this has happened the normal daily domestic responsibilities and skills that otherwise would have been naturally taught and nurtured are today largely absent. Many young women today do not possess the domestic skills necessary to manage a household. The simple ebb and flow of basic household routines now seems unmanageable. The proper balancing of children, husband, household management, local church involvement, and personal life appear impossible to many of these young, untrained women. Will a video or Web site take care of this problem? Minimally. These women need someone they can talk with in person or call in the middle of the night.

They need someone who can come over to their household, observe their patterns, and offer godly wisdom. They need to be able to spend time in the older woman's household to observe her patterns and see how she "loves her husband and children." Many women are involved in multiple Bible studies but have no personal mentor in their life who can speak redemptively to her and offer the instruction, encouragement, and correction that is so crucial for spiritual formation and the development of a godly pattern of life. This primarily happens when there is much personal interaction, not just a "talking head" in a video on an iPod.[3]

Paul is definitely concerned with content, but the context is equally important. Notice how he keeps pressing in on the household. It is here where a young woman should give her attention, not because of culture or tradition, but as Paul says, so "that the word of God might not be reviled" (Titus 3:5). It is a proper response to the fact that "the grace of God has appeared," which is preparing us for "the appearing of the glory of our great God and Savior Jesus Christ, who gave himself for us to redeem us from all lawlessness and to purify for himself a people for his own possession who are zealous for good works" (Titus 2:11, 13–14). The church should make sure that it is encouraging a certain relationality between the older and younger women. Note how Paul encourages the whole church to treat "older women

---

3. This is certainly not to say that this type of instruction is unhelpful or unnecessary. It just cannot supplant the personal interaction that Paul is advocating, particularly with the cultural situation in the United States with so much of this type of domestic instruction being neglected in our homes today.

as mothers, younger women as sisters," (1 Tim. 5:2). How will this take place unless there is a great deal of intentionality from the church? Intentionality will be aided if church leaders can establish and convey that the biblical motivation for doing and encouraging this is in response to God's grace so that the word of God will be honored and good works will be done.

With regard to men, some similar observations can be noted. In many churches across the country, men regularly get together for all sorts of activities. There are golf outings, wild game banquets, conferences, and let's not leave out the fellowship breakfasts with a dry guest speaker who is there to convince the men that this effort to get together was really worthwhile.

Now, of course, none of these things is inherently bad and many men are encouraged and edified by a number of these events. However, it seems to have been ineffective in truly forging men together as bands of brothers who will hold one another accountable, encourage one another to good works, and challenge one another to do great things for God. As I have traveled all over the country speaking to men, I have found that most men do not have even one close friend and do not feel really connected to any of the men in their church.

My proposal is to stop talking about ministry *to* men and to start talking about ministry *by* men. How are the hearts of men forged together? They are forged by some activity that involves hardship, sacrifice, mutual suffering, or a shared challenge that is solved together. Think about it. Men do not build strong relationships with one another strictly by getting together and talking. They don't really trust one another until they have worked together for some agreed-upon goal. What man doesn't think fondly of moments shared with other men as they participated on a sports team, military unit, building project, mission trip, or other organized effort? This is when a man decides who he will trust and to whom he will turn in a time of need. Proverbs 27:17 makes this point clear, that men are sharpened like "iron sharpens iron." It requires a collision. It needs solid objects crashing against one another. Most churches fall short in providing men with these kinds of opportunities. Men are problem solvers. They fix stuff. They build stuff. They are made for hard things, for rugged things, for dirty things, and for ugly things. Give them problems and tell them to figure it out. Then when the work is done, tell them to get together and pray for one another, encourage one another, exhort one another, and even admonish one another and see how these men will become more and more robust for the gospel and the local church.

Churches Will Train Parents to Apply the Scriptures

In a recent study, it was discovered that today's Christian parents do not look primarily to God's Word for their parenting plan. Parents who attend religious services weekly are particularly likely to emphasize faith in God. Yet only 24 percent of parents who attend religious services weekly identify faith in God as a mark of parenting success. Eight out of ten parents believe they should be the people most responsible for their children's spiritual development. Yet only 35 percent say their religious faith is one of the most important influences on their parenting.[4]

> "With rare exception, most of today's Christian parenting resources fail to emphasize what is perhaps the most important aspect of true biblical parenting—*how to relate the Bible to the disciplinary process in practical ways.* Think about it. With all of your training, do you really know how to use the Bible for *doctrine, reproof, correction, and instruction in righteousness* with your children?"
>
> ✦✦
>
> Lou Priolo, *Teach Them Diligently*

Churches would do well to be much more intentional about how they train parents to utilize the Scriptures. Most parents have had the encounter when their child sins and the parent asks in frustration, "Why did you do this?" Of course, the child gives that well-worn answer, "I don't know." There is a reason why they say this: because they don't know. They have to be taught. They have to be given biblical categories. When children are given biblical categories, they are well on their way toward becoming responsive to biblical solutions for their sin. It honors God when His Word is centralized in this way.[5]

Churches Will Show Parents How to Talk about the Gospel Day by Day

One of the most difficult things for many parents to do is to be creative and natural in talking to their children about God on a daily basis.

---

4. Rodney Wilson, Selma Wilson, and Scott McConnell, *The Parent Adventure: Preparing Your Children for a Lifetime with God* (Nashville: B&H, 2008), 127–135.

5. For other resources that would help in this regard, see William P. Farley, *Gospel-Powered Parenting: How the Gospel Shapes and Transforms Parenting* (Phillipsburg, NJ: P&R, 2009); Rob Rienow, *Visionary Parenting: Capture a God-sized Vision for Your Family*, (Nashville: Randall House, 2009); Tedd Tripp, *Shepherding a Child's Heart* (Wapwallopen, PA: Shepherd Press, 1995); and Tedd and Margie Tripp, *Instructing a Child's Heart* (Wapwallopen, PA: Shepherd Press, 2008).

Frankly, this is true because many parents are so compartmentalized in their own faith that they rarely think about God themselves during most of their own day. However, if churches will help place the burden on parents, and then equip them in this task, the parents will even begin to seek out the Lord throughout the day and will themselves more naturally acknowledge their need for God and His presence in their life and activities. While most pastors are faithful to call their congregations to a daily walk with God, there is still the need for instruction and training. Yes, but how is a question that we need to answer in both words and example. The faith once for all delivered to the saints will not be faithfully passed along if children are not taught to understand how God is involved in every aspect of their lives and then practice the skill of conversing about it on a daily basis.

Churches Will Teach Men to Lead in Family Discipleship

Churches should be aware that when most men hear phrases like "family devotion," "family worship," or even "faith talk," some degree of panic sets it. Men think that they may have to lead a condensed version of the church service, replete with hymn leading, orders of worship, and—of course—a sermon. Yet a regular time of pulling the family together, reading the Scriptures, and praying for one another is one of the most effective and fruitful means of building an authentic commitment to the gospel into your family. Much like a man would receive some basic training at the start of a new job, so churches should provide intensely practical instruction on how to call your family together for regular worship. This kind of training should include a live demonstration and then opportunities for men to practice and be observed in the process. Most men just need a clear plan with detailed instructions. The church is perfectly equipped and positioned to offer this kind of help.

> **How is your church equipping men to teach their families?**
> "Every man in the church should be intentionally developing and practicing his teaching skills, because every man is at least a husband or potential husband, and God has commanded husbands to be teachers in the home (Deut. 6:6–7; Eph. 5:25–27; 6:4)."
>
> ❦
>
> Wayne A. Mack and David Swavely, *Life in the Father's House*

Churches Will Build a Culture of Family Discipleship

Creating a particular culture in your church can be challenging. Most people are looking for programs with books and videos and meetings. Building a culture is different. It has to be owned by the leaders of the church and then reinforced in every venue of the church. So in Bible studies, the leader should be asking at every meeting, "Who has a testimony about a conversation you had about God with one of your children this week?" There may even be opportunities for some congregations to do this in their worship services. Pastors should regularly use illustrations that reinforce the family-equipping culture. He might begin an illustration by saying, "This week when we were having a family devotion . . . ," or "I got the most interesting response from my son when I asked him if he could eat a cheeseburger to the glory of God this week." Each time this is done, church members are reminded that this is important. They get ideas for their own household and become more confident, comfortable, and committed to this holistic way of imparting the faith to the generations. A church should make sure that classes are offered to train, books are recommended to encourage, and many opportunities are given for parents to encourage one another in this process.

FROM GENERATION TO GENERATION

Most pastors would agree that in Western culture today we are experiencing great confusion in marriages, ambivalence regarding the values of motherhood, the growing claims of legitimacy for illicit and perverse sexual relationships, the upsurge of physical and emotional abuse in the family, and the breakdown in the structure of the local church. A denial or neglect of the biblical teaching on men and women will lead to an increase in these and many other problems in our households, churches, and society at large. We should be praying that believers around the world will embrace the beauty of God's good design and live out and teach the biblical view of men and women, equal in the image of God, different in role and function. We should also be praying that as this occurs, fathers will have the courage to lead their families in the fear and admonition of the Lord and that mothers will embrace their role as homemakers, nurturers, and helpers in this enormous gospel task. As this takes place the faith will be more adequately passed down from generation to generation and the gospel will be multiplied to every tribe, every tongue, and every nation to the glory of God in Christ (Rev. 7:9–12).

5

THE COMPASSION
OF TRUTH

Homosexuality
in Biblical Perspective

R. Albert Mohler Jr.

H omosexuality is perhaps the most controversial issue of debate in American culture. Once described as "the love that dares not speak its name," homosexuality is now discussed and debated throughout American society. Behind this discussion is an agenda, pushed and promoted by activists, who seek legitimization and social sanction for homosexual acts, relationships, and lifestyles.

The push is on for homosexual "marriage," the removal of all structures and laws considered oppressive to homosexuals, and the recognition of homosexuals, bisexuals, transsexuals, and others as "erotic minorities" deserving special legal protection. The larger culture is now bombarded with messages and images designed to portray homosexuality as a normal lifestyle. Homoerotic images are so common in the mainstream media that many citizens have virtually lost the capacity to be shocked.

Those who oppose homosexuality are depicted as narrow-minded bigots and described as "homophobic." Anyone who suggests that heterosexual marriage is the only acceptable and legitimate arena of sexual activity is lambasted as outdated, oppressive, and outrageously out of step with contemporary culture.

The church has not been an outsider to these debates. As the issue of homosexual legitimization has gained public prominence and moved forward, some churches and denominations have joined the movement—even becoming advocates of homosexuality—while others stand steadfastly opposed to compromise on the issue. In the middle are churches and denominations unable or unwilling to declare a clear conviction on homosexuality. Issues of homosexual ordination and marriage are regularly discussed in the assemblies of several denominations as well as many congregations.

> → How can the family-equipping congregation prepare parents to raise their children in ways that reflect God's creation order, appreciating and rejoicing in the divinely designed distinctions between men and women? ←

TRUSTING GOD'S WORD ON THE NATURE OF MARRIAGE, FAMILY, AND SEXUALITY

This debate is itself nothing less than a revolutionary development. Any fair-minded observer of American culture and the American churches must note the incredible speed with which this issue has been driven into the cultural mainstream. The challenge for the believing church now comes down to this: *Do we have a distinctive message in the midst of this moral confusion?* Our answer must be *yes*. The Christian church must have a distinctive message to speak to the issue of homosexuality, because faithfulness to Holy Scripture demands that we do so.

The affirmation of biblical authority is thus central to the church's consideration of this issue—or any issue. The Bible is the Word of God in written form, inerrant and infallible, inspired by the Holy Spirit and "profitable for doctrine, for reproof, for correction, for instruction in righteousness" (2 Tim. 3:16 NKJV). This is the critical watershed: those churches which reject the authority of Scripture will eventually succumb to cultural pressure and accommodate their understanding of homosexuality to the spirit of the age. Those churches that affirm, confess, and acknowledge the full authority of the Bible have no choice: we must speak a word of compassionate truth. And that compassionate truth is this: homosexual acts are expressly and unconditionally forbidden by God through his Word, and such acts are an abomination to the Lord by his own declaration. Professor Elizabeth Achtemeier of Richmond's Union Theological Seminary states the case clearly: "The clearest teaching of Scripture is that God intended sexual intercourse to be limited to the marriage relationship of one man and one woman."[1] That this is so should be apparent to all who look to the Bible for guidance on this issue. This assessment of the biblical record remained completely uncontroversial throughout the last nineteen centuries of the Christian church. Only in recent years have some biblical scholars come forward to claim that the Bible presents a mixed message—or a very different message—on human sexuality.

The homosexual agenda is pushed by activists who are totally committed to the cause of making homosexuality a sanctioned and recognized form of sexual activity as well as the basis for legitimate family relationships. In their view, every obstacle which stands in the way of progress toward this agenda must be removed, and Scripture stands as the most formidable obstacle to that agenda.

We should not be surprised, then, that apologists for the homosexual agenda have arisen even within the world of biblical scholarship. Biblical scholars are themselves a very mixed group, with some defending the authority of Scripture and others bent on deconstructing the biblical text. The battle lines on this issue are immediately apparent. Many who deny the truthfulness, inspiration, and authority of the Bible have come to argue that Scripture sanctions homosexuality—or at least to argue that the biblical passages forbidding homosexual acts are confused, misinterpreted, or irrelevant.

APPROACHES TO SANCTIONING HOMOSEXUAL RELATIONSHIPS IN LIGHT OF SCRIPTURE

To accomplish this requires feats of exotic biblical interpretation worthy of the most agile circus contortionist. Several decades ago, the late J. Gresham Machen remarked that "the Bible, with a complete abandonment of all scientific historical method, and of all common sense, is made to say the exact opposite of what it means; no Gnostic, no medieval monk with his fourfold sense of Scripture, ever produced more absurd biblical interpretation than can be heard every Sunday in the pulpits of New York."[2] Dr. Machen was referring to misuse and misapplication of Scripture which he saw as a mark of the infusion of a pagan spirit within the church

---

1. Elizabeth Achtemeier, quoted in Mark O'Keefe, "Gays and the Bible," *The Virginian Pilot* (Norfolk, Virginia), February 14, 1993, C-1.
2. J. Gresham Machen, "The Separateness of the Church," in *God Transcendent*, ed. Ned Bernard Stonehouse (Grand Rapids: Eerdmans, 1949; repr., Edinburgh: Banner of Truth Trust, 1982), 113.

in the early twentieth century. Even greater absurdity than that observed by Machen is now evident among those determined to make the Bible sanction homosexuality.

Outright Rejection of Biblical Authority

Different approaches are taken toward this end. For some, an outright rejection of biblical authority is explicit. With astounding candor, William M. Kent, a member of the committee assigned by United Methodists to study homosexuality declared that

> the scriptural texts in the Old and New Testaments condemning homosexual practice are neither inspired by God nor otherwise of enduring Christian value. Considered in the light of the best biblical, theological, scientific, and social knowledge, the biblical condemnation of homosexual practice is better understood as representing time and place bound cultural prejudice.[3]

This approach is the most honest taken among the revisionists. These persons do not deny that the Bible expressly forbids homosexual practices; they acknowledge that the Bible does just that. Their solution is straightforward: We must abandon the Bible in light of modern "knowledge."

The next step taken by those who follow this approach is to suggest that it is not sufficient for the authority of the Bible to be denied; the Bible must be *opposed*. Gary David Comstock, Protestant chaplain at Wesleyan University, charges: "Not to recognize, critique, and condemn Paul's equation of godlessness with homosexuality is dangerous. To remain within our respective Christian traditions and not challenge those passages that degrade and destroy us is to contribute to our own oppression." Further, Comstock argues that "these passages will be brought up and used against us again and again until Christians demand their removal from the biblical canon, or, at the very least, formally discredit their authority to prescribe behavior."[4]

---

3. William M. Kent, *Report of the Committee to Study Homosexuality to the General Council on Ministries of the United Methodist Church* (Dayton: General Council on Ministries, August 24, 1991).

4. Gary David Comstock, *Gay Theology Without Apology* (Cleveland: Pilgrim Press, 1993), 43.

Appeals to the Ignorance of the Human Authors of Scripture

A second approach taken by the revisionists is to suggest that the human authors of Scripture were merely limited by the scientific immaturity of their age. If they knew what we now know, these revisionists claim, the human authors of Scripture would never have been so closed-minded. Victor Paul Furnish argues:

> Not only the terms, but the concepts "homosexual" and "homosexuality" were unknown in Paul's day. These terms like "heterosexual," "heterosexuality," "bisexual," and "bisexuality" presuppose an understanding of human sexuality that was possible only with the advent of modern psychology and sociological analysis. The ancient writers were operating without the vaguest idea of what we have learned to call "sexual orientation."[5]

And indeed, Paul and the other apostles *do* seem ignorant of modern secular understandings of sexual identity and orientation—and this fact is fundamentally irrelevant. Scripture must not be subjected to defend itself in light of modern notions. Instead, modern notions of sexual orientation must be brought to answer to Scripture. Neither the apostle Paul nor the Holy Spirit will apologize to Sigmund Freud or the American Psychological Association. The faithful church must call this approach what it is: a blatant effort to subvert the authority of Scripture and to replace biblical authority with the false authority of modern secular ideologies.

Denial That Biblical Passages Actually Refer to Homosexual Behavior

A third approach taken by the revisionists is to deny that biblical passages actually refer to homosexuality at all, or to argue that the passages refer to specific and "oppressive" homosexual acts. For instance, some argue that Paul's references to homosexuality are actually references to sexual abuse of young boys, to homosexual rape, or to "noncommitted" homosexual relationships. The same is argued concerning passages such as Genesis 19

---

5. Victor Paul Furnish, *The Moral Teachings of Paul: Selected Issues,* 2nd ed. (Nashville: Abingdon Press, 1985), 85.

and Leviticus 18:22 and 20:13. Yet, in order to make this case, the revision-ists are forced to deny the obvious and to argue for the ridiculous.

Likewise, some argue that the sin of Sodom was not homosexuality, but inhospitality. Author John J. McNeill makes this case, arguing that the church oppressively shifted the understanding of the sin of Sodom from inhospitality to homosexuality.[6] The text, however, cannot be made to play this game. The context indicates that the sin of Sodom is clearly homosexuality—and without this meaning, the passage makes no sense. The language and the structure of the text are clear. Beyond this, Jude clearly linked the sin of Sodom with sexual perversion and immorality, stating that "just as Sodom and Gomorrah and the cities around them, since they in the same way as these indulged in gross immorality and went after strange flesh, are exhibited as an example, in undergoing the punish-ment of eternal fire" (Jude 7 NASB).

Leviticus 18:22 speaks of male homosexuality as an "abomination"—the strongest word used of God's judgment against an act. The most exten-sive argument against homosexuality is not found in the Old Testament, however, but in Romans 1:22–27, a passage which is found within Paul's lengthy introduction to his Roman letter:

> Professing to be wise, they became fools, and exchanged the glory of the incorruptible God for an image in the form of corruptible man and of birds and four-footed animals and crawling creatures.
>
> Therefore God gave them over in the lusts of their hearts to impu-rity, so that their bodies would be dishonored among them. For they exchanged the truth of God for a lie, and worshipped and served the creature rather than the Creator, who is blessed forever. Amen.
>
> For this reason, God gave them over to degrading passions; for their women exchanged the natural function for that which is unnatural, and in the same way also the men abandoned the natural function of the woman and burned in their desire toward one another, men with men committing indecent acts and receiving in their own persons the due penalty of their error. (NASB)

As Romans 1 makes absolutely clear, homosexuality is fundamentally an act of unbelief. Paul wrote that the wrath of God is revealed against all those "who suppress the truth in unrighteousness" (NASB). God the

---

6. John J. McNeill, *The Church and the Homosexual*, rev. ed. (Boston: Beacon Press, 1988).

Creator has implanted knowledge of himself in every human being, and all are without excuse. This is the context of Paul's explicit statements on homosexuality.

Paul's classic statements in Romans 1 set the issues squarely before us. Homosexuality is linked directly to idolatry, for it is on the basis of idolatry that God gave them up to their own lusts. Their hearts were committed to impurity, and they were degrading their own bodies by their illicit lusts. Their idolatry—exchanging the truth of God for a lie and worshipping the creature rather than the Creator—led God to give them over to their degrading passions. From here, those given over to their degraded passions exchanged the natural use of sexual intercourse for that which God declared to be unnatural. At this point Paul explicitly deals with female homosexuality or lesbianism. This is one of the very few references in all ancient literature to female homosexuality, and Paul's message is clear.

The women involved in homosexuality were not and are not alone, however. Men, too, have given up natural intercourse with women and have become consumed with passion for other men. The acts they commit, they commit without shame. As a result, they have received God's condemnation.

Paul's message could not be more candid and clear, but there are those who seek to deny the obvious. Some have even claimed that Paul is here dealing only with those *heterosexual* persons who commit *homosexual* acts. The imaginative folly of this approach is undone by Scripture, which allows no understanding that any human beings are born anything other than heterosexual. The modern—and highly political—notion of homosexual "orientation" cannot be squared with the Bible. The only "orientation" indicated by Scripture is the universal human orientation to sin (Rom. 3:9–20).

MARRIAGE AND FAMILY: DIVINELY DESIGNED CREATIONAL STRUCTURES OR ARTIFICIAL SOCIAL CONSTRUCTIONS?

Homosexual acts and homosexual desire are rebellion against God's sovereign intention in his creation and gross perversions of God's good and perfect plan for his created order. Paul made clear in Romans 1 that homosexuality—whether among males or females—is a dramatic sign of rebellion against God and against God's intention for the created order. Those about whom Paul writes have worshipped the creature rather than the

Creator. For this reason, men and women have forfeited the natural complementarity of God's intention for marriage and have turned to members
of their own sex, burning with illicit desires that are both degrading and
dishonorable.

This is a very strong and clear message. The logical progression in
Romans 1 is undeniable. Paul shifted immediately from his description of
rebellion against God as Creator to an identification of homosexuality as
the first and most evident sign of a society upon which God has turned his
judgment. Essential to understanding this reality in theological perspective
is the recognition that homosexual behavior is an assault on the integrity
of creation and of God's intention in creating human beings in two distinct
and complementary sexes.

Here, the confessing and believing church runs counter to the cultural tidal wave. Even to raise the issue of gender is to offend those who
wish to eradicate sexual distinctions, arguing that these are merely socially
constructed realities and vestiges of an ancient past. Scripture will not,
however, allow this attempt to deny the structures of creation. Romans 1
must be read in light of Genesis 1 and 2. As Genesis 1:27 makes apparent,
God intended from the beginning to create human beings in two sexes (or
genders): "Male and female he created them." Both man and woman were
created in God's image. They were and are distinct, and still inseparably
linked by God's own design. The sexes are different, and the distinction
goes far beyond mere physical differences, yet the man recognized in the
woman "bone of my bones and flesh of my flesh" (2:23).

The bond between man and woman is marriage, and marriage is not
a historical accident or the result of socialization over time. To the contrary, marriage and the establishment of the heterosexual covenant union
is central to God's intention—both before and after the initial fall of humanity into sin. Immediately following the creation of man and woman
come the instructive words: "For this cause a man shall leave his father
and his mother, and shall cleave to his wife; and they shall become one
flesh. And the man and his wife were both naked and were not ashamed"
(2:24–25 NAS).

Evangelicals have often failed to present this biblical truth straight-
forwardly. As a result many of our churches and members are unarmed for
the ideological, political, and cultural conflicts that mark the contemporary landscape. The fundamental axiom upon which evangelical Christians
must base every response to homosexuality is this: God alone is sovereign,
and he has created the universe and all within it by his own design and for

his own good pleasure. Furthermore, he has revealed to us his creative intention through Holy Scripture—and that intention was clearly to create and establish two distinct but complementary sexes or genders.

The Genesis narratives demonstrate that this distinction is neither accidental nor inconsequential to the divine design. "It is not good that the man should be alone; I will make [for] him a helper suitable for him," determined God (2:18). And God created woman. God's creative intention is further revealed in the cleaving of man to the woman ("his wife") and their new identity as "one flesh." This biblical assertion, which no contorted interpretation can reasonably escape, clearly places marriage and sexual relations within God's creative act and design.

> → Widespread confusion characterizes the roles expected of men and women in contemporary Western society. "The feminist movement aspired to nothing short of a total social, moral, and cultural revolution. Along the way, feminism redefined womanhood, marriage, motherhood, and the roles for both men and women. . . . Instead of producing a vast expansion of happiness among women, the feminist movement must now answer for the fact that women, by their own evaluation, appear to be less happy than before the revolution" (R. Albert Mohler Jr., "Feminism Unfulfilled," http://www.albertmohler.com). "Many of the most significant man-making institutions of our society are either gone or in big trouble. Military service is now both voluntary and no longer male-only. Organizations like the Boy Scouts attract more opposition and fewer boys" (R. Albert Mohler Jr., "Masculinity in a Can, Fight Club at Church, and the Crisis of Manhood," http://www.albertmohler.com). In this cultural context, how can family-equipping congregations help parents to speak with their children about these issues with clarity and compassion? ←

The sexual union of a man and a woman united in covenant marriage is thus not merely allowed but commanded as God's intention and decree. Sexual expression is limited to this heterosexual covenant, which in its clearest biblical expression consists of one man and one woman united for as long as they both shall live. Any sexual expression outside that heterosexual marriage covenant is illicit, immoral, and outlawed by God's command and law. Adultery, rape, bestiality, pornography, and fornication are, therefore, also forbidden by Holy Scripture. The fundamental truth that sexual expression is limited to heterosexual marriage runs counter not only to the homosexual agenda but also to the rampant sexual immorality of the age.

THE CLARITY OF THE BIBLICAL TESTIMONY

As E. Michael Jones argues, most modern ideologies are, at base, efforts to rationalize sexual behavior. In fact, he identifies modernity itself as "rationalized lust."[7] We should expect the secular world, which is at war with God's truth, to be eager in its efforts to rationalize lust, and to seek legitimacy and social sanction for its sexual sins. We should be shocked, however, that many within the church now seek to accomplish the same purpose, and to join in common cause with those openly at war with God's truth.

In other letters, Paul indicated that homosexual persons—along with those who persist in other sins—will not inherit God's kingdom. The term that Paul uses in 1 Corinthians 6:9–10 and 1 Timothy 1:10 is *arsenokoites*, a word with a graphic etymology. Some modern revisionists have attempted to suggest that this refers only to homosexual rapists or child abusers. This argument will not stand even the slightest scholarly consideration.[8] The word does not appear in any other Greek literature of the period. As New Testament scholar David F. Wright has demonstrated, the word was taken by Paul directly from Leviticus 18:22 and 20:13, and its meaning is homosexuality itself.[9]

The biblical witness is clear: Homosexuality is a grievous sin against God and is a direct rejection of God's intention and command in creation. All sin is a matter of eternal consequence, and the only hope for any sinner is the redemption accomplished by Jesus Christ, who on the cross paid the price for our sin, serving as the substitute for the redeemed.

Our response to persons involved in homosexuality must be marked by genuine compassion. But a central task of genuine compassion is telling the truth, and the Bible reveals a true message that we must convey. Those seeking to contort or subvert the Bible's message are not responding to homosexuals with compassion. To lie is never compassionate—and their lie leads unto death.

---

7. E. Michael Jones, *Degenerate Moderns: Modernity as Rationalized Sexual Misbehavior* (San Francisco: Ignatius, 1993).
8. For a response to one recent attempt to revise the meaning of this term, see Gary Jepsen, "Dale Martin's 'Arsenokoites and Malakos' Tried and Found Wanting," *Currents in Theology and Mission* 33, no. 5 (2006): 397–405.
9. David F. Wright, "Homosexuals or Prostitutes? The Meaning of *Arsenokoitai* (1 Cor. 6:9; 1 Tim. 1:10)," in *Vigiliae Christianae* 38 (1984): 125–53.

PART 2

COVENANTS AND COMMUNITY

Family Discipleship in Christian History

Every family has a story. The family of believers in Jesus is no exception. The household of God has a history, and this history is inescapably theological. At the core of Christian faith stands the assertion that, in Jesus Christ, God personally intersected human history in a unique and consummate way at a particular time in a particular place. When we confess that Jesus was "born of the Virgin Mary," "suffered under Pontius Pilate" and arose "on the third day," we declare that members of God's household share a common history and that this history matters.

Certain documents from this history—the texts of Holy Scripture—continually and authoritatively *form* and *reform* the church even now. Other historical documents and traditions *inform* the church. These secondary truths and traditions are not authoritative for the family of faith, but they do provide important insights into how God has worked among his people in the centuries that separate us from the apostles. In this section of *Trained in the Fear of God*, C. Michael Wren Jr., C. Jeffrey Robinson Sr., Kevin L. Smith, and W. Ryan Steenburg present the church's story from the late ancient period to the present age with a focus on Christian formation in the context of families.

6

AMONG YOUR COMPANY AT HOME

Family Discipleship in Late Ancient and Medieval Households

C. Michael Wren Jr.

How much more, then, should it not suffice for your spiritual profit that you hear the divine lessons in church, but among your company at home you should engage in sacred reading, even several hours, at night, when the days are short,"[1] declared Caesarius of Arles, a bishop in southern Gaul in the sixth century AD.

These words from Caesarius represent a commitment to family discipleship that is a credit to the medieval Western church. At the same time, in the millennium that stretches from the late ancient period to the Renaissance, one also finds much testimony that reflects poorly upon the church's partnership with families.

With the dawning of imperial favor in the fourth century AD and the crumbling of the Roman Empire in the fifth, the primary locus of Christian practice drifted from homes to dedicated institutional structures. Especially in the early Middle Ages, generations grew less literate, and training in Christian traditions increasingly became the domain of professional clergy in ecclesiastical institutions. Still, reformers and pastors ranging from Caesarius in the sixth century to Jean Gerson in the fifteenth

---

1. Caesarius of Arles, *Sermons*, volume 1 (1–80), The Fathers of the Church, vol. 31, trans. Mary Magdeleine Mueller (New York: The Fathers of the Church, Inc., 1956), 46. For more on Caesarius, see William E. Klingshirn, *Caesarius of Arles: the Making of a Christian Community in Late Antique Gaul*, Cambridge Studies in Medieval Life and Thought (Cambridge: Cambridge University Press, 1994).

century boldly called upon churches to improve their efforts at bringing discipleship into the household.

To understand the theology and practice of family discipleship throughout this era, it is necessary first to look carefully at Augustine of Hippo, whose work proved to be the reference point for so many medieval theological discussions. From this vantage point, the contributions of medieval theologians and the practices of medieval churches will become far clearer.

THE TESTIMONY OF AUGUSTINE OF HIPPO

"She Was Bringing My Eternal Salvation to Birth": Monica's Role in Augustine's Salvation

By anyone's reckoning, the North African pastor Augustine of Hippo was the most important theologian in the minds of the medieval scholars. Prominent alongside the searching spiritual narrative of Augustine's *Confessions* are his remarks about the influence of his mother, Monica. According to Augustine's testimony, Monica was reared by Christian parents with the aid of a wise older maidservant.[2] Although her husband was not yet a Christian, Monica had Augustine signed with the cross and rubbed with salt at birth.[3]

Even as Augustine became an adherent of a false religion known as "Manichaeism," Monica refused to give up her concern for her son's soul, weeping more for him "than ever mothers wept for the bodily death of their children." Her prayers for her son seemed to have been answered in a dream; in Monica's dream, a voice told her, "Where you are, he will be." Confident that the Lord had assured her of her son's eventual salvation, she shared this dream with Augustine. Although Augustine suggested that his mother had misunderstood the message, Monica steadfastly denied any misunderstanding. Her prayers for him continued, even after he moved to Italy to advance his teaching career.

Of course, the Lord did not leave Augustine in that state. After he moved from Rome to Milan, Augustine began to listen to the sermons

---

2. Augustine, *Confessions* 9.8.17.
3. This was a rite which was at the time given to catechumens, only later in history to be used during the service of baptism. See John K. Ryan, "Notes to Book 1," in Augustine, *The Confessions of St. Augustine*, trans. John K. Ryan (New York: Doubleday, 1960), 373; Augustine, *Confessions* 1.11.17, in *The Confessions, The Works of Saint Augustine: A Translation for the 21st Century*, Part 1, vol. 1, trans. Maria Boulding, ed. John E. Rotelle (Hyde Park, NY: New City Press, 1997), 51.

of Ambrose—not because of any interest in Christian faith but because of Ambrose's renowned rhetorical skills. Eventually, Augustine was converted, and Monica lived to see Ambrose baptize her son.

Augustine never specifically mentioned any attempts by his mother to provide formal instruction for her son in the Christian faith. Yet, whether or not Monica attempted to teach her son the Apostles' Creed or the Lord's Prayer, or even to read Scripture to him, her influence upon his spiritual life is undeniable. Her prayers, dreams, and confidence in God's sovereignty had an obvious impact upon Augustine's pilgrimage to faith. Perhaps as a testimony to his mother's influence, when Augustine taught on marriage as pastor of the church in Hippo he frequently emphasized the important role that a parent plays in the discipleship of children.

"Their Development . . . Is Due to Your Good Will and Ability": Marriage and the Discipleship of Children in the Theology of Augustine

Marriage was a controversial topic in Augustine's day. Asceticism, the physical discipline of the body and denial of bodily desires, was a popular approach to sanctification. Theologians were suspicious about the wholesomeness of sexual intercourse, even within the context of marriage. Jerome, a prominent churchman and controversialist, had written a scathing response to a Roman Christian named Jovinian, simply because Jovinian contended that marriage and lifelong virginity were equal in holiness. Jerome's response to Jovinian was so harsh that many considered his tirade to be an attack upon the institution of marriage itself.

Augustine's view of marriage, though still negatively influenced by the asceticism of his day, was more measured than Jerome's.[4] According to Augustine, God ordained marriage before humanity's fall into sin for the purpose of begetting children. Ever since humanity's fall into sin, intercourse—even between a husband and wife—has been tainted by lust and sin.[5] This does not, however, negate the value of marriage. Marriages, Augustine stated, can produce children honorably, lawfully,

---

4. For the background on Augustine's treatises on marriage, see David Hunter, "Introduction," in Augustine, *Marriage and Virginity*, *The Works of Saint Augustine: A Translation for the 21st Century*, part 1, vol. 9, trans. Ray Kearney, ed. David G. Hunter (Hyde Park, NY: New City Press, 1999).

5. For Augustine's important works on marriage, see Augustine, *Marriage and Virginity*, *The Works of Saint Augustine*. See also Augustine, *De Civitate Dei* 14.10–26.

and chastely "in a social role. . . . They educate those children without favoritism, soundly, and perseveringly."[6] Despite disagreement with Augustine's view of sexual relations between a husband and wife, contemporary evangelicals can still glean wisdom from Augustine: At a time when many Christians elevated asceticism above marital relations, Augustine saw value in this relationship precisely because marriage provided an opportunity for parents to educate children in the Christian faith.

Augustine's understanding of the importance of the parents' role in training children is further underscored by a treatise that he wrote to provide encouragement to a widow whose daughter had decided to remain a virgin for life. All the widow's children had evidently turned out well. "They were," Augustine declared, "born because of your fertility, they live because of your good fortune, but their development like that is due to your good will and ability. . . . In [your daughter] you participate in something you do not have."[7] According to Augustine, the widow received spiritual benefit from the daughter's commitment because the widow had worked to develop her daughter spiritually. Though Augustine believed that virginity was a state deserving special merit, he demonstrated that parenthood also provided an opportunity for a worthy endeavor of another kind: the discipleship of children. Surely his own mother's unwavering dedication had not been forgotten.

FAMILY DISCIPLESHIP IN MEDIEVAL THEOLOGY

Augustine's theological teachings greatly influenced the intellectual life of the church of the early and high Middle Ages. Whether the topic was the Trinity, the sacraments, the interpretation of Scripture, or the doctrine of the church, theologians and commentators referenced the fifth-century overseer of Hippo first and most often. The question often became not whether Augustine was correct on a subject, but whether or not the current generation was interpreting Augustine correctly.[8]

---

6. Augustine, *Holy Virginity*, in *Marriage and Virginity, The Works of Saint Augustine*, 74.
7. Augustine, *The Excellence of Widowhood*, in *Marriage and Virginity, The Works of Saint Augustine*, 124.
8. For a discussion on Augustine's influence on medieval theology, see Jaroslav Pelikan, *The Christian Tradition: A History of the Development of Doctrine*, vol. 3, *The Growth of Medieval Theology* (600–1300) (Chicago: University of Chicago Press, 1978), esp. 1–49.

Medieval writings on the institution of marriage certainly reflected Augustine's influence. Unfortunately, Augustine's emphasis upon the value of discipling one's children was not often a focus of attention. No major medieval theologians seem to have produced any works exclusively devoted to the subject of spiritual training in the context of a family. The subject of the family was most often broached within the context of the sacrament of marriage, and even within those discussions, many theologians failed to replicate Augustine's concern for discipleship within the context of the Christian household.

Gregory the Great and Hugh of St. Victor

Gregory the Great was one such church leader whose teaching fell short in recognizing the value of parents' role in training their children. As overseer of the Roman church in the late sixth and early seventh centuries, he played an important role in establishing the papacy as an influential office in the medieval church. Like Augustine, he argued that intercourse was appropriate only for the purpose of procreating. Unlike Augustine, he did not include the discipleship of one's children among the virtues or values of marriage. The work of Hugh of St. Victor is in the same vein. His work *On the Sacraments of the Christian Faith* describes marriage as a sacrament that is integrally related to the union of Christ and the church. Even before the fall, God prescribed the duty of sexual intercourse for the purpose of procreation. Humanity's fall into sin left this marital privilege tainted by sinful passions and desires.[9] Hugh, however—like Gregory and unlike Augustine—bypassed the positive role that parents play in providing Christian formation for their children.

Thomas Aquinas

The thirteenth-century theologian Thomas Aquinas echoed Augustine more accurately, at least with respect to the place of family discipleship. Consistent with what had been written before him, Thomas described the

---

9. Hugh of St. Victor, *On the Sacraments of the Christian Faith*, in *A Scholastic Miscellany: Anselm to Ockham*, trans. and ed. Eugene R. Fairweather, Library of Christian Classics, vol. 10 (Philadelphia: Westminster, 1956), 318.

purpose of marriage before the first sin to have been the procreation of children. After the first sin, he asserted, the purpose became twofold: the procreation of children and the safeguarding of Christians against sexual sin.

Unlike Gregory and Hugh, Thomas articulated an important place for the education of children. The duty of marriage, he explained, was to produce offspring, but by the term "offspring," he intended not only "the begetting of children, but also their education, to which as its end is directed the entire communion of works that exists between man and wife as united in marriage." For Thomas, producing offspring was the principal goal of marriage, and educating them was the secondary goal.[10]

Thomas produced a manual of instruction, *The Catechetical Instructions of St. Thomas Aquinas*. Scholars describing family life in the Middle Ages have commented that the church during this period produced no catechisms.[11] If by the term "catechism" one means a document in question-and-answer format designed for the direct instruction of children, no such documents were produced during the Middle Ages. Augustine, however, had produced a work entitled *Catechizing of the Uninstructed*, which offered a framework for pastors and teachers to provide basic doctrinal teaching. Faithful to that tradition, Thomas published an instruction manual for pastors that offered simple explanations of the Apostles' Creed, the Lord's Prayer, the Hail Mary, the Ten Commandments, and the seven sacraments. While the document was not intended to be used in the household, it at least provided a much-needed resource for church leaders that would encourage attention to the young. The only other major church leader to produce such a work during the Middle Ages was Jean Gerson in the fifteenth century.[12]

---

10. Thomas Aquinas, *Summa Theologica*, vol. 5, trans. Fathers of the English Dominican Province (Allen, TX: Thomas More Publishers), 2702, 2726.
11. See, for instance, Bernard Hamilton, *Religion in the Medieval West*, 2nd ed. (London: Arnold; New York: Oxford University Press, 2003), 79; also André Vauchez, *The Laity in the Middle Ages: Religious Beliefs and Devotional Practices*, trans. Margery J. Schneider, ed. Daniel E. Bornsten (South Bend: University of Notre Dame Press, 1996), 90.
12. Joseph B. Collins comments that Thomas deserves a place in the history of Catholic catechetical instruction among Augustine, Gerson, Charles Borromeo, Peter Canisius, and others. Interestingly, the only medieval figure on the list is Gerson. Thomas Aquinas, *The Catechetical Instruction of St. Thomas Aquinas*, trans. Joseph B. Collins (Catholic Primer, 2004), 10, http://www.scribd.com/doc/3243405/Catechism-of-St-Thomas-Aquinas (accessed February 8, 2010). Also accessible at http://catholicprimer.org/home/works/aquinas/cat.

Jean Gerson

Gerson made a concerted effort to improve discipleship in the family during an age in which many were crying out for a reform of the church at
all levels. Gerson became chancellor of the University of Paris in 1395
and quickly concerned himself with bringing much needed reform to the
church. He saw that the church needed more than a reform at the top. The
faith and morals of the people needed reform as well, and this had to start
with the education of children. In a number of sermons preached before
crowds at the university, he called upon parents to disciple their progeny.

Like Augustine and Aquinas before him, Gerson stated that marriage
was ordained not only for the procreation of children but also for their
education. Parents who neglected to disciple their children "will be held
more accountable than if they let their offspring die of hunger."[13] This process, he argued, involved both moral and spiritual formation. Parents must
ensure that children are reared in an environment that is morally pure and
should inculcate virtuous speech and work habits.

To address the spiritual needs of families, Gerson published a manual
for priests, much like those of Augustine and Aquinas before him, which
explained what he perceived to be the basic components of Christian
training: the Lord's Prayer, the Hail Mary, the Apostles' Creed, the seven
sacraments, the seven grades of holy orders, and the six branches of pen-
ance. His manual is more extensive than those of his predecessors, including comments on ethics and spirituality. Gerson clearly saw that the
proper discipleship of children was important—not only for the welfare of
families but also for the welfare of the entire church. And so, he created a
resource to forge a partnership between training at church and training in
the context of Christian households.

In the Middle Ages, interest in the institution of marriage often centered on the function and negative impact of sexuality within the institution. The discipleship of children was overlooked entirely by some of the
most influential writers of the period. Thomas Aquinas and Jean Gerson
were clearly exceptions.

Simply because many of the major thinkers of the church were not
writing on the topic of family discipleship does not, however, mean that
nothing was being done to train children in the fear of God. Outside the

---

13. Jean Gerson, quoted in D. Catherine Brown, *Pastor and Laity in the Theology of Jean Gerson*
   (New York: Cambridge University Press, 1987), 238–42.

halls of the medieval universities and monastic cloisters, some pastors and preachers in direct contact with laypeople *were* making an effort to bring Christian discipleship into the household.

FAMILY DISCIPLESHIP
IN THE MINISTRIES OF MEDIEVAL PASTORS

The Challenge of Christian Training in the Middle Ages

One factor that influenced family discipleship during this period was the state of the clergy. Not all clergy during the medieval era served as pastors. In fact, large numbers of clergy had no ministry whatsoever among laypeople. Monasticism had grown in popularity throughout the Middle Ages, and many monks lived their lives within the confines of cloistered communities. The primary responsibility for teaching laypeople the doctrines and practices of the church fell to the "secular clergy"—to the priests who served as pastors in communities. Yet many of these secular clergy were poorly trained and ill-equipped for their ministries. Boniface, an Anglo-Saxon missionary in the eighth century, found secular clergy living in drunkenness, sexual sin, and ignorance regarding the most basic matters of Christian faith.

In the late eighth and early ninth centuries, even the requirements that church reformers laid upon the secular clergy were very basic: bishops should ensure that priests understood the Apostles' Creed and the Lord's Prayer, could conduct a proper baptism and mass, and could sing certain psalms. Complaints about the ignorance and hypocritical lifestyles of the clergy continued into the Reformation era.[14]

Preaching was often limited to bishops, who were better educated, especially in the early medieval period. Few among the laity had access to the Bible or even the capacity to read. Laypeople encountered Scripture only as it was read during weekly liturgies, and then typically in Latin. Families seeking an encounter with God through Scripture could often do so only at the church during the liturgy—and then only if they understood Latin! During the later centuries of the Middle Ages, the frequency of access to preaching did increase as educational levels improved and as mendicant preaching orders began to make their rounds.

---

14. Joseph H. Lynch, *The Medieval Church: A Brief History* (New York: Longman, 1992), 77–80, 89–90, 339.

Since families had little or no access to the Bible, the spiritual lives of families might often depend upon the liturgy and ceremonies of the church. Baptism and confirmation were particularly important moments for parents in the spiritual lives of their children. Confirmation developed because of the desire to distance infants and younger children from participation in Holy Communion. Confirmation provided priests with the opportunity to examine the understanding of youths, to communicate the basics of the Christian faith, and to affirm

> ### Mendicant Orders
> ❧
> In the Middle Ages, monks in mendicant orders (from Latin, *mendicans,* begging) served the poor and relied on donations for their livelihood. Mendicant preachers traveled among ordinary people and, in some cases, seem to have called parents to engage actively in their children's Christian formation. The Dominicans and Franciscans were both mendicant orders.

the individual's standing in the community.[15] These more extensive requirements may have kept some from participating. The rite of baptism, then, became even more important, both in the eyes of the church hierarchy and in the eyes of parents. In many cases, the emphasis on the one-time act of baptism seems to have resulted in de-emphasis on processes of Christian training and discipleship.

Godparents and Godchildren in the Middle Ages

In the seventh century, Caesarius had advocated the use of the Apostles' Creed and the Lord's Prayer for the discipleship of the laity. Caesarius had said, "You yourselves learn especially the creed and the Lord's Prayer, and teach them to your children. Indeed, I do not know whether a person should even be called a Christian if he neglects to learn a few words of the creedy."[16] He moved beyond words to action as he preached simple sermons expounding upon the words of both statements. Further, he urged

---

15. Kathryn Ann Taglia, "The Cultural Construction of Childhood: Baptism, Communion, and Confirmation," in *Women, Marriage, and Family in Medieval Christendom: Essays in Memory of Michael M. Sheehan, C.S.B.,* ed. Constance M. Rousseau and Joel T. Rosenthal (Kalamazoo, MI: Medieval Institute Publications, 1998), 276–83; Linda E. Mitchell, *Family Life in the Middle Ages* (Westport, CT: Greenwood Press, 2007), 173.
16. Caesarius of Arles, *Sermons,* vol. 1, 100.

parents to teach these statements to their children and baptismal sponsors to teach them to their godchildren when they reached a suitable age.

Building upon Caesarius's methodology, reformers during the reign of Emperor Charlemagne required the sponsors of infants at baptism to commit to teach their godchildren the Creed and the Lord's Prayer. They made this requirement more practical by promoting translations of both statements into the language of the common people. This practice eventually became the standard approach in regions that had once comprised the Western Roman Empire. Documents from medieval England reveal that this practice definitely took hold there as well. Manuals intended for the training of priests in England contain admonitions that godparents should be charged with the spiritual upbringing of children, teaching them the Lord's Prayer, the Apostles' Creed, and the Hail Mary. The responsibility for the selection of godparents in these manuals apparently rested partly upon parents, who were urged not to accept as sponsor anyone who did not know these prayers.

Given the educational levels of both clergy and laity and the limited access to the Scriptures, use of these prayers was a practical solution to the problem of promoting a deeper understanding of the Christian faith among the masses. Further, admonishing baptismal sponsors to teach them provided the church with an official avenue to promote at least a basic level of discipleship. Unfortunately, the church had no means to hold parents and baptismal sponsors accountable to this task. In fact, no documentary evidence exists to reveal whether or not medieval godparents even taught the children these prayers. In some cases mothers took this task upon themselves.[17]

> ### Godparents
> ➤◄
> In late ancient and medieval churches, godparents voiced the confession of faith on behalf of infants who were being baptized. Sixteenth-century reformers such as Ulrich Zwingli and John Calvin encouraged parents to voice the confession, rather than relying on godparents, and to participate more actively in their children's Christian formation.

---

17. Regarding godparents, see Barbara Hanawalt, *The Ties That Bound: Peasant Families in Medieval England* (New York: Oxford University Press, 1986), 246; also Peter Fleming, *Family and Household in Medieval England* (New York: Palgrave, 2001), 62; and Joseph H. Lynch, *Godparents and Kinship in Early Medieval Europe* (Princeton, NJ: Princeton University Press, 1986), 312–19. Numerous scholars make the argument that mothers trained their children in Christian faith, including Mitchell, *Family Life in the Middle Ages*, 171;

Medieval Resources for Family Discipleship

Although discipleship within the family seems to have been promoted primarily by local priests and revolved around parents and godparents teaching their children basic doctrinal statements and prayers, evidence reveals that other resources were available for some. In the Netherlands and Belgium, for example, several "household codices"— manuscripts containing the Apostles' Creed, the Ten Commandments, the Lord's Prayer, and other prayers that were deemed important for the faith and morals of the family—have survived. In a few cases, resourceful pastors or laypersons may have produced manuals for family discipleship.[18]

John Bromyard, a fourteenth-century Dominican friar in Hereford, produced a work that was intended as an aid for Dominican preachers in their mission. Bromyard called upon parents to discipline their children appropriately, to teach them God's commandments, and to teach them to restrain their tongues. Bromyard scolded parents for caring more for their children's physical well-being than for their spiritual vitality: "If they should see them poor they are saddened and sigh. If they see them sinning, nobody is sad." To make matters worse, he complained, wealthy parents send their children to the courts of nobles to complete their education and training but neglect to provide for the education of their souls, "rejoicing to see them led to the gallows of hell with oaths, fopperies, bad manners and dissolute company, grieving and weeping when they see them learning the art of a good life."[19]

Such challenges undoubtedly encouraged family discipleship. If Bromyard's preaching was representative of other Dominican preaching, then perhaps the Dominican order was a useful resource for encouraging family discipleship in the late Middle Ages.

A number of factors made the promotion of family discipleship a

Mary Martyn McLoughlin, "Children and Parents from the Ninth to Thirteenth Centuries," in *Medieval Families: Perspectives on Marriage, Household, and Children*, ed. Carol Neel (Toronto: University of Toronto Press, 2004), 47; Vauchez, *Laity in the Middle Ages*, 91; and Jennifer Ward, *Women in Medieval Europe, 1200–1500* (New York: Longman, 2002), 58.

18. Anneke B. Mulder-Bakker, "The Household as a Site of Civic and Religious Instruction: Two Household Books from Late Medieval Brabant," in *Household, Women, and Christianities in Late Antiquity and the Middle Ages*, ed. Anneke B. Mulder-Bakker and Jocelyn Wogan-Browne (Turnhout, Belgium: Brepols, 2005), 199.

19. John Bromyard, quoted in G. R. Oust, *Literature and Pulpit in Medieval England: A Neglected Chapter in the History of English Letters and of the English People*, 2nd ed. (Oxford: Basil & Blackwell, 1966), 463–66.

challenge for the medieval church. Certainly the most significant challenge was illiteracy. Not only were many fathers and mothers illiterate, low
literacy rates made the production of books, and especially Bibles, expen-
sive. This was a problem peculiar to medieval Europe, since literacy rates
and educational levels in the regions that had once comprised the eastern
Roman Empire were considerably better.[20] The poor state of preparation
among many parish priests did not help the situation. Further complicating
matters, a large number of the clergy—and many of its best educated—
were far removed from parish life because of their service in monasteries.
They were not involved in the spiritual development of families and produced very little to aid those who were. While in some cases a few other
resources were available, many times the church's main effort to promote
family discipleship consisted of encouraging parents and godparents to
teach children basic truths and prayers.

"LAZY HANDS ARE BOUND TO HAVE A LEAN YEAR"

Much has changed since the Middle Ages. Unlike most medieval theologians, the Protestant Reformers of the sixteenth century refused to see
sexual expression within marriage as inherently tainted by sin. In the
Protestant Reformation, then, the institution of marriage became much
more important to the spiritual health of the church. As a consequence,
the discipleship of children also became important, and the Reformers
and their successors placed a greater priority on producing literature for
this task. Rising literacy rates and improved educational levels in the late
Middle Ages and Reformation era meant that many parents became more
capable to teach their children biblical truths.

Contemporary evangelical churches approach the task of family discipleship much differently than medieval churches did. Our theology of
the family and sexuality is obviously different—but the differences don't
end there. The educational resources available to parents in contemporary

---

20. At age seven, children in Constantinople were sent to study at a neighborhood school,
    where they would study the Psalms, various selections from the Bible (especially Prov-
    erbs and Ecclesiastes), and Homer. Parents assisted children as they learned these
    lessons. Marcus Rautman, *Daily Life in the Byzantium Empire* (Westport, CT: Greenwood
    Press, 2006), 54. By the sixth century, schools were open to educate a large propor-
    tion of the children of freedmen. In the eleventh century, Emperor Alexius Comnenus
    opened free schools for all, regardless of social class. Tamara Talbot Rice, *Everyday Life
    in Byzantium* (New York: Dorsett Press, 1967), 192.

literate societies are also much greater. Families in the Middle Ages had little or no access to the Scriptures, much less a Bible in their own language.

> ✦ Fourteenth-century Dominican preacher John Bromyard called parents to repent because they focused on making certain their children were well-educated and well-to-do while neglecting their children's formation in Christian faith. Six centuries later, a LifeWay Research survey of parents revealed that having children who become "happy adults" tied for first place as the most common goal for parenting. By comparison, only nine percent of parents mentioned godliness or faith in God (Mark Kelly, "Faith in God Ranks Low in Definition of Successful Parenting," http://www.lifeway.com/article/168964/). Consider the parents in your congregation. What is their primary goal for their children? What should be their goal? How can you guide these parents toward God's goal for their children? ✦

They possessed few pieces of printed literature, and they often had no consistent preaching to challenge them. These facts make the efforts of persons like Caesarius and Gerson worthy of high commendation. Without printed resources or frequent preaching of Scripture, these men searched for pathways to establish discipleship practices in Christian households. Their example makes the task of partnering church and family all the more urgent for Christians today with such a wealth of resources. This should also call many of us to develop creative ways to help less literate persons to disciple their children. With great resources comes great responsibility.

Martin Luther, urging German cities to establish Christian schools, put it this way:

> Buy while the market is at your door; gather in the harvest while there is sunshine and fair weather; make use of God's grace and word while it is there! For you should know that God's word and grace are like a passing shower of rain which does not return where it has once been. . . . Paul brought it to the Greeks; but again when it's gone it's gone, and now they have the Turk. Rome and the Latins also had it; but when it's gone it's gone, and now they have the pope. And you Germans need not think

that you will have it forever, for ingratitude and contempt will not make it stay. Therefore, seize it and hold it fast, whoever can; for lazy hands are bound to have a lean year.[21]

Luther's admonition applies to all who are charged with discipling children, whether in the classroom in the congregation or in the family. Parents must take advantage of this season of blessing by utilizing the abundant resources available to them to become primary faith-trainers in their children's lives.

---

21. Martin Luther, "To the Councilmen of All Cities in Germany That They Establish and Maintain Christian Schools" (1524), in Martin Luther, *The Christian in Society II*, *Luther's Works*, American edition, vol. 45, ed. Helmut T. Lehmann (Philadelphia: Fortress Press, 1962), 352.

7

THE HOME IS AN EARTHLY KINGDOM

Family Discipleship among Reformers and Puritans

C. Jeffrey Robinson Sr.

The sixteenth-century Protestant Reformation profoundly altered the shape of Christianity. Martin Luther worked to restore the primacy of the doctrine of *sola fide*—justification by faith alone—in the proclamation of the gospel. Luther also asserted the principle of *sola Scriptura*, which identified Scripture as the locus of authority for the church. In Geneva, John Calvin further expounded these principles and posited a theological perspective that emphasized the sovereignty of God and the radical corruption of humanity. These theological emphases of the Reformation have received massive scholarly attention over the centuries. Another critical consequence of the Reformation—no less important—has received far less emphasis: what have been the implications of this movement for ministry to families?

The Reformers, particularly Luther and Calvin, developed a robust vision for Christian training in the household and called parents to disciple their children. The Puritans in England and America cultivated this Reformation vision and brought it to its fullest flower in the form of consistent family worship and discipleship.

"BRING THEM UP TO SERVE HIM": MARRIAGE AND THE TRAINING OF CHILDREN IN MARTIN LUTHER'S THEOLOGY

The medieval church had drawn a sharp distinction between secular and spiritual estates. Persons who took upon themselves the counsels of perfection—poverty, chastity, and obedience—were perceived to possess higher righteousness than those immersed in the daily affairs of the world. Luther rejected this dichotomy and asserted the priesthood of all believers. Further, Luther argued that everyone is born as someone's child and "educated as someone's pupil, governed as someone's subject, supplied as someone's customer, married as someone's spouse, nurtured as someone's parishioner," and at last became a parent of one's own children.[1] Thus, the home must be initial staging ground for the advance of the gospel; in each home, parents are priests, and it is their sworn duty before God to set the gospel before the entire family.

Luther did not merely proclaim the practices of marriage and parenthood; Luther lived them. On June 13, 1525, Luther the ex-monk married runaway nun Katharina von Bora before a group of friends and witnesses. Throughout his marriage as much as his theology, the German reformer radically changed the way that many Christians viewed marriage and family. "Luther's monastic revolt and subsequent marriage represent for his ethics what the nailing of the theses and his defense at Worms represent for his theology."[2]

Luther and Katharina bore six biological children and adopted four more from relatives. By all accounts, the Luther home bustled with activity and joy: Martin sang songs with his children and serenaded them with music played on his lute. The Luther home was filled with teaching and learning, not only about the things of God but also about games and ordinary issues of life.[3] Martin Luther partnered with Katharina in the care of their children, dealing daily with everything from diapers to disciplinary matters.

Luther broke with the Roman Catholic Church by refusing to treat marriage as a sacrament. Marriage and the family it creates was a divine gift and is one of the three basic institutions ordained by God alongside the church and the state. According to Luther,

> Marriage is not a thing of nature but a gift of God, the sweetest, the dearest, and the purest life above all celibacy and singleness, when it

---

1. Martin Luther, quoted in Jane E. Strohl, "The Child in Luther's Theology," in *The Child in Christian Thought*, ed. Marcia J. Bunge (Grand Rapids: Eerdmans, 2001), 139.
2. William H. Lazareth, *Luther on the Christian Home: An Application of the Social Ethics of the Reformation* (Philadelphia: Muhlenberg, 1960), 1.
3. Roland H. Bainton, *Here I Stand: A Life of Martin Luther* (New York: Meridan, 1995), 226–37.

turns out well, though the very devil if it does not. . . . If then these three remain—fidelity and faith, children and progeny, and the sacrament— it is to be considered to be wholly divine and blessed estate. . . . One should not regard any estate as better in the sight of God than the estate of marriage.[4]

The household, as Luther expressed it, was to operate as "an earthly kingdom" where parents train children in the commandments of God.[5] For Luther as for medieval theologians, marriage did function as a safeguard against sexual sin—but that was not the primary function of the marriage relationship. The purpose of marriage was to raise godly offspring:

> The best thing in married life, for the sake of which everything ought to be suffered and done, is the fact that God gives children and commands us to bring them up to serve Him. To do this is the noblest and most precious work on earth, because nothing may be done which pleases God more than saving souls.[6]

From Luther's perspective, parenting is not a secular duty but a holy vocation and a divine calling. The family is the preeminent estate of life— an estate that preceded the fall of humanity and functions as the fundamental component of social order within every culture: "Thus all who are called masters stand in the place of parents and must derive from them their power and authority to govern."[7]

And who is to lead spiritually in the household, this society from which all other societal powers gain their power and authority? The parents, Luther, argued—but a special calling falls to the head of the household, the father. In his preface to the *Larger Catechism*, Luther urged fathers to lead the entire household in regular, substantive training in the Christian faith: "It is the duty of every head of a household at least once a week to examine the children and servants one after the other to ascertain what

4. Martin Luther, *Christian in Society II, Luther's Works*, American edition, vol. 45, ed. Helmut T. Lehmann (Philadelphia: Mulenberg/Fortress Press, 1955), 47.
5. Martin Luther, *The Large Catechism* in *The Book of Concord: The Confessions of the Evangelical Lutheran Church*, ed. Robert Kolb and Timothy J. Wengert, trans. Charles Arand (Minneapolis: Augsburg Fortress Press, 2000), 410.
6. Martin Luther, "Sermon on Married Life," quoted in Leland Ryken, *Worldly Saints: The Puritans as They Really Were* (Grand Rapids: Zondervan, 1986), 239n3.
7. Luther, *Large Catechism* in *Book of Concord*, 406.

they know or have learned of it, and, if they do not know it, to keep them faithfully at it."[8]

"THE OFFICE OF A GOOD HOUSEHOLDER": JOHN CALVIN AND THE CHRISTIAN TRAINING OF CHILDREN

Unlike Martin Luther, the French reformer John Calvin did not have the privilege of raising children from infancy to adulthood. Calvin and his wife, Idelette de Bure, had one son; this child died shortly after a premature birth in July 1542. Idelette had two children from a previous marriage. After Idelette's death in 1549, Calvin helped to raise these children.

Also unlike Luther, Calvin provided little information about how he interacted with children in his household. Still, Calvin's preparation of ordinances for regulation of the church in Geneva, his two catechisms, as well as his promotion of education in the establishment of the Geneva Academy suggest that he was deeply concerned about the education of children. The subtitle of one of Calvin's catechisms was "a form of instruction for children."[9]

In Calvin's thinking, children were simultaneously objects of God's wrath and heirs of God's covenant. As heirs of the covenant, infants of believing parents were to be baptized into church membership. These same children, however, lacked any natural desire to submit to God.[10] Parents— and particularly fathers—were responsible to train these children toward godliness. "Constant conversation should be held . . . with their children, in order that fathers should diligently attend and apply themselves to the duty of instruction."[11] Father Abraham could be considered "a good householder" because he was a father who instructed his family in faithfulness to God (Gen. 18:19).[12] Ulrich Zwingli held a similar perspective on the role of parents in the Christian formation of children.[13]

---

8. Luther, Preface, *Large Catechism* in *Book of Concord*, 383.
9. John Calvin, *Tracts and Letters, Volume* 2, trans. Henry Beveridge (Edinburgh: Banner of Truth Trust, 2009), 33.
10. John Calvin, *Institutes of the Christian Religion: 1536 Edition*, trans. Ford Lewis Battles (Grand Rapids: Eerdmans, 1975), 97.
11. John Calvin, *Harmony of Exodus, Leviticus, Numbers, Deuteronomy* (1563) in *Calvin's Commentaries*, vol. 2, trans. Charles William Bingham (Grand Rapids: Baker, 1999), 367.
12. John Calvin, *Genesis* (1554) in *Calvin's Commentaries*, vol. 1, trans. John King (Grand Rapids: Baker, 1999), 481.
13. W. P. Stephens, *The Theology of Huldrych Zwingli* (Oxford: Oxford University Press, 1986), 194.

Yet parents did not stand alone in their training of children. Members of the larger community of faith bore a responsibility to equip parents and to partner with parents in children's instruction:

> It has ever been the practice of the Church, and one carefully attended to, to see that children should be duly instructed in the Christian religion. That this might be done more conveniently, not only were schools opened in old time, and *individuals enjoined properly to teach their families,* but it was a received public custom and practice, to question children in the churches.[14]

More mature believers in the church were also urged to teach the young: "Let the aged guide the insufficiency of youth with their own wisdom and experience wherein they [surpass] the younger, not railing harshly and loudly against them but tempering their severity with mildness and gentleness."[15]

"EVERY HOUSE A HOUSEHOLD OF FAITH": FAMILY WORSHIP AMONG THE PURITANS

Martin Luther and John Calvin articulated clear theological foundations for discipleship in the context of the Christian household. In the generations following the Reformation, the rise of common-language Scripture translations and mass-printed books led to increased possibilities for discipleship in the Christian household. By the dawning decade of the seventeenth century, the English Puritans were taking full advantage of these new means. In the process, these Puritans and their heirs developed some of the most mature expressions of the theology and practice of what came to be known as "family worship." The term "Puritan" was first coined in 1580 as a slur to describe persons who were seeking to purify Anglican liturgy. The term is employed in much the same way within contemporary popular literature as a synonym for a long-faced fundamentalism: "Puritanism is," one twentieth-century journalist claimed, "the haunting fear that someone, somewhere may be happy."[16]

---

14. Calvin, *Tracts and Letters, Volume 2,* 37 (emphasis added).
15. Calvin, *Institutes of the Christian Religion,* 28.
16. H. L. Mencken, quoted in Ryken, *Worldly Saints,* 1.

Such sweeping generalizations miss the mark at every level. Puritans were people of great passion, joy, even romance. They were the theological heirs of Calvin's reforms, yet they "regarded the Reformation as incomplete and wished to model English church worship and government according to the Word of God."[17] Their commitment to theologically driven evangelism and Scripture-saturated piety serve as excellent models for the church today. Most important for the purposes of this chapter, the Puritans' devotion to Scripture compelled them to develop a vital emphasis on consistent worship of God within the family.

"Every Father a Priest in His Own Family": Puritanism and the Purpose of the Family

For the Puritans, every household was to be "a household of faith; every father a priest in his own family." "It is no small mercy to be the parents of a godly seed," Puritan pastor Richard Baxter wrote, "and this is the end of the institution of marriage"— with "end" referring in this context to an "endpoint" or "goal."[18] Much like Luther, the Puritans refused to separate life into "sacred" and "secular" categories. Every aspect of an individual's life, whether deliberately chosen or circumstantial—which is to say, from a Puritan perspective, *providential*—was part of that person's "particular calling."[19] The domestic calling of men included marriage and child rearing; the entire particular calling for women entailed homemaking.[20]

> ➔ From the Puritan perspective, every Christian household was to be "a household of faith; every father a priest in his own family." In your congregation, what would change if every member viewed his or her home in this way? How can you equip believing fathers for a pastoral role in their households? How can you support and help wives whose husbands are not believers? ◂

A key task in these particular callings was the training of children to love and to obey God. The family was, after all, "the seminary of church

---

17. Horton Davies, *The Worship of the English Puritans*, 2nd ed. (Morgan, PA: Soli Deo Gloria, 1997), 1.
18. Richard Baxter, *The Practical Works of Richard Baxter, Volume 1: A Christian Directory* (1673; repr., Morgan, PA: Soli Deo Gloria, 2000), 20.
19. J. I. Packer, *A Quest for Godliness: The Puritan Vision of the Christian Life* (Wheaton, IL: Crossway, 1990), 271–72.
20. Ibid., 270.

and state and if children be not well principled there, all miscarrieth."[21] Puritans endowed all family activities and roles with dignity, and they understood Scripture to teach a divinely ordained order of responsibility within the household. This order acknowledged the father as the person primarily responsible for the training of children in Christian faith. Fathers were consistently called to "keep up the government of God in your families: holy families must be the chief preservers of the interest of religion in the world."[22]

A Headship of "Love and Complicated Interest": The Father's Role in the Puritan Household

When his child was baptized, the Puritan father promised to supervise and to nurture this child in Christian faith; the father was duty-bound to teach his children the Scriptures and to lead them in prayer and praise. At minimum, Puritan fathers were expected to lead their families in prayers twice each day and to expound the catechism and a Scripture text with their families every Lord's Day.

Both husband and wife were viewed as equal in value and in essence. Yet, functionally, God had ordained the husband to be the head.[23] The husband's headship, according to the Puritans, was not a permit to please himself but a charge to take responsibility for others. Headship did not entitle a husband to "lord it over his family"; his authority was, after all, a derived authority.[24] All authority, including the husband's, is ordained, delegated, and regulated by a greater head, one to whom the father will give an account. The husband's headship was a solemn privilege of loving servanthood built on the example of Jesus Christ. Such love for one's wife was "like Christ's to his church: holy for quality, and great for quantity."[25] Richard Baxter put it this way:

> Your authority over your wife is but such as is necessary to the order of your family, the safe and prudent management of your affairs, and your comfortable cohabitation. The power of love and complicated interest

21. John Geree, *The Character of an Old English Puritaine, or Nonconformist* (1646), quoted in Packer, *Quest for Godliness,* 270.
22. Ibid., 271–72.
23. Packer, *Quest for Godliness,* 262–63.
24. Ryken, *Worldly Saints,* 76.
25. Ibid.

must do more than magisterial commands. Your authority over your children is much greater; but yet only such as, conjunct with love, is needful to their good education and felicity.[26]

A wife's submission is, in the words of John Winthrop, "her honor and freedom . . . Such is the liberty of the church under the authority of Christ."[27]

> "The women was made of a rib out of the side of Adam; not made out of his head to top him, not of his feet to be trampled by him, but out of his side to be equal with him, under his arm to be protected, and near his heart to be loved."
>
> ⊁⊰
>
> Matthew Henry

"To Propagate the Fear of God from Generation to Generation": The Father's Duties in Family Worship

Richard Baxter devoted a major portion of his *Christian Directory* (1673) to the duties of the father in family worship, arguing that if worshippers in the Old Testament made sacrifices twice a day—in the morning and evening—and were commanded to learn the ways of God in the family, believers in Jesus had an even greater duty to give God a sacrifice of praise daily in their households.[28] Baxter visited regularly the homes of his entire congregants to make certain that they were learning the catechism.[29]

For Baxter, as for all the Puritans, time and eternity were at stake. For the father to abdicate his solemn vocation of ministry in the home was to surrender his family to the whims of the world, the flesh, and the devil. Baxter included one chapter in his *Christian Directory* specifically to provide "special motives to persuade men to the holy governing of their families." In this chapter, the minister of Kidderminster pointed out that "a holy and

---

26. Baxter, *Christian Directory*, 2.
27. John Winthrop and James Savage, *The History of New England from 1630 to 1649* (Boston: Little and Brown, 1853), 39.
28. Baxter, *Christian Directory*, 507.
29. Baxter details his ministerial activities and sets forth a comprehensive pastoral vision in his classic work, Richard Baxter, *The Reformed Pastor* (1656; repr., Carlisle, PA: Banner of Truth, 1974). Also, the entire section on family, including the duties of fathers, mothers and children, was recently published in a single work, Richard Baxter, *The Godly Home*, ed. Randall J. Pederson (Wheaton, IL: Crossway, 2010).

well-governed family doth tend to make a holy posterity, and so to propagate the fear of God from generation to generation" and that "a holy, well-governed family is the preparative to a holy and well-governed church."[30]

The Lord's Day held a major place in the theology and ethics of the Puritans. Most viewed it as a remembrance that stood in continuity with the Jewish Sabbath. In addition to attendance of corporate worship with God's people, families were expected to spend their day first preparing for corporate worship, then worshipping God in their homes. The Puritan head of the family began the day with family prayers; after the corporate gathering, family members reconvened to sing a psalm of praise. Fathers rehearsed with their children the major points of the pastor's sermon. The father might also have read from Scripture or another "profitable book," followed by prayer "with all the holy seriousness and joy which is suitable to the work and the day."[31] After supper, the father typically examined children and servants on what they had learned during the day, perhaps even reviewing the catechism. The day concluded with family prayer.

> ✦ Suppose that, at least once each year, a pastor or deacon visited each family in your church and simply asked, "How are you doing when it comes to family worship or devotional times? Are there any particular struggles that you're facing? How might we help you?" How might this help your congregation to move toward a family-equipping ministry model? ✦

This pattern also formed the paradigm for weekday worship in the home: the father led, typically both morning and evening, in devotional exercises that would consist in Scripture reading, catechesis, singing, and prayer. In the event that the husband was unavailable to lead family worship, the wife did so.

It is crucial to note, however, that family worship was not intended to serve as the sole expression of the parents' duty among the Puritans and their heirs. "The whole of family religion is not to be placed in acts of *worship*, properly so called," one Reformed Baptist pastor reminded his church members,

> It includes family government, and discipline; the daily reading of the scriptures . . . , and at some times, especially on the Lord's Day, other

---

30. Baxter, *Christian Directory*, 422–31.
31. Ibid., 573.

practical books; watching over the ways of our household, catechizing children, instructing servants; reproving, admonishing, and correcting for irregularities of temper and conduct; and more especially for sins against God. But family worship is the most important part, and will have a great influence to promote the regular and useful discharge of the rest.[32]

From the perspective of these heirs of the Puritans, ministry within the family entailed far more than a mere practice of family devotions; family ministry was a whole-life experience that included "watching over," disciplining, and differentiating between children's "irregularities" and "sins."

Such devotion spawned a golden age of catechisms and devotional works designed to be used in the teaching of children and in family worship. Separatists in the Puritan tradition, particularly Baptists, wrote catechisms to be used in teaching children. Benjamin Keach, a Particular Baptist preacher in London, abstracted the doctrines of the *Second London Confession* into a catechism.[33] John Bunyan produced a work pointedly titled *Instruction for the Ignorant: Being a Salve to Cure That Great Want of Knowledge, Which So Much Reigns Both in Young and Old.*[34] More conversational than most catechisms, Bunyan concluded with a call to repentance: "Bring thy last day often to thy bedside, and ask thy heart, if this morning thou wast to die, if thou be ready or no."[35]

"Taking Our Turns in Such Devotions": Age-Organized Gatherings among the Puritans[36]

For Puritans in England and New England alike, every Christian household was "a household of faith; every father a priest in his own family." Worship, both in the home and in the church, was largely intergenerational. These practices did not, however, prevent church leaders from gathering age-organized groups for the purpose of teaching biblical truths. Cotton

32. Job Orton, *Religious Exercises Recommended*, American ed. (Bridgeport: Backus, 1809), 66
33. The full text of this catechism has been republished in Tom Nettles, *Teaching Truth, Training Hearts: The Study of Catechisms in Baptist Life* (Amityville, NY: Calvary Press, 1998).
34. John Bunyan, *Instruction for the Ignorant*, in *The Works of John Bunyan, Vol. 2*, ed. John Offor (Edinburgh: Banner of Truth, 1999), 675–90.
35. Ibid., 690.
36. Portions of this section are drawn from Timothy Paul Jones, "A History of Age-Organized Ministry" (course lecture, Models of Student and Family Ministry, The Southern Baptist Theological Seminary, Louisville, Kentucky, 2010–2011).

Mather spoke of belonging to a young people's group that, each Sunday evening, "prayed, and sang a psalm, taking our turns in such devotions."[37]

In 1674, a resident of Roxbury, Massachusetts, recalled the restoration of his church's "primitive practice" of "training up . . . male youth" by gathering them on Sundays to "examine their remembrance" of the sermon and to hear them recite portions of the catechism. Female youth gathered for a similar meeting on Mondays. Church records from Norwich, Connecticut, in 1675 and from Plymouth in 1694 suggest that such practices may have been widespread in New England.[38]

The goal of these age-organized gatherings seems to have been *to reinforce young people's relationship with* the larger community of faith—not *to separate young people from* the congregation. The content of these discussions and devotions was apparently drawn from the pastor's message on the Lord's Day and from catechisms that had been learned at home. The intent was to review and to apply, in an age-organized context, words that were already being proclaimed in intergenerational settings.

"A Little Church and Commonwealth": Household Life and Family Worship in the Ministry of Jonathan Edwards

Jonathan Edwards was the last and most noteworthy of the American Puritans. Edwards's Calvinistic theology formed his framework for family ministry.[39] For Edwards, the Christian family was "a little church and commonwealth by itself," and "the head of the family has more advantage in his little community to promote religion than ministers have in the congregation."[40]

Discipling the Devil's Children

From Edwards' pserspective, the fountainhead of genuine revival was the grace of God working to transform households and to renovate the

---

37. Cotton Mather, quoted in Frederick DeLand Leete, *Christian Brotherhoods* (Cincinnati: Jennings and Graham, 1912), 209.
38. *Publications of the Colonial Society of Massachusetts, Volume 21* (Massachusetts: The Colonial Society of Massachusetts, 1920), 259–65. Young people also gathered, as early as 1717, in "singing schools." Francis Otis Erb, *The Development of the Young People's Movement* (Chicago: University of Chicago, 1917), 16–17.
39. For works on the Edwards' home, see Elisabeth Dodd, *Marriage to a Difficult Man: The "Uncommon Union" of Jonathan and Sarah Edwards* (Laurel, MS: Audubon: 2004); and Edna Gerstner, *Jonathan and Sarah: An Uncommon Union* (Morgan, PA: Soli Deo Gloria, 1996)..
40. Jonathan Edwards, "Living to Christ," in *Sermons and Discourses, 1720–1723*, The Works of Jonathan Edwards, vol. 10, ed. Wilson H. Kimnach (New Haven: Yale University Press, 1992), 577.

hearts of fathers.[41] Children were separated from God—"little snakes" and "children of the devil," Edwards called them—by nature and by choice,[42] and parents bore a special responsibility for evangelizing their own children.[43] For this to occur, children desperately needed to see the gospel treasured within the father's affections.[44]

Jonathan Edwards diligently read Scripture with his eleven children each day and taught them the catechisms. Each Saturday, he carefully prepared them for worship on the Lord's Day.[45] His wife, Sarah, oversaw finances and daily operations in the Edwards home. By all accounts, Edwards's own children profited from their father's ministry, embracing the gospel and committing themselves to lives of holiness.[46]

Local Church and "Little Church"

The churchly function of the household never, however, eclipsed the importance of the gathered people of God. The local church provided the lens through which Edwards viewed the functions of the "little church," the family; Edwards proclaimed certain tasks and purposes for the Christian family precisely because God had already assigned these purposes to the larger gathering of the saints.[47] The household represented a parallel outworking of the life of the local congregation, with the father functioning as pastor within this model of the church in miniature.[48]

These emphases persisted for many decades not only among the direct heirs of the Puritans but also among others, including the Methodists. In the latter half of the eighteenth century, John Wesley declared to husbands and fathers that

---

41. Jonathan Edwards, "The Importance of Revival Among Heads of Families," in *Sermons and Discourses, 1720–1723*, Works of Jonathan Edwards, vol. 22, 451.
42. Jonathan Edwards, quoted in John H. Gerstner, *Jonathan Edwards: Evangelist* (Morgan, PA: Soli Deo Gloria, 1995), 34–35.
43. Ibid.
44. Edwards, "Importance of Revival Among Heads of Families," 453.
45. Beck, *Little Church*, 3.
46. Iain H. Murray, *Jonathan Edwards: A New Biography* (Carlisle, PA: Banner of Truth, 1987), 214.
47. Peter Beck, "The 'Little Church': Raising a Spiritual Family with Jonathan Edwards" (paper presented at the Southeastern Regional Meeting of the Evangelical Theological Society, Temple Baptist Seminary, Chattanooga, TN, April 3, 2009). Published under same title by *Puritan Theological Journal* 2, no. 1 (January 2010).
48. Edwards, "Importance of Revival Among Heads of Families," 451.

the person in your house that claims your first and nearest attention, is, undoubtedly, your wife; seeing you are to love her, even as Christ hath loved the Church. . . . Next to your wife are your children; immortal spirits whom God hath, for a time, entrusted to your care, that you may train them up in all holiness, and fit them for the enjoyment of God in eternity. This is a glorious and important trust; seeing one soul is of more value than all the world beside. Every child, therefore, you are to watch over with the utmost care, that, when you are called to give an account of each to the Father of spirits, you may give your accounts with joy and not with grief.[49]

Edwards and Age-Organized Gatherings

Like his Puritan forebears, Jonathan Edwards was willing to gather the children of the church in age-organized groups to reinforce the catechisms that they were learning in their homes as well as the messages that they heard on Sundays. Edwards described this practice to an acquaintance in 1743:

At the conclusion of the public exercise on the Sabbath, I appointed the children that were under sixteen years of age to go from the meeting-house to a neighbor house, that I there might further enforce what they had heard in public, and might give in some counsels proper for their age. . . . About the middle of the summer, I called together the young people that were communicants, from sixteen to twenty-six years of age, to my house; which proved to be a most happy meeting. . . . We had several meetings that summer of young people.[50]

When a teenager named Billy Sheldon died, Edwards gathered a group of young people to proclaim a message to them, emphasizing the need to seek salvation now: Billy "was cut off at such a time," said Edwards, "to make you take full advantage of our opportunity." Edwards's exposition

---

49. John Wesley, "On Family Religion," Sermon 94 in *Sermons on Several Occasions*, Second Series (1872; repr., Christian Classics Ethereal Library), http://www.ccel.org/ccel/wesley/sermons.vi.xli.html?. Based on the 1872 text, this edition was originally published in four volumes in 1771.

50. Jonathan Edwards to the Reverend Thomas Prince of Boston, Northampton, Massachusetts, December 12, 1743, National Humanities Institute, http://www.nhinet.org/ccs/docs/awaken.htm.

of the text is very brief, but his evangelistic application to the lives of the youth is long and pleading.[51]

> "For what end do you send your children to school? 'Why, that they may be fit to live in the world.' In which world do you mean—this or the next? Perhaps you thought of this world only and had forgot that there is a world to come; yea, and one that will last forever! Pray take this into your account, and send them to such masters as will keep it always before their eyes. . . . Surely, if you live or fear God yourself, this will be your first consideration: 'In what business will your son be most likely to love and serve God? In what employment will he have the greatest advantage for laying up treasure in heaven?' I have been shocked above measure in observing how little this is attended to, even by pious parents! Even these consider only how he may get most money; not how he may get most holiness! . . . Upon this motive they fix him in a business which will necessarily expose him to such temptations as will leave him not a probability, if a possibility, of serving God. O savage parents! Unnatural, diabolical cruelty—if you believe there is another world."
> → John Wesley, Anglican cleric and founder of Methodism ←
> *"On Family Religion," Sermon 94*

WHERE REVOLUTION MUST BEGIN

A pastor wrote the following words, bemoaning the breakdown of the families around him, pointing out that marriage was being entered into casually with no concern for raising godly offspring:

> I have observed many married couples coming together in such great passion that they were ready to devour each other for love, but after a half-year the one ran away from the other. I have known people who have become hostile to each other after they had five or six children and were bound to each other not merely by marriage but also by the fruits of their union. Yet they left each other.[52]

The pastor was not someone in twenty-first century Europe or North America. It was Martin Luther, and the era was the early sixteenth century.
Then, as now, the revolution in family relationships cannot begin in

---

51. Edwards, quoted in Gerstner, *Jonathan Edwards: Evangelist*, 35.
52. Martin Luther, sermon on Matthew 19:10–12, quoted in Ryken, *Worldly Saints*, 73.

the church. It must begin in the Christian household. A new reformation must begin with fathers taking responsibility for training their children in righteousness and with mothers who partner with their husbands in pursuing this vision. It will require these fathers and mothers to love and to train children whose parents are unbelieving or uninvolved in their spiritual development. It will require churches to equip single parents and to connect them with other families who can assist them in tasks of family discipleship. But the revolution cannot begin with church activities or programs; the revolution begins with your household and mine.

8

THE CHALLENGE OF MATRIARCHY

Family Discipleship and the African American Experience

Kevin L. Smith

D id God give fathers a special and specific command to be responsible for the godly training of their children? That's precisely what Paul declared in his letter to the Ephesian church: "Fathers, do not provoke your children to anger, but bring them up in the discipline and instruction of the Lord" (6:4). But where has the black church stood on this issue? And in what ways do the dynamics of the black church differ from the challenges faced by Christian brothers and sisters with different cultural backgrounds? These are the questions that form a vital background as we consider the interaction between churches and African American fathers, mothers, and children in the Christian formation of present and future generations.

The black church has functioned as a central organizing institution in the African American experience.[1] As such, the history of the black church coincides with the general flow of the lives of former Africans in North America: slavery, Reconstruction, segregation, the Civil Rights

---

1. The term *black church* functions here as a historical designation rather than a theological or ecclesiological reference. Black churches—like other churches—fall into the theological categories of fundamentalist, moderate, and liberal. *Evangelical* is not a popular term in some segments of the black church due to the political assumptions sometimes associated with the term.

Movement, and the post–Civil Rights era.[2] Each of these periods influenced the African American family in ways that often undercut the influence of fathers and established de facto matriarchal structures. Necessary and well-intended family leadership from mothers, grandmothers, and aunts unintentionally created a legacy of "fatherlessness" in the African American family and—by extension—in the black church.

> ✦ Regardless of the dominant racial demographic in your congregation, recognize that separation of Christians by race or ethnicity falls far short of God's ideal of drawing together blood-purchased people from "every tribe, every language, every people, every nation" (Rev. 5:9 Knox). How can your congregation pursue this divinely inspired vision here and now? ✦

THE AFRICAN AMERICAN FAMILY FROM SLAVERY TO CIVIL RIGHTS

Former Secretary of State Condoleezza Rice has referred to slavery as America's national "birth defect."[3] Her graphic description provides a beginning point for examining the long-term effects of the early Africans' plight in North America and how their plight influenced the trajectory of African American families. The slave was primarily an object in the system of chattel slavery; therefore, all other aspects of the slave's life, including family structures, were secondary. In most cases, it would have been impossible for slaves to have practically or functionally prioritized family roles, particularly fatherhood.

African American Family Structures
Prior to the American Civil War

Slaveholders held little or no regard for family relationships among their slaves. Even before reaching America, many slaves had been terribly

---

2. James Oliver Horton and Lois E. Horton, *Hard Road to Freedom: The Story of African America* (New Brunswick, NJ: Rutgers University Press, 2001); John Hope Franklin and Alfred A. Moss Jr., *From Slavery to Freedom: A History of Negro Americans*, 6th ed. (New York: McGraw-Hill, 1988); and Darlene Clark Hine, William C. Hine, and Stanley Harrold, *The African-American Odyssey* (Upper Saddle River, NJ: Prentice Hall, 2000).

3. Condoleezza Rice, interview by *Washington Times*, March 28, 2008, quoted in "Condoleezza Rice on Race: America's 'Birth Defect'," DiversityInc, posted April 1, 2008, http://diversityinc.com/content/1757/article/3347/.

destabilized and "broken" in order to be resocialized into the slavery system.

> The human cargo which [the slave traders] collected were the remnants of various tribes and clan organizations. The manner in which men and women were packed indiscriminately in slave ships during the Middle Passage tended to destroy social bonds and tribal distinctions. The process of "breaking" the Negroes into the slaves system in the West Indies, where they often landed before shipment to the colonies and the United States, tended to efface the memories of their traditional culture. In the colonies and later in the southern United States, the slaves were widely scattered on comparatively small plantations where there was little opportunity to reknit social bonds or regenerate the African culture.[4]

Until the early nineteenth century, male slaves outnumbered female slaves. In many cases, male slaves had sexual encounters with Native American women; these encounters resulted in children without functioning fathers, outcasts from the communities both of their fathers and of their mothers. Female slaves were subjected to their masters' sexual whims. In some cases, their biracial children received a measure of status from their slaveholding fathers; in other cases, the children remained unrecognized and unwanted, except as living property.

In an economy where property was currency, masters often sold or traded slaves. In what certainly laid the foundation for matriarchal family structures, mother-child relationships were protected in many of these transactions while husband-wife relationships held no dependable status. On some economically stable plantations, it *was* possible for slaves to develop family structures that mirrored the family of the plantation patriarch. Such situations seem to have been rare, however. Some manumitted slaves did develop

> ✦ The slave was primarily an object in the system of chattel slavery; therefore, all other aspects of the slave's life, including family structures, were secondary. In most cases, it would have been impossible for slaves to have practically or functionally prioritized family roles, particularly fatherhood. ✦

---

4. E. Franklin Frazier, "The Negro Family in America," in Ruth Nanda Anshen, *The Family: Its Function and Destiny*, rev. ed. (New York: Harper & Row, 1959), 65.

reasonably stable family structures. The families of these "freed blacks" manifested a peculiar form of patriarchy that differed from the typical patterns that characterized the century leading up to the American Civil War.

African American Family Structures during Reconstruction and Segregation

After the American Civil War, one might have expected the newly freed slaves and families to have flourished. In reality, there were still many challenges to be faced. If the slavery era of African American history represented a time of general instability for families, the era after the Civil War brought about total destabilization.

Slaveholders had bought and sold slaves without regard for marital status. Now, what could the previously sold male do when he returned to his previous plantation to reclaim his wife, only to find that she had remarried? How could a man reunite his family when he had fathered children on different plantations in different states? These were real-life questions that faced many former slaves in the aftermath of the American Civil War.

Matriarchal leadership was deeply entrenched by this point in African American history. For example, many freedmen were afraid to offer public support for Ulysses S. Grant in the 1868 presidential election. Their wives, however, proudly wore their husbands' pins and pictures of Grant. If husbands refused to hand over these items, wives were known to defy their husbands, boldly marching into town to buy their own.[5] For these women, emancipation provided confirmation of the spirit of self-sufficiency that they had learned in slavery.[6] The mother was "the supreme authority in the household," so much so that daughters were reluctant to leave their mother's household to live with their husbands.[7]

After decades in which slaveholders had ignored marital relationships among slaves, former slaves viewed marriage as a means of economic cooperation instead of a covenant rooted in God's creation and a fundamental basis for societal structuring. Wives described their marital arrangements not in terms of a lasting covenant but as "working with a man." Such perspectives did little to promote meaningful roles for husbands and fathers.

---

5. "The Matriarchate" in E. Franklin Frazier, *The Negro Family in the United States* (Chicago: University of Chicago Press, 1939), 125.

6. Ibid., 125.

7. Ibid., 144.

Until "the Great Migration" of African Americans to northern cities in the opening decades of the twentieth century, an overwhelming number of former slaves remained in the South. For these persons, tenant farming often replaced slavery. During the Great Migration, close to two million African Americans moved north. Nearly one-fourth of the migrants relocated in one of three cities—Chicago, Philadelphia, or New York City.[8]

Unfortunately, northern cities lacked the familial folkways and community structures—such as the church and the lodge—that had marked the rural South. Rates of illegitimacy increased. Unwed urban mothers were not viewed as having the same innocence as their southern counterparts in previous generations. In this context, communities generally expressed stronger disdain for illegitimacy, resulting in higher rates of desertion among fathers.

Patterns in African American Marriage and Family Life: An African Heritage or a Creational Structure Distorted by Slavery?

It is important to point out that scholarship focusing on African American history has held differing views on the family history that I have described here.[9] The two primary perspectives are associated with the work of E. Franklin Frazier and Melville J. Herskovits in the mid-twentieth century.

> Frazier's main contention is that the Negro family contains no appreciable African influences and is a product of the condition of slavery and racial discrimination in the United States, . . . Herskovits views [African American family structures] as rooted in West African cultures; Frazier views matriarchy as a sign of social disorganization, Herskovits views it as playing an essential role in the survival of the black community in America.[10]

Frazier's thesis criticized high rates of illegitimacy and female headship in African American families as well as patterns of male headship that included overinvolved mothers-in-law. In contrast, Herskovits's thesis ascribed a certain nobility to the very patterns that Frazier considered to be maladies in

8. Horton and Horton, _Hard Road to Freedom_, 216–17.
9. The works cited of sociologist E. Franklin Frazier represent a view counter to that put forth by Melville J. Herskovits, _The Myth of the Negro Past_ (New York: Harper & Brothers, 1941).
10. John H. Bracey Jr., August Meier, and Elliott Rudwick, eds., _Black Matriarchy: Myth or Reality?_ (Belmont, CA: Wadsworth, 1971), 1–2.

African American families—high rates of illegitimacy and a dominant role for mothers with a resulting passive role for fathers. According to Herskovits, "the responsibilities of upbringing, discipline, and supervision are much more the province of the mother than of the father,"[11] and these patterns are holdovers from a West African past. Where Frazier saw weakening and harmful patterns of family life, Herskovits saw a heritage from Africa.

Because some see matriarchy and looser marital structures as remnants of Africa, the pursuit of biblical manhood and womanhood may be perceived by some as an attempt to rob African American families of their cultural past. This has been a particular challenge because the black church has institutionally borne a burden of cultural preservation and protection that has competed at times with gospel priorities.

> ✦ Despite the biblical command that fathers must train their children in godliness (Eph. 6:4) and in spite of male spiritual leadership in the household being a qualification for local church leadership (1 Tim. 3:4–5), the black church has been historically influenced by matriarchy in ways that have hampered its ability to produce a generation that has been "trained in the fear of God." ✦

In this context, it is crucial that pastors proclaim biblical manhood and womanhood with charity, clarity, and conviction. Even if some patterns in African American family life *are* relics from Africa—a claim that is far from certain!—biblical expectations for men and women are rooted in divine creation, not in cultural innovation or historical heritage. It was God, not culture, who designed marriage as an institution to unite one male with one female for life. It was God, not culture, who wisely designated particular roles for men and women. It was God, not culture, who commanded the man to "hold fast to his wife" and to "become one flesh" (Gen. 2:24).

African American Family Structures during the Civil Rights and Post–Civil Rights Era

After more than three centuries of slavery and state-enforced segregation, African Americans began to gain legal protections during the Civil Rights

---

11. Herskovits, *Myth of the Negro Past*, 169.

era. Unfortunately, during this same era, African American families were the first to suffer from the "sexual revolution," which was contiguous with pathologies that were already prevalent. As a result, when assistant secretary of labor Daniel Moynihan issued a report on the African American family in 1965, the report did not paint a healthy picture: "That the Negro American has survived at all is extraordinary—a lesser people might have simply died out, as indeed others have."[12] Despite misconceptions to the contrary, he clearly noted that there were great discontinuities in family structures in the United States. White households differed from African American households and, just as importantly, African American middle-class families differed from those found in the African American lower class.

Independent black churches emerged in an environment where matriarchy was already embedded, due to prevailing societal circumstances. Nothing in subsequent history has altered this fact. Over time, this matriarchy became the accepted norm. At this same time, emerging theological trends were further undermining practices of biblical manhood and womanhood in black church families. Broader opportunities for theological training became available. In some cases, the agendas of radical feminism—as well as other perspectives that weakened biblical perspectives on marriage, family, and sexual ethics—increasingly infiltrated black churches.

The Public Emasculation of the Black Church

The decade surrounding the turn of the twenty-first century was a decade of public emasculation for the black church. The downfall began in 1997. Rev. Henry J. Lyons—president of the National Baptist Convention—was exposed as an adulterer and indicted on charges of fraud, extortion, money laundering, conspiracy, and tax evasion.

As the most prominent male African American church leader was plunging into disgrace, women were ascending to the top. In 2000, the African Methodist Episcopal Church—the oldest independent African American denomination—elected Rev. Vashti M. McKenzie as its first bishop. In 2000, Dr. Suzan Johnson Cook was elected the first woman president of the Hampton University Minister's Conference, the largest interdenominational gathering

---

12. Daniel P. Moynihan, *The Negro Family: The Case for National Action* (Washington, DC: Government Printing Office, 1965), chap. 4. Originally published by the Office of Planning and Research, US Department of Labor; commonly known as the Moynihan Report.

of African American clergy. Evangelist Joyce Rodgers has become one of the premiere preachers of the Church of God in Christ.

MOVING TOWARD FAMILY MINISTRY IN THE BLACK CHURCH

Despite the biblical command that fathers must teach and train their children in godliness (Eph. 6:4) and in spite of male spiritual leadership in the household being a qualification for local church leadership (1 Tim. 3:4–5), the black church has been historically influenced by matriarchy in ways that have hampered its ability to produce a generation that has been "trained in the fear of God."

So, should pastoral leaders in black churches simply give up? By no means! Historical challenges to the black family in America should in no way discourage the black church or its leaders from faithfully pursuing God's design for the family and discipleship. The power of God beyond us and within us is greater than the power of history behind us. Our overarching metanarrative is not slavery and Jim Crow, segregation and Civil Rights. As believers in Jesus Christ, the metanarrative of our lives is creation and fall, redemption and consummation. Long-standing maladies will, however, require healing and correction that only God can give.

Given the biblical truth that matriarchy—whether de facto or de jure—does not reflect God's design for his church, it will be helpful for the pastoral leader to discover what roles are presently in place in the black church before seeking to implement biblical reforms. It is possible to identify at least five roles that women play in black churches. To illustrate each one, I have provided an illustrative parallel from the narrative of Scripture, as well as some suggestions for how a pastor might proceed in this situation.

A Responsible Woman in a Context of Passive and Irresponsible Men

"Deborah . . . was judging Israel at that time," the book of Judges tells us (4:4). Israel was in a state of captivity, slavery, and calamity. That background was the setting for Deborah's leadership as a judge. Later in the narrative, she asserted her leadership by urging Barak into battle against the Canaanites (4:7–9). Barak should have been the hero of the narrative, but Barak remained passive until Deborah agreed to go into battle with him. Because of Barak's failure to lead, the honor of victory went not to the Israelite Barak but to a Canaanite woman named Jael.

Such de facto consequential matriarchs as Deborah are very prominent in the black church. The consequential matriarch might be a single mother, divorced or never married. She may be the responsible caregiver for her aging parents. Increasingly, she could be a grandmother raising the offspring of her irresponsible adult children. Whatever the particulars of her situation may be, there is a single common element in her situation: she is taking a leadership role because the men have failed to do so. She is not, by nature, a usurper. If the men in her world would fulfill their responsibilities, she would gladly step aside; however, she has seen too much male passivity, disobedience, and outright ungodliness. She could be bitter and angry, but she isn't. In many cases, this woman affirms biblical complementarity. The main word to describe this woman is *responsible*.

This woman should not be attacked. She has not created the problem; she has merely responded to the problem. She is probably eager for men to "step up to the plate" and to embrace roles of biblical manhood. Her particular role has emerged over an extended period of time—and the matriarchy of the black church developed over three centuries! Such recognitions should steady the pastoral leader for patient and deliberate course corrections. Congregational life must become a safe haven for the pursuit of a countercultural model of family over an extended time, not only through instruction but also through re-enculturation. Perhaps most important, male discipleship must become a pressing priority in the black church. Instead of focusing on Deborah, the black church must properly situate and disciple Barak.[13]

The One Who Usurps the Pastoral Leader's Authority

King Ahab of Israel "took for his wife Jezebel" and followed her religion (1 Kings 16:31). Thus begins the ancient narrative of an idolatrous queen and her spineless husband. The narrative presents a de jure matrifocality— a setting where a male is present, but he is weak and his office of leadership has been usurped by an influential female. In the examples of Deborah and Sapphira (whom we have not yet considered), the women are simply responding to their circumstances. The sort of woman exemplified in

---

13. For analysis of the black church in particular, see Jawanza Kunjufu, *Adam! Where Are You?: Why Most Black Men Don't Go to Church* (Chicago: African American Images, 1994).

Jezebel is actively shaping her circumstances and aggressively usurping biblical leadership.

Black churches must recognize that this pattern represents active opposition to God's good order. If the true nature of this opposition remains disregarded, the church will lack the necessary boldness for confrontation. This woman must be confronted with truth and love for the sake of the biblical betterment of the church.

Some seem to believe that the black church belongs to the black community instead of Jesus Christ. As such, the pastoral leader must be willing to endure criticism and scorn from persons in the community who may not even be part of the church. Even in this circumstance, every choice must be made deliberately. A particular history with peculiar turns has led to this point. It is likely to take some time before Jezebel is thrown down from her balcony, so to speak (2 Kings 9:30–37).

The One Who Despises Manhood

"When Athaliah the mother of Ahaziah saw that her son was dead, she arose and destroyed all the royal family of the house of Judah" (2 Chron. 22:10). When there was no possibility that Athaliah could unofficially rule the kingdom through her own offspring, she decided to kill all other contenders for the throne and to declare herself queen.

In the context of the black church, this woman is not simply resistant toward biblical manhood: she despises male leadership in any form. She sees men as the problem. She may be reacting in frustration against the sins of male passivity or mistreatment of women. Her hatred of male terminology even extends to negative attitudes toward "Father" and "Son" in the Godhead, distorting her understanding of God and the gospel. For this woman, everything must be viewed in light of whether it promotes or hampers women's issues in the church.

The pastoral leader must be prepared for the potentially hostile nature of this engagement. If the male leader fails to honor biblical guidelines for sexual purity, he may find himself *rightly* hamstrung by an antagonist such as this one. Even leaders who are biblically qualified for their role may struggle to deal with women of the Athaliah variety. Godly females must support and share in this battle for biblical order—but the battle is spiritual, and carnal implements must never constitute the leader's weaponry (2 Cor. 10:4). Otherwise, the leader will have simply stooped to the same level as Athaliah.

The Servant of the Church

"I commend to you our sister Phoebe," Paul wrote to the Romans (16:1), acclaiming a particularly faithful female servant that he would soon be sending to Rome. The black church is filled with many such faithful sisters who love the Lord and graciously and dutifully serve his church. African American women have been described as the "backbone" of the black church. Unfortunately, such women may be the sole servants—and sometimes the primary leaders—in many churches.

The servant has no ill intent; she is seeking to love her God with all her heart, soul, mind, and strength. The problem is not her presence; it is, rather, her disproportionate presence and influence. The lack of a balancing male presence has fostered an unfruitful environment for her ministry. Males must be challenged to become faithful servants in local congregations. In the black church, this involves a recoupling of church membership and discipleship—which assumes a prior recoupling of commitment to Christ with commitment to the body of Christ in its local expression.

Such a shift also will involve highlighting areas of faithful Christian service for men beyond the titled ministries of "pastor" or "deacon." In too many congregations, preachers and deacons are seen as the "men of God"—but every faithful God-honoring brother should be viewed as a man of God. The problem is not the existence of women like Phoebe; the problem is the nonexistence of men like Stephen and Philip (Acts 6:5). The solution is not calling men to become like Phoebe; the solution is calling men to serve in the ways that God has called them to serve, so that Phoebe is not serving alone.

The Woman Partnered with Her Husband

Partnered with their husbands, some women may present particular problems, while others may present positive opportunities. In the book of Acts, Sapphira fits into the problematic category. Her husband sinned by taking from the offering that he had committed to the church. Not only did he sin but his wife also participated in his folly (Acts 5:1–11). Several chapters later, another picture of husband-wife partnership emerges: Priscilla and Aquila were a faithful team that supported missions and corrected inadequate teachings (Acts 18:26; Rom. 16:3–4; 1 Cor. 16:19).

Many wives in the black church mirror their husband's spiritual maturity or lack thereof. Some, like Priscilla, may manifest characteristics in congregational life that reflect how their husbands have edified them. Many women in black churches stand on the legacy of an Aquila-like husband or father who loves his wife as Christ loves the church.

Other wives, like Sapphira, may exhibit characteristics that stem from fear, wounding, or manipulation that has been caused by their husband. These women may not trust the church's leadership because of how sin has characterized their husbands' lives. In order to effect godly transformation, pastoral leaders must acknowledge the oneness of marriage as they seek to disciple both husbands and wives. If a woman has an ungodly or spiritually immature husband, little gospel benefit will be gained by attempting to circumvent the husband in the discipleship process. Even if a woman is celebrated as a faithful model for others, little will be gained if her husband is not somehow called to account in that process.

Such discipleship processes will also require the black church to present a radically countercultural model of marriage and family—a model that reflects biblical truth about gender and marital relationships. The role of the husband must be elevated to the status of a wife's primary human relationship. This will necessarily require the mind of Christ to replace physique, career, and hobbies as the central sources of identity for African American Christian men.

WHERE DO WE GO FROM HERE?

If pastoral leaders desire to implement family-equipping ministries in black churches, they must carefully consider the structures of resistance that they will face. Yes, it is difficult "to perceive the effect that three centuries of exploitation have had on the fabric of Negro society itself."[14] And yet, constrained by Holy Scripture and empowered by the Holy Spirit, the pastoral leader can deliberately, patiently, and effectively call forth men and women in black churches to assume their divinely ordained roles to the glory of God.

---

14. Moynihan, *Negro Family*, chap. 2.

9

GROWING GAPS FROM GENERATION TO GENERATION

Family Discipleship in Modern and Postmodern Contexts

W. Ryan Steenburg with Timothy Paul Jones

It was all about the flux capacitor. That was the lunchbox-sized device in the modified DeLorean that allowed Marty McFly to travel from 1985 to 1955, to 2015, and to 1885.[1] In the *Back to the Future* trilogy, Marty had the unprecedented experience of traveling through time and viewing the various ways that his town of Hill Valley had progressed from one generation to the next, from one century to another. Much like some of Marty McFly's adventures, this chapter will race into the past and then return to the present, albeit without the special effects and certainly without the flux capacitor. The goal of this chapter is to undertake a task that involves taking a look at past generations but requires no modifications to your car—specifically, to seek an answer these questions: How has the Christian household developed over the past two centuries in its approach to the training and discipleship of children? And what has been the church's role in this process?

Whether through AWANA, Royal Ambassadors and Girls in Action, Five-Day Clubs, or the more generic "youth group," contemporary church

---

1. *Back to the Future* trilogy, directed by Robert Zemeckis, produced by Amblin Entertainment, and distributed by Universal Pictures, 1985, 1989, 1990, respectively.

attendees are familiar with curriculum and programs that gather young people on a regular and separate basis, typically with a disproportionately high ratio of youth or children to adults. For many of us, such programs perceived as the primary contexts for the Christian formation of children—but it hasn't always been this way. This is church as the twenty-first century knows it, as the twentieth century refined it, and as the nineteenth century created it.

> ✦ When and why did youth groups and separate children's ministries begin in churches? If you attend a congregation that has been in existence for several decades and if the documents are available to you, look through church records from the early twentieth century through the 1960s and 1970s. See what you can learn about the shift toward segmented-programmatic ministry in your church. ✦

NOTHING NEW UNDER THE SUN

Not only in the present day but also throughout centuries past, Christian leaders have lamented the loss of worship and discipleship practices in households. In 1805—decades before age-segmented programs were popular in churches—one pastor described the situation in these terms:

> It is a complaint, and I fear made with too much justice, that many parents are too negligent respecting the religious education and instruction of their children. . . . I am grieved to add, that I apprehend this declension is much to be attributed to the spiritual weakness, and indulgence of parents.[2]

Francis E. Clark wrote in 1903 that "family religion is the foundation stone of all our religious life in church and state, and family worship lies near the foundation of all family religion" while expressing concern regarding "irreligion in the family."[3] Almost a century later, Dennis Rainey stated that "no church, community, or nation will rise higher than the spiritual condition of its families" but confessed that Christian families were "weak."[4]

---

2. Frederick Smith, *A Letter to Parents* (London: Darton and Harvey, 1806), 4–5.
3. Francis Edward Clark, *The Christian Endeavor Manual* (Norwood, MA: Plimpton, 1903), 196, 198.
4. Dennis Rainey, "Local Church Family Ministry in the New Millennium," in *Building Strong Families*, ed. Dennis Rainey (Wheaton: Crossway, 2002), 15.

From generation to generation, the concern has been the same: children need Christian training, parents should be the primary providers of that training, but practices of family discipleship have been difficult to maintain. These laments are not the unique property of the twenty-first century. Alarms about the downfall of the family may be found even in the Puritan writings of the seventeenth century. Specific concerns about the religious instruction of children in the context of families have been common from the late eighteenth and early nineteenth centuries. With that in mind, let's explore the developments in social structures over the past two centuries that have affected the training of children in Christian households.

THE FAMILY GOES TO THE FACTORY

Prior to the Industrial Revolution, training for a trade, one's general education, and family discipleship were daily activities that took place in a household with support from a local congregation and community. Beginning in the late eighteenth century, the Industrial Revolution radically reshaped families' economic and social contexts.

> The old system of home manufacture, in which personal skill was so large a factor, in which the master and his family were on friendliest terms with journeyman and apprentice, in which the children of the household early made their contribution of labor under the parental eye, and so learned the family trade, was swept away. In its place came largely increased production and the crowding of people about the factories.[5]

---

5. Francis Otis Erb, _The Development of the Young People's Movement_ (Chicago: University of Chicago, 1917), 2. The Industrial Revolution changed the landscape of America from a rural nation whose economy revolved around the seasons to a commercial nation whose economy revolved around the metropolises. Culture and society were also heavily influenced. For a detailed exposition of the Industrial Revolution, see Kevin Hillstrom and Laurie Collier Hillstrom, eds., _The Industrial Revolution in America_, vol. 7, _Communications;_ vol. 8, _Agriculture and Meatpacking_ (Santa Barbara, CA: ABC-CLIO, 2007); and Donald M. Scott and Bernard W. Wishy, _America's Families: A Documentary History_ (New York: Harper & Row, 1982), 219. For effects on Christian education, see Robert W. Pazmiño, _Foundational Issues in Christian Education: An Introduction in Evangelical Perspective_, 2nd ed. (Grand Rapids: Baker, 1997), 129–30; and Roy W. Fairchild and John Charles Wynn, _Families in the Church: A Protestant Survey_ (New York: Association Press, 1961), 34. Diana Garland indicates that the work which used to be a familial affair "increasingly became an individual . . . pursuit." Ultimately, this resulted in the "breadwinner" going "outside the family [to] earn enough to support the rest."

In the Industrial Revolution, goods became cheaper and were manufactured faster. Manufacturing once performed at home by hand shifted to factories, and household "cottage industries" faltered. At first, factories hired entire families to work within the factory. Yet, even when families were employed together their time together was fragmented by the very nature of factory labor.

This is not to suggest, of course, that every family member remained in the household cottage industry into adulthood. Fathers often placed their older boys in other families as apprentices to learn a trade. Even in these circumstances, however, the young man lived within a household that bore responsibility for his physical, moral, and spiritual well-being. All of this changed during the Industrial Revolution.

Faced with increasing industrialization and fragmentation, new social epitomes for families began to take shape: The concept of family moved from a clan, embedded in a community and united by a common covenant, to a nuclear unit commenced by the mutual consent of two individuals to enter into companionship with each other. In an ideal family, the father—once the coordinator of labor and production within the household—would become a breadwinner whose sphere of labor was outside the household while his wife and children remained inside the home. And thus, "in the rise of the factory system, to a large extent the family lost the father."[6] Where a father once might have taught his son a family trade, working side by side, the boy was now left to assist his mother or left to amuse himself. Where schooling and discipleship were once a natural practice on the workshop floor, only a fading family principle could now be found. Families increasingly deferred the education and discipleship of their children to programs and institutions outside the household.

On the American frontier, the fragmentation and nuclearization took a somewhat different form, but the results were no less radical. Cheap land became readily available on the frontier, and fathers moved their families west to rule as sovereigns over their own forests and fields.[7] Unconstrained

Diana R. Garland, *Family Ministry: A Comprehensive Guide* (Downers Grove, IL: InterVarsity Press, 1999), 262–63. For a clear statement of this ideal, see Maginel Wright Enright, "Matrimony, Our Most Neglected Profession," *McClure's Magazine* 38, no. 6 (April 1912): 626, http://books.google.com/books?id=DUhGekiHRWAC.

6. Henry Frederick Cope, *Religious Education in the Family* (Chicago: University Chicago Press, 1915), 20.

7. Steven J. Keillor, *This Rebellious House: American History and the Truth of Christianity* (Downers Grove, IL: InterVarsity Press, 1996), 105–25. See also Scott and Wishy, *America's*

by larger clans and faith communities, frontiersmen tended to disengage from their families spiritually and relationally. For many men, religious responsibilities became constraints to be avoided rather than vital expressions of shared faith.

FAMILY FRAGMENTATION AND FREE FORMAL EDUCATION

Prior to the Industrial Revolution, primary school education did exist—but primarily for the wealthy, using tutors or private teachers. Children from other socioeconomic classes typically received training through their parents. Much of this education might center on working in the family industry or, in later years, learning a trade as an apprentice. As the locus of labor shifted from farms and cottage industries to factories in urban areas, household education became less feasible. In the eighteenth and nineteenth centuries, two very different institutions—the Sunday school and the common school—arose in response to new educational challenges.

"The Most Potent Instrument for Moral and Religious Advancement": Robert Raikes and the Sunday School

The rate of incarceration in Gloucester was high. So were the expectations of factory bosses. Adults and children alike worked six days each week. With many parents imprisoned for petty crimes or exhausted after a week of labor, children ran the streets on Sundays. After disappointing attempts to work with adults in Gloucester, a philanthropist named Robert Raikes concluded that the primary contributing factors to the adults' difficulties were idleness that emerged after childhood and ignorance due to a lack of education during childhood. Sunday schools represented Raikes's response to both problems. Early Sunday schools educated lower-class children and provided semblances of structure in unstructured social contexts.

Sunday schools grew rapidly in England and soon expanded to the United States. Raikes had many allies, but he also had his share of opponents. He had, after all, established a form of secular instruction on Sunday—a day that was strictly reserved for biblical instruction. For many American

Families, 181; and Arlene Skolnick, "Changes of Heart: Family Dynamics in Historical Perspective," in *Family, Self, and Society: Toward a New Agenda for Family Research*, ed. Philip A. Cowan (Hillsdale, NJ: Erlbaum, 1993), 43–68.

opponents of the Sunday school, the establishment of public schools in the mid-1800s came as a welcomed relief.[8] It had been inexcusable, from their perspective, to teach reading on the Lord's Day. Once weekday schooling was established for all, the Lord apparently got his day back.

Weekday education did not, however, lead to the extinction of Sunday schools. Sunday school quickly metamorphosed into a time to gather children and adults alike for the purpose of teaching the Bible. In 1905, little more than a century after Robert Raikes formed the first Sunday school, one writer declared this program to be "the most potent instrument for moral and religious advancement, to be passed on to the twentieth century for a development beyond the dreams of the most sanguine."[9]

"The Great Equalizer of the Conditions of Men": Horace Mann and the Common School

Some have suggested that the establishment of public schooling was partly due to the decline in the behavior of the American child in the aftermath of the Industrial Revolution.[10] Politician and education reformer Horace Mann was, however, driven by far loftier designs. He suggested that Americans should sense a divine compulsion to provide compulsory education for every child. The perception of divinity that compelled Mann's designs was not, however, rooted in the Old or New Testaments. His vision of the divine was deistic at best. For Mann, natural religion trumped revealed religion; as a result, he sought character education without allegiance to any specific faith or creed.[11]

One of the central tasks of the "common school" that Mann envisioned was the teaching of religion—not the perspectives of any particular denomination or faith commitment, but general "Christian morals." Parents might add specific beliefs at home, but the common school would

8. Charles Gallaudet Trumbull, "The Nineteenth-Century Sunday School," in *The Development of the Sunday School* ed. W. N. Hartshorn, George R. Merrill, and Marion Lawrance (Boston: Fort Hill Press, 1905), 8–9, http://www.archive.org/details/cu31924010370801. This was the official report of the eleventh international Sunday-school convention, including the United States and British American provinces, Toronto, Canada, June 23–27, 1905.
9. George R. Merrill, "The Sunday School," in Hartshorn, Merrill, and Lawrance, *Development of the Sunday School*, 6.
10. David Nasaw, *Schooled to Order: A Social History of Public Schooling in the United States* (New York: Oxford University Press, 1979), 7–9.
11. Richard Gable, "Public Funds for Public and Private Schools" (PhD Diss., Catholic University of America, Washington, DC, 1937), 266–67.

take up the formation of children's perspectives on religion and ethics—a task at which many parents were perceived to be failing even in the mid-nineteenth century.

In Mann's mind, there were also national economic motivations for the establishment of common schools. "Education, if equably diffused, will draw property after it by the strongest of all attractions," Horace Mann contended in 1848. "Education, beyond all other devices of human origin, is the great equalizer of the conditions of men—the balance-wheel of the social machinery."[12] Horace Mann and the governor of Massachusetts successfully pressed for the Prussian practice of compulsory school attendance in their state. As other states copied the practices that Massachusetts had inaugurated, Mann began referring to these new systems as "public schools."[13] As late as 1867, Horace Mann still contended that parents were failing to train their children adequately both in general knowledge and in ethics.[14] Mann's solution was for parents to concede more of their educational role to the state.

"To Grow Up a Christian": Horace Bushnell's Vision for the Nurture of Children

Throughout the nineteenth century, Sunday schools and youth societies were—with the best of intentions and, in many cases, because of perceived necessity—providing religious education that had once occurred in the household. Not everyone viewed the religious training of young people as a task that should occur primarily outside the household, however. In 1847, a Congregational pastor named Horace Bushnell called parents to raise their children as Christians from the cradle. From Bushnell's perspective, it was desirable for a child "to grow up a Christian, and never know himself as being otherwise."[15]

---

12. Horace Mann, *Lectures, and Annual Reports on Education* (Cambridge: Mann, 1867), 191–209; Horace Mann, "Report for 1848: The Capacity of the Common-School System to Improve the Pecuniary Condition, and Elevate the Intellectual, Moral, and Religious Character, of the Commonwealth," in *Annual Reports on Education* (Boston: Fuller, 1868), 669.
13. Horace Mann, *Sequel to the So-Called Correspondence between the Reverend M. H. Smith and Horace Mann* (Boston: W. B. Fowle, 1847), 4, 5, 31–33, 39, 40, 45.
14. Mann, *Lectures, and Annual Reports on Education*, 217.
15. Horace Bushnell, *Christian Nurture* (New York: Scribner, Armstrong, 1876), 10, 253–70. Originally published under the title *Views of Christian Nurture, and of Subjects Adjacent Thereto* in 1847.

The liberalism of Bushnell's theology left much to be desired in his definition of "Christianity." Christianity was, for him, primarily an ethical response to transcendent reality rather than life-defining trust in the crucified and risen Lord Jesus. Additionally, much of his work represents a reaction against the emphasis that revival preachers had placed on an emotional experience of personal conversion.

> "We deeply want a revival of domestic religion. The Christian family was the bulwark of godliness in the days of the Puritans, but in these evil times hundreds of families of so-called Christians have no family worship, no restraint upon growing sons, and no wholesome instruction or discipline. How can we hope to see the kingdom of our Lord advance when his own disciples do not teach his gospel to their own children? Oh, Christian men and women, be thorough in what you do and know and teach! Let your families be trained in the fear of God and be yourselves 'holiness unto the Lord'; so shall you stand like a rock amid the surging waves of error and ungodliness which rage around us."
>
> → Charles Haddon Spurgeon ←
> Nineteenth-century Baptist pastor in London
> "The Kind of Revival We Need"

Still, Horace Bushnell did recognize this truth: parents, despite their apparent lack of qualifications, have been divinely designated to nurture their children's religious orientation. Furthermore, he called churches to equip parents for this task. In the end, however, it was not Horace Bushnell's vision that would most strongly shape the churches of the late nineteenth and twentieth centuries.

"MORE USEFUL" AND "MORE EFFICIENT": THE RISE OF YOUNG PEOPLE'S SOCIETIES

In the aftermath of the Industrial Revolution, affinity-based associations and societies emerged to fulfill roles that congregations, clans, and communities once filled. Some of the earliest of these mutual-improvement associations were unions to educate laborers and to care for family needs if a laborer died unexpectedly.

In 1824, David Naismith began organizing societies for the "religious improvement" of young men in England. Fifteen years later, after establishing thirty such associations in the United States, Naismith gave up on the societies and predicted their rapid demise. Naismith's skepticism about the effectiveness of these societies may have been well placed, but his prediction of their demise proved faulty. The religious improvement societies persisted. Many of them affiliated with the new Young Men's Christian Associations (YMCA) that began in 1844.

The original YMCA was far more than a catchy tune, complete with hand motions, that's played after the sixth inning at the local ballpark. These associations provided technical training and job preparation for young men as well as providing a safe atmosphere in urban settings where Christian conversion and commitment might take place.

The Society for Christian Endeavor, unlike YMCA, neither provided vocational training nor succeeded in inspiring a disco tune. Christian Endeavor societies began in 1881 with a single-minded focus on deepening Christian commitment among young people. Inspired by Theodore Cuyler's Young People's Association, Francis E. Clark launched the first Society for Christian Endeavor in his congregation because several young converts had entered "upon a very critical period of their Christian life, and unless they were set at work for the Master at once and good habits of religious service were inculcated, their whole future lives would suffer loss, and many would take their places among the drones in the church hive."[16]

Like Horace Bushnell, Clark contended that young people should be nurtured toward Christian faith from their childhood. Unlike Bushnell, Clark held to an orthodox, evangelical understanding of Christianity; also unlike Bushnell, Clark did not view the family as a central context for Christian growth. Instead, Clark bypassed the parents and aimed directly for the youth. At a time when many persons argued that youth should not even be admitted to church membership, Clark called young people to a high standard so that they might become "more useful in the service of God and more efficient in church work, and thus establish them in the faith and practice of the Gospel."[17]

Four principles marked the pledge of the Society for Christian Endeavor: (1) confession of Christ, (2) service to Christ, (3) loyalty to Christ's church, and (4) fellowship with Christ's people. Endeavorers fulfilled the first principle through weekly confessions of Christ at prayer meetings. Christian Endeavor committees were seen as a "systematic and efficient" way to

---

16. Clark, *Christian Endeavor Manual*, 12.
17. Ibid., 11.

accomplish the second priority.[18] While encouraging loyalty to the church and fellowship with other believers, Christian Endeavor meetings occurred apart from the church where Endeavorers served themselves, prayed by themselves, and were led in all of this by their peers. Older church members were invited to the societal meetings but were requested not to participate. The pastor might speak a few words from time to time but, for the most part, the youth of Christian Endeavor were discipling themselves.

From the perspective of efficiency and numeric growth, Christian Endeavor was wildly successful. Youth societies already existed in thousands of churches; in many cases, what Christian Endeavor provided was a worldwide federation to draw these disparate societies together. In a mere ten years, Christian Endeavor grew from one group with fifty-seven young people embracing the pledge to 16,274 societies with nearly one million youth enrolled.[19] Throughout his 1903 manual, Francis E. Clark highlighted the efficiency of these groups. He suggested that such societies provided an efficient system for the church to minister to young people, an efficient means for establishing the young people in the Christian faith, and an efficient method for creating converts.[20] These societies, while always intending to support the ministry of local churches, seem to have isolated the Christian formation of many young people from their congregations and, just as importantly, from their families.

One student minister depicted the relationship between the youth group and the rest of the congregation as a "one-eared Mickey Mouse."[21] The head of the cartoon mouse represented the church as a whole, and the ear represented youth ministry. His point was simply this: Although the student ministry and the larger congregation were technically linked, the two operated on separate tracks, with each one pursuing its own purposes and passions. Like the ear of the renowned rodent on Walt Disney's drawing board, youth ministries were barely connected to the rest of the body. The birth of the one-eared Mickey Mouse has sometimes been placed in the era of Elvis Presley and the Beatles; however, a survey of the

---

18. Ibid., 26–27, 88.
19. Leonard Woolsey Bacon and Charles Addison Northrop, *Young People's Societies* (New York: Lentilhon, 1900), 30.
20. Clark, *Christian Endeavor Manual*, 11, 105, 109–10.
21. Chap Clark, "From Fragmentation to Integration," forMinistry, American Bible Society, October 24, 2006, http://www.forministry.com. Also, portions of this paragraph have been drawn from lectures by Timothy Paul Jones, (course, Models of Student and Family Ministry, The Southern Baptist Theological Seminary, Louisville, Kentucky, 2010–2011).

Christian Endeavor societies reveals a somewhat different picture. The economic boom that followed the Second World War *did* enable many churches to professionalize the mutant mouse as they hired age-focused ministers. From the young people's societies of the nineteenth century until the Young Life organization began hiring youth ministers in the mid-twentieth century, youth ministry had been a volunteer endeavor. In the 1950s and 1960s, youth ministry shifted to a paid profession, solidifying the youth group's segmentation from the rest of the congregation. Yet the separation between youth and adults in the churches was already present in the society system of the late nineteenth century, preceding Presley's 1956 "Heartbreak Hotel" by more than half a century.

PIG-IRON AND CHURCH PROGRAMS: WHAT HAPPENED WHEN EFFICIENCY WENT TO CHURCH

The early twentieth century saw the rise of the "efficiency movement." Proponents of this movement suggested that everything could improve if organizations would empower consultants to identify problems and to implement solutions. What followed was a period of intensive scientific analysis in every field from medicine and engineering, from city planning to factory design, to determine the most efficient ways to regulate society. Expert consultants developed scientific principles and rules for efficiency which began to govern practices within their spheres of study.

Great emphasis was placed on specialization, professionalization, and standardization. According to efficiency proponent Frederick Winslow Taylor, ordinary workers were incapable of understanding how to be efficient; therefore, expert managers were responsible to enforce practices of efficiency. "The man who is," Taylor declared in his testimony to the House of Representatives, "physically able to handle pig-iron and is sufficiently phlegmatic and stupid to choose this for his occupation is rarely able to comprehend the science of handling pig-iron."[22] One result of this pattern was the advent of a "deferral culture." Individuals and organizations increasingly deferred responsibilities to persons perceived as having expertise in particular areas.

---

22. Frederick Winslow Taylor, quoted in *Hearings before Special Committee of the House of Representatives to Investigate the Taylor and Other Systems of Shop Management*, vol. 3 (Washington, DC: Government Printing Office, 1912), 1397.

Churches readily embraced many aspects of the efficiency movement. In 1915, W. A. Hobson, editor of the *Florida Baptist Witness*, dubbed efficiency in Christian service "the true test of orthodoxy" and declared evangelism and efficiency "the two great fundamental things in the teaching of Christ and his apostles."[23] In churches, the movement toward efficiency led to increased centralization and professionalization of ministries. According to an article from 1909, a church needed three trained "experts" in addition to the pastor: a director of religious education, a director of social work, and a church visitor. The purpose of this church staff was to do what church members "have not the technical training to do as it ought to be done."[24] Put another way, ordinary church members—like handlers of pig-iron in the factories—lacked the skills to understand what they were doing, so trained experts would now take over and do ministry "as it ought to be done." This trend seems to have contributed to the shape of ministry to children and youth in the twentieth and twenty-first centuries.

MINISTRY TO FAMILIES IN THE MODERN AGE

So how did churches attempt to partner with parents in the Christian formation of their children in the nineteenth and twentieth centuries?

Or did they?

The good news is that many churches *did* attempt to minister to families. In fact, it is possible to identify three primary approaches to ministry in the nineteenth and twentieth centuries. Sometimes these attempts drew families together and equipped parents to disciple their children. In other instances, well-intended approaches to ministry seem to have pulled the generations apart.

Samuel W. Dike's "Home Department":
A Comprehensive-Coordinative Approach

Meagerly represented in the twentieth century, the comprehensive-coordinative model was an attempt to reestablish the household as a primary

---

23. W. A. Hobson, "Editorial," *Florida Baptist Witness*, February 4, 1915, 6–7. See also Elmer T. Clark, *The Church Efficiency Movement* (Nashville: Publishing House of the M. E. Church, 1915), 4–9.
24. Richard Morse Hodge, "What Should Be the Training of Pastor's Assistants?" *Religious Education* 3, no. 4 (October 1908): 152; see also rest of article, 151–57.

context for the Christian training of children. Comprehensive-coordinative approaches attempted to equip parents by coordinating practices of household discipleship with existing church programs.

Samuel W. Dike is best known for his writings on marriage and divorce in the early twentieth century. He was also known, however, as the founder of "the Home Department." Dike's purpose was to call parents back to their God-ordained role as disciple-makers in their children's lives.[25] Through his Home Department, ministers and laypeople were trained to visit the homes of church members, providing curriculum and equipping parents to engage in family worship and the teaching of Bible stories. According to Dike, churches of the nineteenth century had been

> enriching [their own programs] of centralized activities at the expense of the home's chance to cultivate family religion. Sunday-school sessions, missionary societies, temperance and other reformatory meetings, young people's meetings, brotherhoods and guilds—each as it came in seized on some Sunday or week-day hour and appropriated it for the use of its own church-centered activity. The churches, in fact, have done for religious training what the factories had done for industrial training. They have taken it out of the home.[26]

Dike did not desire to do away with church societies or Sunday schools. The full name of his effort was, in fact, "the Home Department *of the Sunday School*." His desire was to align existing church programs with Christian training in homes.

Unfortunately, many churches mistook the Home Department for a further development of what W. A. Duncan had established as "home classes"—an attempt to increase Sunday school numbers by counting shut-ins who received curriculum and who agreed to study the curriculum at least thirty minutes each week.[27] By

> What aspects of your church could move toward comprehensive-coordinative family ministry? Which aspects would be the hardest to change? Why?

25. Samuel W. Dike, "The Message of the Home Department of the Sunday School," in Hartshorn, Merrill, and Lawrance, *Development of the Sunday School*, 262.
26. Edmund Morris Fergusson, *Church-School Administration* (New York: Fleming H. Revell, 1922), 124–25.
27. P. E. Burroughs, *The Present-Day Sunday School, Studies in Its Organization and Management* (New York: Fleming H. Revell, 1917), 142.

the 1920s and 1930s, the Home Department had faded into a literature distribution program in most churches. "Schooling had become the
model for religious education and efficiency the standard by which it was
judged."[28] At a time when efficiency, centralization, and professionalization were the watchwords, equipping parents to serve as amateur educators in their homes did not seem particularly practicable.

A Separate Ministry for Every Member of the Family: A Segmented-Programmatic Approach

Even before the Second World War, the pledge-based youth societies of
the late 1800s and early 1900s were fading. Many societies were shifting
to church-based gatherings intended to foster fellowship with God and
with one another. Sunday schools had become "the chief instrument of the
church for training the young in religion."[29] At the same time, parachurch
organizations were emerging to evangelize unchurched youth.

By the late 1940s and 1950s, the widespread availability of secondary
public education had coupled with the euphoria of postwar economic re-
covery to birth a new series of American ideals. These ideals included a sup-
position that, in the most respectable families, youth could be exempted
from any responsibility to assist their families through meaningful labor.[30]
Perhaps most important, the youth of this era became the first generation in American history to receive sufficient spending money to affect the
economy in significant ways. Eventually, not only teens but also children became targets of marketing campaigns that centered on the perceived needs
of particular age-groupings. A family's needs could be satisfied by purchasing
a product for each family member that was aimed at his or her age group.

In some sense, that's how the segmented-programmatic church
attempted to minister to the family. The segmented-programmatic
church emerged as the society structures of the nineteenth century became professionalized in the twentieth century. By the mid-twentieth century, local churches were imitating parachurch ministries such as Young
Life and Youth for Christ by hiring professional ministers whose primary

---

28. Mark H. Senter III, *When God Shows Up: A History of Protestant Youth Ministry in America* (Grand Rapids: Baker Academic, 2010), 63.

29. Robert S. Lynd and Helen Merrell Lynd, *Middletown: A Study in American Culture* (New York: Harcourt, Brace, 1929), 393–98.

30. Stephanie Coontz, *The Way We Never Were: American Families and the Nostalgia Trap* (New York: Basic Books, 1992), 13–14.

purpose was to engage adolescents. The first Young Life manual declared that "the Leader is it!" in the youth club.[31] Likewise, throughout the new wave of church-based youth groups in the 1950s and 1960s, the capacity of the youth minister to attract and to retain adolescents became central. In earlier times, youth societies had been directed by the young people themselves or by volunteers. Now, age-organized ministry was quickly becoming professionalized. Soon, churches were calling specialized ministers to oversee programs for other age-groupings as well.

Table 9.1. Modern Trends in Family Ministry[32]		
Comprehensive-Coordinative	**Segmented-Programmatic**	**Educational-Programmatic**
Comprehensive-coordinative family ministry equips parents to function as primary disciple-makers in their children's lives by partnering with parents and by providing resources and training in their households. Promoted by Samuel W. Dike in the late 1800s and early 1900s, the "Home Department of the Sunday School" faded, primarily due to confusion of purpose and the rise of the efficiency movement. In the late twentieth and early twenty-first centuries, many aspects of comprehensive-coordinative ministry were revived in family-integrated, family-equipping, and (to a lesser extent) family-based congregations.	Segmented-programmatic ministry to families means a separate and specific program for each member of the family. Influenced by a variety of earlier factors—including young people's societies, the efficiency movement, the rise of age-focused associate ministers, and the rise of professional youth ministers—the segmented-programmatic approach dominated the last half of the twentieth century. Family-based ministry, promoted by Mark DeVries in the late twentieth century, represented a reorientation of segmented-programmatic structures to empower parents to participate actively in the discipleship of children and adolescents.	The educational-programmatic or Family Life Education approach to family ministry establishes ambulance programs to assist families in crises and guardrail programs to strengthen healthy families. Reggie Joiner refers to this approach as "departmental family ministry."[33] In the twenty-first century, Family Life Education continues in many congregations, typically in the form of distinct programs for family education and counseling.

31. First Young Life manual, quoted in Senter, *When God Shows Up*, 219.
32. Timothy Paul Jones, "Models for Family Ministry" in *A Theology for Family Ministry*, ed. Michael Anthony and Michelle Anthony (Nashville: B&H, 2011, forthcoming).
33. Reggie Joiner, *Think Orange: Imagine the Impact When Church and Family Collide* (Colorado Springs: David C. Cook, 2009), Concentrate 6.2.

Ministry to families came to mean having a separate ministry for each member of the family. These ministries tended to exist in "silos," perhaps united around a common goal but organizationally separated. In many segmented-programmatic congregations, it became possible to attend church regularly without ever rubbing shoulders with anyone—except perhaps a teacher or two—from a generation other than one's own.

The segmented-programmatic approach dominated the organization of evangelical churches in the twentieth and even into the twenty-first centuries. At best, this approach allows each family member to experience Christian training in age-appropriate ways in the context of the faith community. The problem is, parents may never spiritually engage with their children. Adolescents receive their training in youth group, children go to children's church, and adults have Bible studies and worship celebrations tailored to their particular preferences. At worst, this approach can function like "an octopus without a brain."[34] The various programs may loosely connect with one another, but each one works independently of the others.

Help for Hurting Families, Training for Healthy Families: An Educational-Programmatic Approach

In some churches, educational-programmatic family ministry functions as an additional "arm" in the segmented-programmatic approach. Often known as "family life ministries" or "family life education," educational-programmatic programs train families to deal with relational issues. Particularly near the midpoint of the twentieth century, churches and colleges developed counseling programs and instructional materials for families in distress as well as preventative training to strengthen healthy families.[35] The focus of family life education may be the formation of family-like relationships within the church or counseling and support services for family well-being. Even in the opening decades of the twenty-first century, educational-programmatic family ministry remains a popular partner with existing segmented-programmatic structures in many churches.

---

34. Chap Clark, *The Youth Workers Handbook to Family Ministry: Strategies and Practical Ideas for Reaching Your Students' Families* (Grand Rapids: Zondervan, 1997), 24.
35. Margaret E. Arcus, Jay D. Schvanefeldt, and J. Joel Moss, "The Nature of Family Life Education," in *Handbook of Family Life Education: Foundations of Family Life Education*, vol. 1, ed. Margaret E. Arcus, Jay D. Schvaneveldt, and J. Joel Moss (Thousand Oaks, CA: SAGE, 1993), 9.

"MAKE IT A GOOD ONE"

To a large extent, churches still live in the shadow of the age of efficiency. It is easier to hire a professional expert to disciple the emerging generation than it is to train parents for this task. Yet God has called parents to function as the primary disciple-makers in their children's lives. The church should not try to do the work *of* the parents or *for* the parents; instead, every effort of the church should be to *equip* the parents for this momentous task.

In the past couple of decades, three different family ministry models—*family-based, family-integrated*, and *family-equipping*—have emerged with that very purpose in mind. Leaders in all three of these movements have recognized that a few hours in church each week are insufficient to train children and youth. With 168 hours in a week—supposing 8 hours of sleep each night and 9 hours at school for five days every week—about 67 hours of prospective time remains every week for parents' relationship with their children. Churches must partner with mothers and fathers so that parents learn to make the most of these hours.

> ✦ If your church is segmented-programmatic or educational-programmatic in its approach to family ministry, develop an outline that clearly demonstrates how your church might transition toward a comprehensive-coordinative approach. Within the comprehensive-coordinative approach, the three primary models are *family-integrated, family-equipping*, and *family-based*. ✦

If Marty McFly's experiences are accurate, much has yet to happen in the twenty-first century. Not only will our kids soon be using skateboards with no wheels, but we will also be operating flying cars and our clothing will automatically adjust for proper fit. Let's face it, though: none of this appears to be likely anytime soon. The producers in the 1980s completely missed the technology we *have* gained—who would have imagined e-mail, cell phones, and pay-at-the-pump gas stations?—and most of what they did imagine is decades from fruition.

The *Back to the Future* trilogy ends with a conversation between Doc Brown, Marty McFly, and his girlfriend Jennifer Parker. "Your future has not been written yet," Doc Brown declares to Jennifer. "No one's has. Your future is whatever you make it. So make it a good one." Doc Brown wasn't quite correct, of course. God has, in fact, already written every detail of our future. And yet, there is something to be said about our human responsibility to "make it a good one." For believers in Jesus Christ, making our future "a good one" is not defined by buildings, budgets, or warm bodies in the pews. It is defined instead by faithfulness to a divine story of creation and fall, redemption and consummation—a story that, from the beginning, has called parents to train their children so that God's glory extends throughout the earth.

PART 3

GROWING THE FAMILY OF GOD

Guiding a Congregation toward Theologically Grounded Family Ministry

When it comes to doing family ministry in the local church, what real-life needs and struggles will you face? And what about parents who are not training their children in the fear of God? What do they need to know about family ministry? This final section of *Trained in the Fear of God* gathers pastors and parents, professors and practitioners, to explore the practical implications of family-equipping ministry for families and churches.

David Prince demonstrates why family ministry doesn't begin in a church staff meeting—it begins in the pastor's home. Peter R. Schemm shows what habits might mark a gospel-centered household, while Brian Haynes focuses on milestones that parents, children, and churches can celebrate together. George Willard Cochran Jr. and Brian Richardson outline the need for parental involvement in light of the latest brain research. Carolyn McCulley and Lilly Park look at the roles of women and singles. Finally, Michael S. Wilder presents a case for families serving together, and Jay Strother shows how churches can make the transition from segmented programs to comprehensively coordinated family-equipping ministry.

10

THE PASTOR'S HOME AS PARADIGM FOR THE CHURCH'S FAMILY MINISTRY

David Prince

As a young, newly married man with no children yet, I listened intently to what sounded like a helpful idea for the small congregation where I served at the time.

"I really want to see our church minister to families," my pastor declared, "and I want my family to connect with families as well!"

To meet this goal of leading the church toward more family-oriented ministry, the pastor presented this plan: he put out a jar with small slips of blank paper beside it; families in the church could write their names and telephone numbers on a slip of paper if they were willing for the pastor's family to come over for a visit and then place that piece of paper in the jar.

Each week the pastor reached into the jar, pulled out a slip of paper, called the number listed on it, and took his entire family over for a visit on Sunday afternoon. The idea was well received, and the jar filled up quickly. It had been a long time since this church had been pastored by a man who so sincerely desired such a personal connection with families in the congregation.

Within a few weeks, something began to happen that was a bit awkward for the entire congregation—something that worked against the pastor's intention of leading the church toward family-oriented ministry. The little slips of paper began to disappear from the large jar, but *not* because the pastor was working overtime at making those visits. After four or five weeks, the jar that was so full at the beginning only included a few lonely papers—and even those slips, rumor had it, weren't deposited by the families whose names were written on them but by others in the church.

Why was this happening?

The pastor and his family were well liked; the problem was that his family was not well-ordered. It hadn't taken long for news to spread that if the pastor's family came to visit, your valuables might not be safe—and your children might not be safe either. The pastor was a kind, warmhearted servant—and his popularity never waned during the course of the ordeal—but he lost his credibility in attempting to lead the church toward family-oriented ministry.

People were looking for someone who could practice in his own family what he was preaching from the pulpit.

HOW DO WE GET FROM *HERE* TO *THERE?*

In the 1980s and 1990s, discontent with segmented-programmatic ministry began to simmer in many evangelical churches.[1] In the dominant segmented-programmatic approach, families functionally said goodbye after exiting the car in the church parking lot and greeted one another again when they climbed back into the car to return home. In the worst cases, ministry environments were so tightly tailored to the preferences of individual groups that there was nothing to discuss on that car ride home.

In the opening decade of the twenty-first century, this simmering discontent boiled over into a full-scale movement in many evangelical churches—a family ministry movement that is now sweeping across a broad range of methodological and ecclesiological boundaries. This movement toward comprehensive-coordinative family ministry is not a program or a denominational campaign; it is made up of local churches coming to grips with the failure of segmented-programmatic ministry and then searching the Scripture for a more biblical alternative.[2]

---

1. The conversation was predominately taking place in youth ministry circles. The youth ministries were the most radically segmented from the church as a whole and often functioned as a completely separate entity with their own worship, leader, name, and ministry focus. For a seminal early volume in this movement, see Mark DeVries, *Family-Based Youth Ministry* (Downers Grove, IL: InterVarsity Press, 1994).

2. From a pragmatic perspective, it might be difficult to call a segmented-programmatic approach a failed ministry philosophy because of the numerical success that has so often accompanied the approach. The failure instead is seen when the fruit of the approach is examined. Two of the more odious fruits of the segmented-programmatic

I praise God for this movement, but I also recognize that every church desiring to move toward a comprehensive-coordinate family ministry model must answer a single crucial question: how do we get from *here* to *there*? In answering that question, there is a key component, often overlooked, that will be essential: no church will effectively establish any form of comprehensive-coordinative family ministry unless the pastor's family models the change that the congregation is seeking.[3] If the pastor's family does not reflect the desired change, you can be assured that the slips of paper in the family ministry jar will quickly begin to disappear.

Fathers as Shepherds

Fathers are called to be pastors in their homes. "What the preacher is in the pulpit," Lewis Bayly declared, "the same the Christian householder is in his house."[4] The idea of fathers as the pastors of their homes is not one constructed artificially; it arises from the testimony of Scripture. The word *pastor* comes from the Latin word for "shepherd"—and every father is called to serve as a shepherd in his home.[5]

Sheep are mentioned in the Bible more than any other animal, and

---

approach are (1) parents who are subtly taught that they are not the primary people responsible for the discipleship of their children as well as (2) the cultivation of a *narcissistic* preoccupation with age and cultural preferences. When catering to individual preferences becomes a methodological presupposition, the casualty is a call to self-sacrificial spiritual maturity. However, it must also be noted that some family ministry advocates have had an unhealthy response to these problems and have cultivated an equally self-oriented attitude in the opposite direction by failing to acknowledge the unique authority of the local church. This attitude of antiecclesiastical authority can produce an almost idolatrous attitude regarding familial authority.

3. The Greek words *poimen* (pastor), *presbyteros* (elder), and *episkopos* (overseer) are used interchangeably to refer to the same office in the church (Acts 20:17, 28; Eph. 4:11–12; 1 Tim. 3:1–7; Titus 1:5–9; 1 Peter 5:1–2). While the Bible indicates that it is normative for a local church to have a plurality of pastors (Acts 16:24, 20:17, 21:18; Titus 1:5; James 5:14), the primary focus of this chapter is the pastor who is called to the congregation's preaching ministry.
4. Lewis Bayly, quoted in David E. Prince, "Family Worship," Council of Biblical Manhood and Womanhood, http://www.cbmw.org/Resources/Articles/Family-Worship (accessed March 12, 2010).
5. For an extensive treatment of the biblical use of the shepherd language and imagery see, Timothy S. Laniak, *Shepherds after My Own Heart: Pastoral Traditions and Leadership in the Bible* (Downers Grove, IL: InterVarsity Press, 2006).

shepherds appear in the text more than one hundred times.[6] Any examination of pastoral responsibilities must begin with the Lord who revealed himself as "the God who has been my shepherd all my life long" (Gen. 48:15; see also Ps. 23:1). When many contemporary evangelicals consider what it means to be a shepherd, their minds conjure pictures of an effeminate Jesus gazing longingly at a sheep as he strokes its wool. In the ancient Near East, however, shepherds were rugged warriors who bore scars from protecting their sheep. To identify God as a shepherd suggests that he is the authoritative head of his people, the one who directs, disciplines, and defends his own. The psalmist Asaph celebrated God's redemption of his people from Egypt by singing, "You led your people like a flock" (Ps. 77:20). This same event was described by the Israelites as a time when God went to war on their behalf (Exod. 15:3).

David made the case to Saul that he could defeat Goliath by appealing to his experiences as a shepherd:

> Your servant used to keep sheep for his father. And when there came a lion, or a bear, and took a lamb from the flock, I went after him and struck him and delivered it out of his mouth. And if he arose against me, I caught him by his beard and struck him and killed him. Your servant has struck down both lions and bears, and this uncircumcised Philistine shall be like one of them. (1 Sam. 17:34–36a)

In the context of the Old Testament, the compassionate care offered by a good shepherd was costly and sacrificial. The mark of an unfaithful shepherd was that he served himself and did not sacrifice himself for his sheep (Jer. 23; Ezek. 34). Jesus fulfilled the ancient promises of a Shepherd-King (Matt. 2:6) and identified himself as "the good shepherd" who "lays down his life for the sheep" (John 10:11).[7] In the end, it is Jesus who will defeat the enemies of God's people, wiping away his flock's every tear, precisely because he is "their shepherd" (Rev. 7:17).

When the triumphant Shepherd-King ascended to the Father, he extended his care to his people as "the chief Shepherd" by providing the gift

---

6. Leland Ryken, James C. Wilhoit, and Tremper Longman III, "Sheep, Shepherd," *Dictionary of Biblical Imagery* (Downers Grove, IL: InterVarsity Press, 1998), 782.

7. Leon Morris is correct to note the uniqueness of Jesus' role as shepherd in that his death for the sheep did not mean disaster for them but rather life through his resurrection. Leon Morris, *The Gospel According to John*, rev. ed., New International Commentary (Grand Rapids: Eerdmans, 1995), 454.

of "under-shepherds"—elders or overseers who would direct, discipline, and defend local communities of believers (Eph. 4:11; 1 Tim. 3:1–7). The apostle Peter commended these church leaders to "shepherd the flock of God" (1 Peter 5:1–2).

Peter warned elders about those who abandon the sheep rather than leading and protecting the sheep, just as Jesus before him had warned about the person who is "a hired hand and not a shepherd" while establishing the fact that he was "the good shepherd" (John 10:12–14). Peter wrote that elders were to honor the good shepherd by "exercising oversight, not under compulsion, but willingly, as God would have you; not for shameful gain, but eagerly; not domineering over those in your charge, but being examples to the flock" (1 Peter 5:2b–3).

Likewise, the apostle Paul referred to the church at Ephesus as "the flock" and described how he counted his ministry among them as more dear than his own life (Acts 20:17–38).[8] His intent was that the Ephesian elders—and, by extension, that all pastors—would follow his example.[9] Pastors bear the weighty responsibility to reflect Jesus, the good shepherd, by leading, guiding, directing, teaching, disciplining, and defending the flock of God gathered in local churches.

But the application of the shepherding imagery does not end with the call for elders to reflect the ministry of the good shepherd in the local church. Scripture also draws parallels between the responsibility of Christian fathers to pastor their families and the responsibility of called men to shepherd the local church.[10] Paul had this to say about anyone who might become an elder: "He must manage his own household well, with all dignity keeping his children submissive, for if someone does not know how to manage his own household, how will he care for God's church?" (1 Tim. 3:5).

---

8. Ben Witherington notes that Paul's reference to "the flock" (v. 28) makes it clear that "[t]he Ephesian elders are not being called to shepherd the church universal, but to oversee all of the flock of which the Spirit has made them leaders." He also points out that Ezekiel 34 seems to lie in the background of the warnings of those who would harm the flock of God from within. Ben Witherington, *The Acts of the Apostles: A Socio-Rhetorical Commentary* (Grand Rapids: Eerdmans, 1998), 624.

9. David G. Peterson, *The Acts of the Apostles*, Pillar New Testament Commentary (Grand Rapids: Eerdmans, 2009), 568.

10. For an excellent lecture on the parallels between pastoring the local church and pastoring a family, see D. A. Carson, "The Pastor as Father to His Family and Flock," Desiring God 2008 Conference for Pastors, February 5, 2008, http://www.desiring-god.org/resource-library/conference-messages/the-pastor-as-father-to-his-family-and-flock (accessed March 15, 2010).

Shepherding the "Little Flock"

"Leaders must be good shepherds of their little flocks at home before they are qualified to serve as shepherds of God's flock, the church."[11] Every man in a local church should be able to look to his pastor's ministry as a model of faithful shepherding to be imitated on a smaller scale in his own home. If the congregation's pastor is shepherding the church but not his family, his influence is muted and his model is one of tragic hypocrisy.

A family is not a church; every Christian believer, as an individual, functions under the authority of the congregation. Yet the principles of directing and caring for the church and the household are the same.[12] Paul called local churches "the household of God" (1 Tim. 3:15) and uses family imagery to exhort these congregations (1 Tim. 5:1–2; 1 Cor 4:15–16; 1 Thess 2:11). The interplay in the Scripture between the household of God and familial households, as well as the interplay between pastors and fathers, should arrest the reader's attention.

> → If you are a pastoral leader, honestly ask yourself, "Am I doing what I am asking my congregation to do? Do I disciple my children? Am I consistently guiding my wife toward Christian maturity?" If you are a church member, consider this question: "Does my congregation provide our pastoral leaders with sufficient family time to disciple their families?" ←

"The church is the family of God," Randy Stinson asserts, "and family relationships represent a divinely ordained paradigm for God's church—which is why it is so important for our relationships in the family and in the church to reflect God's ideal."[13] It is common today for families to have the mentality that the church exists to serve the family. In reality, such a view needs to be turned on its head. Our households exist to portray to the world the church, the household of God. The congregation, then, is to be conformed to the Word of God and be determined to know nothing but Christ and him crucified (1 Cor. 2:2)—and to call families to do the same. The Scripture makes an

---

11. Timothy Z. Witmer, *The Shepherd Leader: Achieving Effective Shepherding in Your Church* (Phillipsburg, NJ: P&R, 2010), 164.

12. Laniak writes, "Authority is a feature of the shepherd's role, but one comprehensively qualified by the reminder that elders are caring for the flock *of God.*" Laniak, *Shepherds after My Own Heart*, 233. Likewise, the elder must exercise the same sort of caring authority in the home as he leads his little flock for God.

13. Randy Stinson, "Family Ministry and the Future of the Church" (foreword), in *Perspectives on Family Ministry: 3 Views*, ed. Timothy Paul Jones (Nashville: B&H, 2009), 3.

unequivocal and vital link between an elder's calling to pastor a local church and a man's responsibility to pastor his family. Pastors reflect Jesus in the church by directing, disciplining, and defending the flock of God, and fathers must do likewise with the little flock God has entrusted to them.

The Well-Equipped Father and the Family-Equipping Church

A family-equipping church desires every father in the congregation to acknowledge and to embrace his role as the shepherd of his family. To live out this role every father must begin to see himself as a rugged, shepherd-warrior who leads his family like a flock—enduring whatever sacrificial hardships are necessary for his family's provision, protection, and care. A father's oversight is costly—but this is to be expected, because he is a shepherd.

A father is the head of his home, the spiritual leader, who has the responsibility to feed his family the Word of God on a daily basis. He also must know that, even though he is the shepherd of his little flock, "the chief Shepherd" has graciously placed him under the authority of the church and its shepherds, "the flock of God" (1 Peter 5:2, 4). Therefore, each father leads his family to the church as a vital partner as he guides his family. He should be able to say, with the apostle Paul, that he ministers night and day with tears, declaring the whole counsel of God and refusing to count his life more dear than his ministry to his family (Acts 20:17–38). The church that implements coordinative-comprehensive family ministry must have fathers who understand these shepherding responsibilities not as preferential matters but as essential spiritual warfare.

Far too often, Christian fathers define success according to self-generated standards, forsaking their role as the shepherds of their home in an ambitious pursuit of power or achievement, material possessions or personal acclaim. Other fathers, typically young adults in what has been appropriately dubbed "Generation Me,"[14] simply forsake their role as the family shepherd in the quest for self-pleasure and trivial pursuits. While it is common for evangelical pastors to bemoan the passivity of men in their congregation—passivity exhibited through a lack of paternal leadership in the home—too often the passivity they critique is nurtured by the very leadership model they present to families in the congregation! When the

---

14. Jean M. Twenge, *Generation Me: Why Today's Young Americans Are More Confident, Assertive, Entitled—and More Miserable than Ever Before* (New York: Free Press, 2007).

pastor of a church possesses an aggressive mentality in leading his congregation—one in which he will do whatever it takes to cultivate measurable success at the church—but then takes a secondary role in shepherding his own family—as though he is his wife's helper—his poor example effectively drowns out his homiletic rhetoric. Likewise, when a pastor organizes his life around golf outings and college sporting events in the name of "ministry"—all while his wife raises the children—then the men in the church hear that daily "sermon" delivered with far greater clarity than the one delivered from the pulpit on Sunday.

For a church to move toward a family-equipping model of ministry, the pastor of the church must daily equip his own family. Every elder has the responsibility to lead by example. Sadly, this means that many churches will not move toward a family-equipping model of ministry simply because they cannot do so with integrity. The pastor of such a church is unable to say with authenticity, "Be imitators of me, as I am of Christ" (1 Cor. 11:1) when he calls men in the congregation to become genuine family shepherds.

> "The Bible says the 'husband is the head of the wife, as also Christ is the head of the church' (Eph. 5:23). Paul most emphatically does *not* say that husbands *ought* to be heads of their wives. He says that they *are*."
>
> ✴
>
> Douglas Wilson, *Reforming Marriage*

I do not mean, of course, that a pastor must have a perfect home—or that he must pretend to have such a home—in order to lead the church toward family-equipping ministry. He *must*, however, be an intentional shepherd who "manage[s] his own household well" (1 Tim. 3:4). In fact, the way a God-called elder manages the challenges of home life will be invaluably instructive for the other fathers in the congregation. In the pastor, the men of the congregation must see a father who makes no excuses as he intentionally feeds, leads, serves, and sacrifices himself for his household, declaring with Paul that "I die every day!" in self-sacrificial service for his home, as well as the church (1 Cor. 15:31).

The Centrality of Jesus in a Family-Equipping Church

What must not be overlooked in all of this, however, is that the most important reality in the life of the family is not the family but Jesus Christ. The entire cosmos was created by Christ and for Christ (Col. 1:16–18).

All Scripture testifies of him (Luke 24:27; John 5:39); he is the final Word (Heb. 1:2); all the promises of God find their "yes" and "amen" in him (2 Cor. 1:20). It is God's eternal plan to sum up all things in him (Eph. 1:10).

The shepherd of the church who is also the shepherd of a family has the responsibility to "sum up" both family and church in the gospel of Jesus Christ. His family must be one in which this gospel is central to every facet of life. Any family movement in the church that fails to focus on the gospel will produce family-Pharisees who settle for behavioral change, isolation from the world, and idolatrous focus on their own families. Family problems are, however, deeper than behavior; they are issues of the heart for which the only answer is the gospel.[15] A home full of well-behaved, well-mannered children whose obedience is not understood through the lens of the gospel is not holy but hellish.

The pastor's family should function as a daily model of the centrality of the gospel. An elder who is more concerned with the fact that his children's behavior might sometimes embarrass him in public than he is concerned for the condition of their hearts is merely using his family as a prop in his personal public relations campaign. Such prideful obsession proclaims to the congregation what many already believe—that mere external changes are an acceptable goal for their families and their Christian lives. Likewise, the pastor who allows the whims of his children to determine his direction of his family perpetuates the prideful exaltation of self that is already too rampant in the pews.

> "I fear that the cross, without ever being disowned, is constantly in danger of being dismissed from the central place it must enjoy, by relatively peripheral insights that take on far too much weight. Whenever the periphery is in danger of displacing the center, we are not far removed from idolatry."
>
> ♦♦
>
> D.A. Carson, *The Cross and Christian Ministry*

The root problem with both scenarios is not that they lead to disastrous practical consequences; the problem is that they work against the gospel. The gospel deals with the internal transformation of the heart and demands self-sacrificial humility before the Lord Jesus Christ. If a pastor desires to lead a church in family-equipping ministry, he must not trade a segmented-programmatic approach to church ministry—one in which the desires of

---

15. Tedd Tripp, *Shepherding a Child's Heart* (Wapwallopen, PA: Shepherd Press, 1995).

each individual stand at the center—for an approach in which the family is drawn to the proper center. The cross of Jesus must stand at the center both of church ministry and of family life; anything more or less is idolatry.

Co-championship in the Family-Equipping Church

One's commitment in all things to the centrality of Jesus Christ, the head of the church, should naturally lead to a love of the church, which is his body (1 Cor. 12:12; Eph. 1:22, 5:23; Col. 1:18, 24). In fact, Christ so closely identifies himself with the church that Paul writes that the church is Jesus' "body, the fullness of him who fills all in all" (Eph 1:23).

A family-equipping church seeks to champion both family and church. Marriage pictures the relationship between Christ and the church, and the family unit pictures the family of God—the church, the household of faith (Eph. 2:19, 5:22–33; 1 Tim. 3:15; 1 Peter 4:17). The following observations from Steve Wright and Chris Graves, although aimed primarily at student ministry, are applicable to all church ministries:

> God created the family. God created the church. And in His wisdom, He created the two to function together. The biblical ideal is one of the family supporting the church and the church supporting the family, but it's not happening today. It has reached such extremes that some parents want to stop all student ministries, and some student pastors want to stop trying to partner with parents. What God has joined together man has separated over time.[16]

Children as Blessings in the Family-Equipping Church

Soon after I accepted the call to become the pastor of one particular local church, my wife began hearing comments that disturbed her greatly. Church members mentioned how the previous pastor's wife repeatedly mentioned that she hoped none of her children would ever follow in her husband's footsteps by going into vocational ministry and that her pastor husband felt the same way. My wife was horrified that a pastor's wife would broadcast such negative attitudes toward the church.

Negative attitudes toward the church create a separation between the church and the family that makes family-equipping ministry impossible. Negative attitudes toward the family have the same effect. When a

---

16. Steve Wright with Chris Graves, reThink: Decide for Yourself, Is Student Ministry Working? (Wake Forest, NC: InQuest Publishing, 2007), 105–6.

church member mentions the possibility of having more children and the pastor rolls his eyes and says, "Not for my wife and me! We've had enough. We are just glad this church has a nursery," the consequences are tragic. Antichild, antifamily jargon sounds more like the words of Pharaoh about the Hebrew children (Exod. 1:8–22) than the word of Christ (Gen. 1:28; Matt. 19:14). God refers to children as a blessing (Ps. 127, 128) and to the church of Jesus Christ as the community of the blessed (Rom. 4:7–8). It is dangerous, even jokingly, to call a curse what God has declared a blessing.

The shepherd who delights in weekly standing before a congregation of Christ's sheep, lovingly preaching the glorious gospel of Jesus in corporate worship, is to be the same shepherd who possesses the same delight before his little flock at home in family worship. In fact, there is a primacy to his responsibility to pastor his family with the Word of God. If he does not shepherd his family, he is not fit to shepherd the household of God (1 Tim. 3:5; Titus 1:6).

THE RESPONSIBILITY OF THE PASTOR IN CALLING PARENTS TO THEIR RESPONSIBILITY

The pastor who desires to lead a family-equipping church must sound a clear note in his own home that he understands it is not the church but parents—and fathers in particular—who are given the primary responsibility for calling the emerging generation to hope in God (Ps. 78:1–8). The church serves a supplementary role, reinforcing the biblical nurture that is occurring in the home. It is not the job of professionals at the church to train believers' children in the fear of God. The family-equipping pastor who is also a family shepherd will not allow Sunday schools, children's ministries, or youth ministries to become substitutes for the household discipleship of his children. This commitment provides a solid platform to call Christian fathers who have abdicated their God-given responsibility to repent and to embrace their role as family shepherds.

What If Parents Feel Inadequate?

When God established Israel as his covenant people, he also established responsibility for parents to nurture their children in the faith. This is a clear charge given by the Lord God to fathers and mothers in Deuteronomy 6:4–7. This text is known in Jewish tradition as the Shema, after the first

Hebrew word in verse 4, an urgent command that is typically translated "hear" but that might also be rendered as "listen" or "obey."

It is interesting to note that it is Moses who is God's instrument to convey this command to his people. When God first called him to speak his words to the children of Israel, Moses responded, "I am slow of speech and slow of tongue" (Exod. 4:10). God quickly reminded Moses that the one who gave him the command was also the one who created his mouth (Exod. 4:11). Many parents need to be reminded that it is *God* who commands them to teach their children divine truth. All of the excuses—"I'm not smart enough," "I don't speak well," or "the pastor is more qualified"—fade in light of the one who gives the command. This truth should call parents to ask themselves, "Who created me? Who is calling me to disciple my children? Who gave me these children in the first place?"

Deuteronomy 6:7 makes it clear that the commands of the Lord, which are to be on the hearts of the parent, should be passed on to the children to be on their hearts as well: "You shall teach them diligently to your children." The Hebrew word translated "teach them diligently" is a word that implies "piercing," "carving," or "whetting." The word picture is graphic. Parents are to engrave God's truth into their children's hearts like an engraver chiseling words into a solid slab of stone.[17] This work of parents' piercing their children's hearts with God's Word should take place when the family is sitting, walking, touching, seeing, coming, and going (Deut. 6:7–9)—in other words, all the time.

One essential starting point in the carving of God's Word into children's lives is a set family worship time that centers on the Word of God and prayer. Just as the larger flock of God needs consistent corporate worship to live God's Word in their daily lives, so too the little flock at home needs consistent family worship as a catalyst to cultivate constant conversations about God. If family worship is established as a priority in the home, then perhaps all of family life can be transformed into a pursuit of God.

What If Parents Feel Too Busy?

The pastor of a family-equipping must teach parents the dangerous consequences for their children if family worship and daily conversations about

---

17. Eugene H. Merrill, *Deuteronomy*, New American Commentary, vol. 4 (Nashville: Broadman & Holman, 1994), 167.

God are not established as a priority. What if you think that you are too busy for such things? Then perhaps you should ask yourself: "Do I eat? Do I provide meals for my family?" If so, you have just admitted that physical food is more important to you than spiritual food. "Do I watch television?" If so, then you have declared entertainment a higher priority than worship. "Do I partake in extracurricular activities?" If so, you are saying that recreation is more important than your children's spiritual well-being. "Do I sleep?" If so, you are telling your children that comfort has a higher priority than godliness. These are dangerous messages to communicate to children.

CALLING ALL MEN

The call for churches to embrace a family-equipping ministry vision begins with a call for men to embrace biblical manhood. In the very beginning, the man received a divine mandate of dominion, to rule the earth under God's authority as his vice-regent, his warrior-shepherd (Gen. 1:28). The woman was a partner in the dominion mandate (2:18), but the man's role in naming God's creatures suggests that the man had a unique responsibility to lead in taking dominion (Gen. 2:19–20; 3:20). The man's responsibility was to subdue the created order and to lead, to protect, and to provide for those within his care—all to the glory of God (see also 1 Cor. 11:8–9).

The fall into sin represented Adam's familial failure as a leader, protector, and provider. He did not provide his wife with the Word of God in her time of need, he led her into rebellion by his passivity, and he left her unprotected from the serpent. And thus, God held him accountable (Gen. 3:9; see also Rom. 5:12–14). Thereafter, the promise of a male seed from the woman who would someday crush the serpent's head only intensified Satan's assault, even as it also ensured his defeat (Gen. 3:15).

That is why pastors must minister to men not simply as one more special-interest group but as heads of households and future heads of households:

> Pastors must . . . find a way to encourage and equip men, as the heads of their respective households, to function in a pastoral way in their homes. The duties of a Christian father are clear in Scripture, and they are *pastoral* in nature. This does not mean setting up a pulpit in the living room or administering the sacraments around the dinner table. But a father *is* to bring up his children in the nurture and admonition of the Lord. A

husband *is* to nourish and cherish his wife, loving her as Christ loved the Church. These duties cannot be performed by anyone else in the church, and their performance (or lack of performance) directly relates to the health of the church. Sound households are the key to a sound church.[18]

The most fundamental way that a pastor can lead his church toward family-equipping ministry is to ensure that his family is a model of what he—and more importantly of what God—desires in the families of the church. This does not mean that the pastor holds his family up as a model of perfection, but his family must represent a model of submission to God's design. Attempting to embrace God's design will lead to frequent repentance for everyone who follows this part. This is not the path of least resistance—far from it! The evil one despises well-ordered, gospel-saturated families. Shepherds must sacrifice and suffer for the sake of their flocks, but the flock is worth any amount of suffering and sacrifice (John 10:14–15).

Jesus once said to his disciples, "Render to Caesar the things that are Caesar's, and to God the things that are God's" (Matt. 22:21). What was Caesar's was indicated by means of an image stamped on the coin; God's image is stamped on our children. As the shepherd of my family I must constantly render my children to God. Anything less turns family-equipping ministry into one more borrowed strategy or program and will yield only short-term interest in the church—or no interest at all. If no attempt is made to partner with parents and to equip them to disciple their children, the very ministry structures that appear successful outwardly will sabotage authentic effectiveness. When the church partners with parents and equips them to disciple their children, generations yet to come will learn to hope in God.

---

18. Douglas Wilson, *Mother Kirk: Essays and Forays in Practical Ecclesiology* (Moscow, ID: Canon Press, 2001), 237.

11

HABITS OF A GOSPEL-CENTERED HOUSEHOLD

Peter R. Schemm Jr.

Envision a household where the gospel stands at the center of life—a place where Scripture, in all its depth and richness, is believed and lived anew each day. This is a household where Christians are formed and reformed daily, where those who have yet to believe can see the influence of the Lord Jesus, morning and evening.

Unfortunately, this sort of household is something that's difficult for many people to envision. A significant number of Christian parents have never been equipped to work toward such a goal. It could even be that you've thought at some point, "Surely there's more to the Christian home than a Veggie Tales video on the television, worship music playing in the background, and an unopened family Bible on the coffee table! What do we do next? How do we train our children in the fear of God?"

Consider how much it would please God if our theology came alive in our kitchens and bedrooms and backyards—in the places where we spend time together. This chapter is about that kind of life. It is about life and doctrine in a gospel-centered household. Although I serve the church as a theologian and a minister, I write this chapter not as a pastor or a professor but as a Christian father who longs to live with daily habits that will lead to rich, gospel-centered community in the life of my family.

This chapter first describes *the spirit of the Christian household*—a gospel-centered community marked by relationships that share daily in repentance and grace. Then, I propose *six habits* through which the gospel may be learned, remembered, and practiced regularly. The chapter concludes with a reminder of *our ultimate goal* in the Christian household.

THE SPIRIT OF THE CHRISTIAN HOUSEHOLD

I once thought that the defining mark of a Christian home was "family worship" in the living room every evening.[1] I would not have put it that way at the time, of course. Yet I have since realized that I was far too invested in performing the act of family worship as a measure of my success as a father. I possessed the spirit of a Pharisee—and few attitudes are more unhelpful to the gospel of Jesus than such a spirit. It is the spirit of one who works to impress God and others through religious achievements. It is the spirit of self-justification. It is not the spirit of a Christian household.

By the spirit of the Christian household, I mean something closer to what Dallas Willard suggests in his book *The Spirit of the Disciplines*. He says,

> The spirit of the disciplines—that which moves us to them and moves through them to prevent them from becoming a new bondage and to deepen constantly our union with the heart and mind of God—is [our] love of Jesus, with its steadfast longing and resolute will to be like him.[2]

Spiritual habits and disciplines are hollow apart from a genuine love and affection for Jesus Christ. They tend to take on a "new bondage" and become a means to seek an evil and enslaving endpoint instead.

---

1. As Scripture clearly teaches parents to instruct and train their children (e.g., Deut. 6; Proverbs; Eph. 6:1–4), with the role of the father being emphasized, it is easy to see why many advocate family worship. I am not opposed to this kind of model, and we regularly incorporate such habits into our family life. I do, however, have some concerns with the read-sing-pray model and with the way it is promoted at times. Some of its advocates seem to assume this model is the best way or even the only way to accomplish spiritual formation in the family. I am also concerned that fathers not equate the read-sing-pray model with leading gospel-centered homes. I propose that we think beyond "family worship" and consider numerous ways to develop a gospel-centered family. My hope is that this chapter encourages fathers and mothers toward that end. For one of the more helpful and responsible treatments of family worship, see J. Ligon Duncan III and Terry L. Johnson, "A Call to Family Worship," in *Give Praise to God: A Vision for Reforming Worship*, ed. Philip Graham Ryken, Derek W. H. Thomas, and J. Ligon Duncan III (Phillipsburg, NJ: P&R, 2003), 317–38.
2. Dallas Willard, *The Spirit of the Disciplines: Understanding How God Changes Lives* (San Francisco: HarperSanFrancisco, 1990), 251.

The spirit of the Christian household is inspired by the love of God whom "we love because he first loved us" (1 John 4:19). It is a disposition that consistently reflects God's love through grace and forgiveness. This disposition moves us *to* and *through* the habits proposed below. Our habits and disciplines, founded on the love of God, become a good means to a greater end. They form and transform our families into redemptive communities. These habits and disciplines train not only children but also fathers and mothers, to repent of specific things such as anger and demanding expectations. Paul Tripp describes it this way: "As we—parents and children alike— face our need as sinners, the family becomes a truly redemptive community where the themes of grace, forgiveness, deliverance from sin, reconciliation, new life in Christ, and hope become the central themes of family life."[3] In a word, the spirit of the Christian household is a spirit of redemption.

HABITS OF A GOSPEL-CENTERED HOUSEHOLD

What habits, then, should be practiced in the context of this redemptive community? The following six habits help us to learn, remember, and practice the gospel regularly. They are intentionally theological and reflect a rich heritage that ties us to the Christians of previous generations. They are simple habits that require no advanced training. And they are helpful at every stage of life—for children and young adults, for parents and grandparents alike.

1. Reciting the Apostles' Creed Together

Christians have historically recited many creeds to express their faith. My favorite is the Apostles' Creed.[4] It is the oldest creed in common use among Christian churches today. Its trinitarian structure, following the

---

3. Paul Tripp, *The Age of Opportunity: A Biblical Guide to Parenting Teens* (Phillipsburg, NJ: P&R, 2001), 66.

4. The Apostles' Creed is so named, not because it was written by the apostles, but because it one of the earliest creedal formulations or summaries of the apostles' teaching. It, like the Nicene Creed, expresses the core message of the apostles. The present form of the Apostles' Creed, according to Karl Barth, "probably derives from the third century and goes back to an original form confessed and acknowledged in the congregation of Rome." Karl Barth, *Dogmatics in Outline*, trans. G. T. Thomson (New York: Harper & Row, 1959), 14. Wayne Grudem discusses the development of the wording of the Apostles' Creed over time, with a helpful discussion particularly concerning the phrase "he descended into hell." Wayne Grudem, *Systematic Theology: An Introduction to Biblical Doctrine* (Grand Rapids: Zondervan, 1994), 586–94.

pattern of Father, Son, and Spirit, as well as its detailed summary of the gospel of Jesus Christ explain why it has served the church so well for over 1,500 years.

Confessional Value of the Creed

The English word *creed* is related to the Latin word *credo*, meaning "I believe." The Apostles' Creed begins this way because it summarizes the faith, or belief, of the apostles who followed Jesus. That same faith—according to the specificity of each line of the Creed—has been once for all delivered to the saints. We join with all who have made this confession of faith in Christ by saying, "I believe." So when recited as a true expression of one's heart and mind, the Creed serves well as a confession of faith in Christ.

It would be a mistake, however, to assume that the Creed is only for those who presently possess faith in Christ. It also serves well to cultivate faith. In other words, learning from an early age to say "I believe" in the triune God and his gospel cultivates a grammar of faith that may one day be invested with genuine, saving faith. And, in addition to preparing one for faith in Christ, it serves to sustain and deepen genuine faith. Christians are as frail and forgetful as anyone. The Creed reminds us all, young or old, to live in accordance with the gospel of God. We never mature beyond saying "I believe."

Historical and Communal Value of the Creed

There is also a historical value in the use of the Creed. Retrieving the tradition of the apostles, through the Creed, enriches our understanding of the gospel. It is well suited to form a "transgenerational" understanding of the gospel because it situates our faith in a rich and lasting heritage. It helps us to realize that ours is an ancient faith, a time-tested faith that crosses geographical and cultural boundaries.[5] All over the world, others believed the gospel long before we did.

This rich sense of heritage and tradition serves to correct the "Me" generation's radical individualism and deep-seated sense of entitlement. The Creed helps us to redeem the fallen self through a sense of holy community. It provides a context of community for the individual, so that the

---

5. For an engaging discussion of the place of the creeds in the Christian faith, listen to Jarsilov Pelikan, "The Need for Creeds," interviewed in 2003 by Krista Tippett, *Speaking of Faith*, American Public Media, October 22, 2009, http://speakingoffaith.publicradio.org/programs/2009/pelikan.

"I" of faith is no longer detached but embedded in the common "I believe" of "the communion of saints." This is the language of a shared tradition.

✦ The Apostles' Creed ✦

I believe in God the Father Almighty;
  Maker of heaven and earth.

And in Jesus Christ, his only (begotten) Son, our Lord;
  Who was conceived by the Holy Spirit, born of the Virgin Mary;
  Suffered under Pontius Pilate, was crucified, dead, and buried;
  He descended into Hell [Hades, spirit-world];
  The third day he rose from the dead;
  He ascended into heaven; and sits at the right hand of God the Father
    Almighty;
  From there he shall come to judge the living and the dead.

I believe in the Holy Spirit;
  the holy catholic [universal] Church;
  The communion of saints; the forgiveness of sins;
  The resurrection of the body;
  And the life everlasting. Amen.[6]

Grand and Cosmic Value of the Creed

Finally, as we rehearse the Creed we are trained to think about the gospel in a grand and cosmic sense. The gospel is more than just "Jesus died for my sins"—though that is certainly true! Yet the gospel is bigger and greater than what happened for me on that Friday afternoon. Our understanding of the gospel ought to include the triune God as well as the world that he made. The Creed helps us to realize how the gospel reaches in scope from the universals to the particulars of God's creation. It does so through both its *shape* and *language*.

Following Ralph Martin, we appreciate the Creed because its shape corresponds to "the shape of the Gospel" itself.[7] It moves from creation, "maker of heaven and earth," to consummation, "life everlasting. Amen." It has a beginning-to-end shape. It sums up the creation, fall, and restoration

---

6. As found in Philip Schaff, *The Creeds of Christendom. Volume 2: The Greek and Latin Creeds*, 6th ed. (New York: n.p., 1877; repr., Grand Rapids: Baker, 1998), 45, with a few modernizations of language and style.
7. Ralph P. Martin, *The Worship of God: Some Theological, Pastoral, and Practical Reflections* (Grand Rapids: Eerdmans, 1982), 12.

of all things. The Creed is not a simplistic expression of the gospel. Rather, it is simple expression of a grand and cosmic gospel.

As to its language, it also has a grand or universal value. We see a universal sense conveyed in the phrase "the holy *catholic* Church." This, of course, is catholic with a lower case *c*, which means "universal" or "worldwide." Some may even prefer to render this phrase as "*universal* church." The point here is that the gospel of Christ has a scope that reaches far beyond any particular church. And that makes sense, since the gospel itself is for all nations—one gospel for all nations down through the ages.

The way the Creed helps us to think about the gospel is all the more significant when we realize that it combines an economy of words with faithfulness to the biblical text. Every line of the Creed was crafted around biblical language. Other than Scripture itself, I know of no better summary of the gospel with which to train our children.

> → **Working the Apostles' Creed into the Life of Your Family** ←
> 1. Memorize the first of the Creed's three main parts.
> 2. Recite the first part as a statement of your faith at the beginning or end of a meal-time prayer.
> 3. A week or two later, add to your prayer the second part of the Creed, a few phrases at a time.
> 4. A week or two later, add part three.

2. Reading Scripture Together

Holy Scripture is the most important source for training in the Christian household. Scripture alone is sufficient to form our understanding of salvation and every aspect of Christian living (see 2 Tim. 3:10–17; Pss. 1, 19, 119). Jesus taught that God's Word is sufficient when he said, "It is written, 'Man shall not live by bread alone, but by every word that comes from the mouth of God'" (Matt 4:4).

Scripture is not our *only source* for improving our understanding of God and Christian doctrine, but it is our *only perfect and ultimate source*. Every other resource we might employ is subject to the authority of Scripture. Because Scripture is the ultimate source of authority in all matters of life and doctrine, we see Scripture as the primary means for Christian formation.

Why Read the Bible in the Christian Household

No one has been more helpful to me in understanding the place of Scripture in the Christian community than Dietrich Bonhoeffer. His modern classic *Life Together* defines the Christian community as "life together under the Word."[8] For Bonhoeffer and for us, reading Scripture must be foundational to life in community. Scripture is, in Bonhoeffer's words, "God's revealed Word for all men, for all times. Holy Scripture does not consist of individual passages; it is a unit and is intended to be used as such."[9] Bonhoeffer went on to explain that some will object to reading and listening to a full chapter of the Old or New Testament in one sitting. Then he added,

> If it is really true that it is hard for us, as adult Christians, to comprehend even a chapter of the Old Testament in sequence, then this can only fill us with profound shame; what kind of testimony is that to our knowledge of the Scriptures and all our previous reading of them? If we were familiar with the substance of what we read we should be able to follow a chapter without difficulty, especially if we have an open Bible in our hands and participate in the reading. But, of course, we must admit that the Scriptures are still largely unknown to us. Can the realization of our fault, our ignorance of the Word of God, have any other consequence than that we should earnestly and faithfully retrieve what has been neglected?[10]

To those who further object that the purpose of "common devotions" ought to be more profound than simply learning the content of Scripture, he replied:

> God's Word is to be heard by everyone in his own way and according to the measure of his understanding. A child hears and learns the Bible for the first time in family worship; the adult Christian learns it repeatedly and better, and he will never finish acquiring knowledge of its story.[11]

What an insightful way to put it! Even as maturing Christians, we learn the Word "repeatedly and better." We never finish learning the story

---

8. Dietrich Bonhoeffer, *Life Together*, trans. John W. Doberstein (San Francisco: Harper & Row, 1954), 17.
9. Ibid., 50–51.
10. Ibid., 51–52.
11. Ibid., 52.

because we never finish living the story. Reading Scripture must always be a priority in the Christian household—no matter what age a believer is, seven or seventy.

How to Read the Bible in the Christian Household

The important thing to note about our second habit is its simplicity. Reading Scripture together is not a Bible study or a lesson. It is quite simply a time to read the Bible together and listen to it—to read and learn as a family. Read Scripture *regularly*—not necessarily daily but consistently. It has been my experience, mostly with fathers, that a daily goal is counterproductive. They fail to meet this goal and then give up altogether. A better goal for the habit of Scripture reading is "life together under the Word." Reading consistently as a family, along with faithful participation in a local church, can accomplish this goal.

Read Scripture *appropriately*. Bonhoeffer suggested that we ought to read the Bible more like novices. Those who are familiar with the Bible often take on the character of the person who is speaking—whether God or a human being. In so doing, they tend to distort the reading of Scripture. Readers become "rhetorical, emotional, sentimental, or coercive" and direct the listeners' attention to themselves instead of toward God's Word.[12] Ironically, it becomes difficult to hear God speak from his own Word. When the Bible is read appropriately, in humility, our families have a better chance of hearing from God.

Read Scripture *in unity*. I recommend the same Bible translation for everyone, children and parents. Bible story books may be helpful at times, but in the end our families ought to learn the Word of God using the same grammar. Of course your seven-year-old is unlikely to grasp the significance of the word *justification* as it is used in Paul's letter to the Romans—but that's not the point. Honestly, who among us understood *justification* the first time we read it? It is our responsibility, as parents, to build a grammar of faith. And we hope to do so in a manner consistent with our belief in the gospel.

3. Practicing Catechesis Together

One of my heroes in the Christian faith is J. I. Packer. I respect Packer because of his clear and substantive approach to theological formation. I

12. Ibid., 56.

think he has it right when he says to pastors, "You have three priorities: teach, teach, and teach. Evangelical churches are weaker than we realize because we don't teach the confessions and doctrine. Set new standards in teaching. Understand the word *catechesis*, and practice that art."[13] Packer could have easily said the same thing about the Christian household. Our households are "weaker than we realize" because fathers and mothers do not teach their children what and how to believe.

One of the best ways to teach the Christian faith is through what Packer calls the "art" of catechesis. I want to emphasize the practice of catechesis as an art since that accords well with the spirit of the Christian home spoken of above. Using a catechism to train our children in a mechanical and less skillful way might easily turn out the next champion at Bible trivia—but mere biblical knowledge is not our goal!

> **The Simple Art of Catechesis**
> ✠
> 1. Select a catechism; consult your pastor for ideas.
> 2. Choose a question in which your family has interest.
> 3. Rehearse the question and answer two or three times.
> 4. Ask someone the question; help when needed in order to keep the answer word perfect.

What Is a Catechism?

A catechism is a summary of Christian doctrine put in the form of questions and answers. It is a tool designed for personal interaction. Catechisms are confessional in nature and thus they represent different Christian traditions—some may be Roman Catholic while others are Protestant—as well as different denominations, including Anglican, Lutheran, Presbyterian, and Baptist. Most Protestant catechisms have their roots in the time of the Reformers and Puritans.

Our family uses *A Catechism of Bible Teaching* (1892) written by John A. Broadus.[14] But that has not always been the case. About a decade ago, I tried to draft my own family catechism. I still have those documents to

---

13. J. I. Packer, quoted in Warren Cole Smith, "Patriarch," *World Magazine*, December 5, 2009, http://www.worldmag.com/articles/16150.
14. John A. Broadus was a widely recognized, highly esteemed Baptist theologian and pastor of the nineteenth century. His work *A Catechism of Bible Teaching* was the first publication projected by the Baptist Sunday School Board (now LifeWay Christian Resources) upon its organization in 1891. See Timothy George, "Introduction to John A. Broadus: A Living Legacy" in *John A. Broadus: A Living Legacy*, ed. David S. Dockery and Roger D. Duke (Nashville: B&H, 2008), 5.

serve as a reminder—a reminder that one should not too quickly try to reinvent the wheel of doctrine. After I came to my senses, I realized that it is more valuable to pass on a heritage to my children than to tweak portions of Professor Broadus's wording into theological alignment with mine.

Here are two sample questions from *A Catechism of Bible Teaching* to give you an idea of what practicing this habit might look like:

Lesson 9: Repentance and Faith[15]

1. What is it to repent of sin?

A. Repenting of sin means that one changes his thoughts and feelings about sin, resolving to forsake sin and live for God.

2. Does not repenting mean being sorry?

A. Everyone who truly resolves to quit sinning will be sorry for his past sins, but people are often sorry without quitting.

The Art of Catechesis

Practicing the art of catechesis is not complicated. It is as simple as selecting a question for the week and enfolding that question into our lives at various times—at church, in the truck, at bedtime, during a backyard conversation, or at the workbench in the garage. Once the routine is established, the weekly question flows naturally in and out of conversations with one another. Over time the warehouse of biblical and theological teaching gets stocked. Even at a modest forty or so weeks per year—allowing for other seasonal commitments and unexpected life events—this is one of the most effective means I know of to be "trained in the words of the faith" (1 Tim. 4:6).

4. Singing Together

This habit is a bit different because not everyone is musically inclined. But almost everyone enjoys some type of music. Our purpose in this habit is to

---

15. Quoted from John A. Broadus, *A Catechism of Bible Teaching* (n.p., 1892), in *Baptist Confessions, Covenants and Catechisms*, ed. Timothy George and Denise George (Nashville: Broadman & Holman, 1996).

help one another see the value in "psalms and hymns and spiritual songs" (Eph. 5:19) and to see how such a habit can form our understanding of the gospel.

Hymns and songs express the biblical and theological language of the church in artistic, poetic, and memorable ways. They make an appeal to the soul on the basis of the beauty of the gospel. The gospel is already a beautiful reality, but through the use of hymns we learn to hear and feel and thus sense more deeply the beauty of God.

Perhaps an illustration will help us here. I have never heard someone say, after rehearsing a catechism answer, "Wow—that was moving and powerful!" I have, on the other hand, seen my own children nodding appreciation after a stirring rendition of "Be Thou My Vision." The same theological idea has been conveyed in both: God is great and we ought to worship him because of his greatness. Yet a catechism does not convey a sense of delight and emotion like a soul stirring lyric accompanied by beautiful music.

Look for hymns and spiritual songs that are theologically rich and memorable. Look for hymns and songs that have theological integrity— that is to say, the mood and style of the music ought to match the theological ideas. A song about the depth of sin should not have a bouncy and happy mood. Look for hymns that are soul-satisfying. Our souls are in need of this, and gospel-centered, theologically rich songs address our human needs according to Scripture.

The practice of this habit, for those of us who are less musically inclined, is best related to the local church. It may be as simple as experiencing a hymn or song together at church, asking one another why that song was so enjoyable, and incorporating a particular phrase from the song into your prayer at lunch on Sunday.

Of course, psalms and hymns and spiritual songs can be used in formal family worship as well, and I would commend that. Yet even for those who are less musically inclined, there are ways to use the great hymns and songs of the faith to cultivate sensitivity toward the beauty of the gospel.

5. Morning and Evening Prayers Together

Scripture includes many examples of those who prayed at the beginning and end of the day, including our Lord Jesus (e.g., Ps. 4:8; 5:3; 57:7–8; 88:13; Mark 1:35; 14:32–42.). One particularly relevant text, Deuteronomy

6:1–9, suggests that it was the role of the fathers in Israel to "repeat" words of faith in God every morning and evening—"when you lie down and when you get up" (v. 7).

Why Pray

Morning and evening prayers train us in the lifelong habit of trusting in God. The purpose of prayer is to glorify God by deepening our trust in him. In the morning we ask God to help us to trust him and glorify him all day long. We rejoice that his mercies are "new every morning" (Lam. 3:22–23)! In the evening we ask him to show us where we have and have not trusted him. We thank him for the times we did trust him; we repent where we have not. Then we close our eyes asking God to preserve us for yet another day.

What to Pray

The content of our prayers may be spontaneous, a reflection of the present concerns of our minds and hearts. But prayers may also be planned and scripted. One of my favorite prayers, "The Gospel Way," contains this appeal: "Glorious Trinity, impress the Gospel on my soul, until its virtue diffuses every faculty."[16] I need that. I long for the day when the virtue of the gospel so permeates my every ability and facility that I am recognizably Christ's.

The best scripted prayers are those written by the inspired writers of Holy Scripture. Some of the commonly prayed texts of Scripture include psalms (e.g., Psalms 1, 4, 5, 19, 23, 90, 121), the Lord's model prayer (Matt. 6:9–13), promises such as Paul's words in Romans 8:26–39), character-forming passages like 1 Corinthians 13 and Galatians 5:16–24, or prayers for the community of faith (e.g., Eph. 1:15–23; Phil. 1:3–11; Col. 1:3–14).

How to Pray

In the morning, consider offering a prayer together as a statement of faith in God. You might recite the Apostles' Creed or the Lord's Prayer together. It is also fitting to set the concerns of the day before the Lord at this time. This may be done in just a few minutes at the breakfast table and it honors God by giving him the "first thoughts" and "first words" of the

---

16. Quoted in Arthur G. Bennett, ed., *The Valley of Vision: A Collection of Puritan Prayers and Devotions* (Carlisle, PA: Banner of Truth, 1975), 62.

day.[17] Other places to start the day in prayer together are the bedroom, the living room, or on the way to school.

Evening time is appropriate for prayers that require reflection on the day. We might ask for insight as to how the day was or was not pleasing to God. Or we may explicitly repent of things that, we know, did not please God. Evening is also a fitting time for exercising faith in God throughout the night. The Lord is the one who "keeps us" and protects us while we sleep—"He who keeps [you] will neither sleep not slumber" (Ps.121:4). Christian children have been praying this short evening prayer at least since the twelfth century:[18]

> Now I lay me down to sleep.
> I pray the Lord my soul to keep.
> If I should die before I wake,
> I pray the Lord my soul to take.

Praying each day, morning and evening, is an important way to train ourselves in the fear of God. It is something we may do alone but we should also consider doing it together.

6. Talking at the Table Together

Perhaps the most underrated means to forming one another in Christ is the daily meal. Sharing a meal together as a family has fallen on hard times.[19] Everything from baseball practice to dance lessons, television to video games, has made missing a meal together a foregone conclusion for many families. We do not make time for it, and we are suffering the consequences. I suggest that we recover one of the most basic, most ancient ways of sharing life together—eating together daily—as a means of spiritual formation in the Christian household.

---

17. Bonhoeffer, *Life Together*, 42.
18. Richard John Neuhaus, *Death on a Friday Afternoon: Meditations on the Last Words of Jesus from the Cross* (New York: Basic Books, 2000), 229–30.
19. While I want to focus on the gospel-forming potential of eating together, the wide-ranging effects of family meals are receiving attention of late in wider circles. For example, documentary filmmaker and journalist Miriam Weinstein advocates that families regularly eat meals together and describes the many benefits that result from such a practice. Miriam Weinstein, *The Surprising Power of Family Meals: How Eating Together Makes Us Smarter, Stronger, Healthier, and Happier* (Hanover, NH: Steerforth Press, 2005).

Encouraged by Martin Luther's example, I refer to meaningful conversation over a meal as "table-talk."[20] The value of table-talk to form the gospel in us builds on the idea that we enjoy talking about what matters to us at mealtime. God created us, as relational creatures, to eat together and to talk to one another; some of the most important conversations we ever have come at meal times. It is not coincidental that some of the most important conversations that Jesus had about the significance of his death were around a table—looking at one another, eye to eye, and eating together (Matt. 26:17–29; Mark 14:12–26; Luke 22:7–23; 24:13–35; see also Exod. 12; Deut. 16; Rev. 19).

→ How to Practice Table-Talk ←

1. Gather for a meal with the entire family present at least three nights per week.
2. Guard the priority of that meal by agreeing on a start time.
3. Identify a topic of meaningful conversation before the meal; use questions; listen carefully to one another.
4. Guide the conversation in meaningful ways; this may mean focusing, expanding, or even ending a conversation at the appropriate time.

Our conversation in table-talk may vary from the mundane to the profound. It is appropriate to talk about the weather and the big game and other shared interests. It is also appropriate to talk about the gospel and repentance and God's faithfulness to us as a family. It should not seem awkward or out of place when we talk about weighty and substantive things. If it does seem awkward, that probably reflects the absence of regular, meaningful conversations. Here are some questions that may help us to form one another through table-talk:

---

20. The English edition of *Luther's Works* dedicates an entire volume to comments made by Luther "at table," which were recorded by those present. John Mathesius, who was often present during the year 1540, described Luther's interaction: "When he wished to get us to talk he would throw out a question, 'What's new?' The first time we let this remark pass, but if he repeated it—'You prelates, what's new in the land?'—the oldest ones at the table would start talking." Luther would often provide "expert and concise answers" to questions on the Bible and theology. And when, on occasion, someone would take exception to Luther, "the doctor was able to bear this patiently and refute him with a skillful answer. Reputable persons often came to the table from the university and from foreign places, and then very nice talks and stories were heard." John Mathesius, quoted in *Luther's Works, Volume 54: Table Talk*, ed. and trans. Theodore G. Tappert (Philadelphia: Fortress Press, 1967), ix–x.

- What was your day like?
- What were the highlights of today?
- What was hard for you today?
- How did God provide for us today?
- Have we honored one another today?
- How can I serve you tomorrow?

These, and other questions like them, can prompt gospel-centered conversations that help us to reflect meaningfully on the daily evidences of God's grace toward us.

THE GOAL OF THE CHRISTIAN HOUSEHOLD

I want to conclude with a reminder of the ultimate goal of the Christian household. We practice these habits together because we long for gospel-centered relationships where the grace of God is rehearsed in our households. Home is the place where we are most often our true selves— whether in gladness or anger, honesty or deceit, love or ill will. It is by God's design, then, that learning and living the gospel at home brings a depth to spiritual formation that is otherwise unlikely if not impossible.

And yet a well-ordered Christian household is *not* our ultimate goal! The Christian household is arguably the most foundational of all Christian communities but it is not the most important or ultimate Christian community.[21] As we seek to bring life and doctrine together, we must think rightly about both the family and the church. The family and the church each has a unique and distinct role in God's economy.

The Christian household, while important, must never become *more* important to us than the church or the kingdom of Christ. Such a belief would undermine the primacy of the gospel of Christ and oppose the plain

---

21. The family is the first institution God created and in which man was made to live in relation to himself (Gen. 1–2). It is the only community that, according to God's good design, portrays the gospel in the marriage relationship of husband and wife (Eph. 5:32). It is the only community from which the next generation of believers may come from an earthly father in a way that directly reflects the creative power and divine purposes of our heavenly Father (Eph. 3:15; cf. Prov. 22:6; Eph. 6:4). And, it is the only community that serves as the decisive, qualifying factor regarding a man's fitness to serve as a spiritual leader in the church (1 Tim. 3:1–15). For these reasons, the Christian home is a unique Christian community and has a unique fitting place in the economy of God.

teaching of Jesus: "Whoever loves father or mother more than me is not worthy of me, and whoever loves son or daughter more than me is not worthy of me" (Matt. 10:37).

The Christian household is where we live now, but it is not our ultimate home. Our ultimate home is with the family of God in the new heavens and the new earth. This is our ultimate hope and goal. This is why we take seriously our responsibilities in our families and in the church, in accordance with the gospel, because we long for Jesus. We long to go home, and we recognize that one day God himself will *be* our home (Rev. 21:3).

12

BUILDING A MILESTONE MINISTRY IN YOUR CHURCH

Brian Haynes

God created the Christian household to serve as a primary context for children's discipleship. The purpose of the comprehensive-coordinative approaches to family ministry is to forge a partnership that equips parents to engage actively in the discipleship of their children. This process must begin not with a program but with the lives of pastoral leaders.

Yet how can pastoral leaders embrace the family-equipping model in light of existing segmented-programmatic approaches that dominate evangelical churches in the Western culture? At first, it seems like an insurmountable endeavor to lead such an adventurous transition. Rites of passage are one way to move the congregation toward family-equipping ministry. Developing rites of passage as a spiritual formation strategy enables churches that once thought of discipleship as class on Sunday to equip the family as the primary faith-training vehicle for the next generation.

So what is a rite of passage? *A rite of passage is a point of spiritual maturity preceded by a period of parental instruction that focuses on specific, age-appropriate biblical truths.* Rites of passage, also known as "milestones," serve as both moments of celebration and catalytic points of entry into a new season of life for the maturing Christ-follower. Developing rites of passages as a central strategy in a family-equipping church deeply benefits both church and family.

> ⭢ Rite of passage:
> A point of spiritual maturity preceded by a period of parental instruction that focuses on specific, age-appropriate biblical truths. ⭢

CONTEXTUAL BASIS FOR RITES OF PASSAGE

The Christian life is a journey filled with celebrations and suffering, the mountaintops and the mundane. All of life, however, provides an opportunity for training children in the fear of God. In the Hebrew context, the Shema of Deuteronomy 6 defines a biblical pattern for using life itself as a context for developing followers of God: "And these words that I command you today shall be on your heart. You shall teach them diligently to your children and shall talk of them when you sit in your house, and when you walk by the way, and when you lie down, and when you rise" (vv. 6–7).

What we recognize in rites of passage is that all of life is a context for learning God's ways. In Hebrew culture, rites of passage offered a spiritual growth strategy tethered to significant milestones.

Circumcision on the eighth day was a milestone (Gen. 17:10–12). Although performed on the child, the practice seems to have focused mostly on parents. This milestone required parents to embrace their responsibility to raise the child in accordance with God's plan.

Another Hebrew rite of passage was the redemption of the firstborn: "Everything that opens the womb of all flesh, whether man or beast, which they offer to the Lord shall be yours. Nevertheless the first born of man you shall redeem, and the first born of unclean animals you shall redeem" (Num. 18:15). At one point in Israel's history, the firstborn son would have served as the priest of the family with the duty of offering sacrifices (Ex. 13:2). After the Passover in Egypt, the Israelites sinned at the golden calf and rendered every firstborn son unclean except for those from the tribe of Levi. Thus God required fathers from other tribes to *redeem* their firstborn sons by paying five shekels to the priest. Jesus experienced this rite of passage in obedience to God: "When time came for their purification according to the Law of Moses, they brought him up to Jerusalem to present him to the Lord (as is written in the Law of the Lord, 'Every male who opens the womb shall be called holy to the Lord')" (Luke 2:22–23).

The bar mitzvah—meaning "son of the commandment"—is a rite of passage celebration commemorating a Jewish boy passing into adulthood. Based not necessarily on biblical precepts but on the Mishnah and long-standing oral traditions, boys celebrate bar mitzvah at age thirteen. In modern Judaism, girls celebrate bat mitzvah—becoming a "daughter of the commandment"—at age twelve. Bar mitzvah often marks the child's public reading of God's instruction for the Jewish people; minimally, the child coming of age recites a blessing before the congregation. In some cases, the young man may make a short speech (*drash*) regarding the Scripture reading; this speech begins with the clause, "Today, I am a man."

Other significant rites of passage in the Hebrew context include marriage, death, and eternal life. In totality these five passages compose the "Jewish life cycle." Though Christians certainly do not need to embrace each of these milestones, it is apparent that one way to live out the expectations of the Shema is to use rites of passage as markers in the maturation process. Rites of passage can provide a framework for parents to train their children in God's ways.

THE IMPORTANCE OF PARENTAL PRACTICES PRECEDING RITES OF PASSAGES

The problem is, most of us do not serve in churches that expect parents to take the lead in the discipleship of children. Pastoral leaders must understand what parental behaviors are needed to lead children spiritually *before* exploring rites of passage.

Why focus on parental behaviors first? The family-equipping model seeks to establish intentional and biblical training of children in Christian homes. Before any rite of passage can be achieved with any integrity, parents must learn to carve God's commands on their children's hearts as they walk along the road, as they lie down, and as they get up. It is crucial to ask, "Beyond bringing children to church how do parents lead their children from one rite of passage to the next?" The answer to this question is found in *formal* and *informal* training for parents.

Formal Training: Faith Talks

God designed the family as the central environment for spiritual formation. Embracing this concept as a parent requires the development of a formal parental platform to disciple children. Sadly, in many Christian homes, this platform of biblical training has been abdicated—and, even worse, the church's segmented-programmatic practices of ministry have perpetuated this parental abdication by implying that the discipleship of children is a task for paid professionals.

For a church to implement family-equipping ministry, the congregation must equip parents to rebuild a formal platform of biblical training in their child's life. This formal platform goes by many names: family devotions, faith talks, family worship, family discipleship. Whatever the name, this formal platform requires time set aside every week to worship as a family and to examine the Scriptures in compelling ways. This parenting behavior is a major step, a necessary step, and a difficult step for many families.

This formal platform is a necessary prerequisite for rites of passage. Here's why: it is during times of family worship or devotions that parents discover which rites of passage their children are maturing towards. Parents can then intentionally lead times of family worship that teach biblical truths necessary for the child to take another step toward the next rite of passage.

So what is the church's role in all of this? First, the church trains parents how to lead effective times of family worship. Second, the church provides or points out tools and resources to help the parents. Most parents lack a healthy model of faith training in the context of the home. The family-equipping church embraces the difficult task of discipling parents so that they become able to lead their children spiritually.

The church must make it clear that the family faith talk or worship time is both possible and *practical*. Family-equipping churches realize that parents need guidance when it comes to developing a formal faith-training platform. This can be done in a number of simple ways. Perhaps the pastor can outline a brief faith talk each week, based in his sermon; this outline can be provided in the weekly worship bulletin. Hearing the sermon on Sunday provides a parent with an understanding of a particular biblical text. Through the sermon, the pastor has filled the parent's spiritual tank. Providing a short faith talk based on the sermon equips parents to lead a discussion based on a truth that is fresh on the parents' minds. Elementary? Yes—but such a practice provides parents with an entry-level opportunity to develop this practice. Using a Bible study curriculum that incorporates a family faith talk component may be another way to establish formal platforms for discipleship in the Christian household. Again, fill the parents' spiritual tank; then provide them with a tool to use at home.

Another effective method of empowering the formal platform at home is to provide a list of faith talk resources organized by particular rites of passage. For example, if one rite of passage is "purity for life" during the early teen years, the church reviews and recommends resources to equip parents for formal faith talks to train their children toward this milestone. This can be as simple as a list on the church Web site or as complex as a resource center where parents preview the tools and purchase them.

Why gather weekly and not daily? Many families have more than one child. Each child is maturing toward a different rite of passage. A weekly faith talk brings the family together around the Scriptures but may be too broad for families that have children in middle school, elementary school, and preschool. Individual faith talks may be needed during the week to center on each child's individual growth process. Focused, individual faith talks throughout the week supplement the weekly family faith talk.

Informal Training: God Moments

An equally important parenting practice involves spiritual training that is informal in nature. This training is not necessarily planned but occurs each day during the ordinary experiences of life. Informal training involves modeling authentic faith and capturing teachable moments.

The precepts of God are to be constantly on our hearts (Deut. 6:6). Likely, the greatest act of Christian parenting lies in the informal model of Christlikeness. Sons learn how to be godly men, husbands, and fathers as they observe their own fathers in daily life. Daughters understand what a woman, wife, and mother looks like as they interact with their mother. Children learn to pray and study the Scripture by observing parents who pray and study the Scripture. Teenagers learn to forgive, repent, and reconcile by observing parents who pursue reconciliation in every relationship. It is almost impossible to overstate the importance of modeling the faith day by day.

Capturing "God moments" or teachable moments is an art that Christian parents must master in training their children. Each day provides a new set of situations that parents can use to teach key truths and to bolster their children's biblical worldview. The family-equipping church trains parents to discern God moments in a child's life and to speak biblical truth in that circumstance. This informal way of teaching is highly effective and memorable for the child. God moments occur often as parents lead a child toward the next milestone.

Passage Celebrations: Milestones

As children grow spiritually, they reach certain rites of passage. When this happens, the family celebrates! Celebrating the work of God in the lives of his people is a timeless and biblical tradition. The family-equipping church partners with families by suggesting possible passage celebrations for each milestone.

RITES OF PASSAGE AS FAMILY-EQUIPPING STRATEGY

From a theological perspective, *discipleship* and *family ministry* are insep-arable. The family is a crucial context for discipleship, and consistent practices of discipleship are essential to family ministry. As a result, our congregation has developed a unified approach to making disciples based on Deuteronomy 6:4–9 and Matthew 28:18–20. In this strategy, spiritual formation is a two-sided coin. One side is the biblical New Testament church and the other side is the equally important discipleship context of family.

The Legacy Milestones

This approach consists of seven legacy milestones representing all stages of life. A milestone is an event preceded by a period of instruction by par-ents and the church to be celebrated as God works in a person's life. Each milestone marks an individual's progression along a life path of spiritual formation. Milestones naturally connect with Christian families in impor-tant seasons of life. The seven milestones align all discipleship ministries—children's ministry, student ministry, adult discipleship ministry—to coor-dinate comprehensively with the family.

For children and teen-agers whose parents engage in this process, their fami-lies become primary vehicles to transport them along the path of milestones. Parents with children on the path anywhere in the first six mile-stones learn to lead weekly faith talks, to capture God moments, and to celebrate

> **→ Seven Legacy Milestones ←**
> Milestone 1: Parent/Baby Dedication
> Milestone 2: Salvation and Baptism
> Milestone 3: Preparing for Adolescence
> Milestone 4: Purity for Life
> Milestone 5: Rite of Passage to Adulthood
> Milestone 6: High School Graduation
> Milestone 7: Life in Christ

milestones in memorable and meaningful ways. Adults in the seventh mile-stone develop in their devotion to Jesus Christ at every phase of adult life. Whether they are senior adult, single adult, a married couple without chil-dren, or parents of children, adults function as disciple-makers, partnering with the church to equip the generations one home at a time. In this way, family ministry becomes ministry for every stage of life. The suggested re-sources and rituals that I present here are the ones that my congregation uses—but these are only suggestions! Your church might use very different curricula or even produce your own resources. The particular resources or even these precise milestones are not nearly as important as the over-arching principle of guiding a child to Christ-centered adulthood by part-nering church and household in significant rites of passage.

What about Single-Parent Households?

Single parents face an enormous burden, parenting children alone. Sometimes single parents feel as if they cannot lead their children spiritu-ally. This is not the case. A single parent is a primary faith trainer just as much as a married parent. We choose to integrate single parents into the equipping strategy of the church not differentiating them from others be-cause of their marital status. Understanding that single parents face unique issues, we offer ongoing counsel and encouragement as well as a seminar twice a year called "Walking the Path as a Single Parent" to support strug-gling single parents.

What about Students Whose Parents Aren't Believers?

Students whose parents do not lead them spiritually really find the church taking the primary role in their spiritual development. The youth ministry works diligently to discover students who have little or zero faith influence at home. Then Sunday school teachers, life group leaders, or small group leaders in the student ministry build relationships with these teenagers, leading them along the path of legacy milestones. Though the situation is not ideal, the bride of Christ steps in beautifully for the family as the primary faith influence of students with unbelieving parents.

1. Parent/Baby Dedication

Many churches already practice some form of infant dedication. Most pas-toral leaders conduct baby dedications in the context of corporate wor-ship. The intent of the parent in this ceremony is typically to seek God's blessing over their infant son or daughter. When practiced as a rite of passage, however, baby dedication becomes more about parents than about the baby. Parents must comprehend the commitment they are mak-ing before God and his congregation as they, often tearfully with joy and sobriety, commit to lead their children "in the training and admonition of the Lord." Asking parents to make such an important commitment without first training them in God's expectations for parents is exasperating for the parent and counterproductive for the church.

A family-equipping church trains parents *before* this significant passage. Infant dedication presents an excellent opportunity for "required training." New parents are anxious to discover how they can most effectively raise their new child. Using this milestone to equip parents for family disciple-ship allows the church to connect with the parents in a natural season of excitement and perhaps anxiety.[1] If your congregation practices infant bap-tism, this milestone may also include the baptism of the newborn child.

Practical Equipping Methods

Many churches offer a required seminar or series of classes designed for parents in preparation for Parent/Baby Dedication. Though each church may design the seminar to fit its unique strategy, certain biblical truths must form the foundational content. Seminars centered around this first milestone should begin with a basic theology of parenting and spiri-tual training. The biblical thread of parental faith training, including such passages as Deuteronomy 6:4–9, Psalm 78:1–8, Proverbs 22:6, Matthew 28:18–20, and Ephesians 6:4, should be traced and applied to the lives of Christian parents. Fathers must be exhorted and equipped to embrace their biblical role as the leader in their households.

The seminar should also demonstrate how the church will partner with the family throughout the child's life. But what can the parent of an infant do today to begin leading his newborn spiritually? The remainder of the sem-inar might address these issues. Teaching parents of infants to begin praying scriptural blessings over their child before they put them in bed gives parents points of intentionality. Offering tools like *Bedtime Blessings* by John Trent or *A Father's Guide to Blessing His Child* by David Michael provide parents with the opportunity to begin the faith-training process immediately following the seminar, even before the child is born.[2] The family-equipping church con-stantly seeks effective and simple tools parents can utilize as they lead their children spiritually. Parents leaving this important seminar understand their role and are equipped to begin the journey in a way that is age-appropriate

---

1. Brian, *Shift: What It Takes to Finally Reach Families Today* (Loveland, CO: Group, 2009), 52.
2. John Trent, *Bedtime Blessings 101 Bedtime Stories and Activities for Blessing Your Child*, vols. 1–2 (Wheaton, IL: Tyndale House, 2009); David Michael, *A Father's Guide to Blessing His Child* (Minneapolis: Children Desiring God, 2010), available in electronic or print at http://www.childrendesiringgod.org.

for their infant son or daughter. In a very real way, they will be able to stand before the church and know biblically and practically what it means to train their children in the nurture and admonition of the Lord.

Important Core Competencies

Every rite of passage by nature demands that a person has grown in knowledge, wisdom, and practical obedience to the Scriptures. A family-equipping strategy utilizing rites of passage will identify key core competencies to understand and apply between milestones. Parent/Baby Dedication has one foundation core competency: the parent is the primary faith trainer. In order to celebrate infant dedication, parents need to first understand and discover how to apply their new role as primary faith trainers.

Celebrating the Passage

Family-equipping churches can repurpose much of what they already practice to celebrate significant rites of passage with the family. Celebrating the first milestone may be as simple as conducting Parent/Baby Dedication in worship. Repurposing this celebration requires the intent of the ceremony to change from a baby blessing to include training the parents and coordinating the congregation to work together to train this new child in the fear of the Lord.

Beginning with a celebration of the child's life, the pastor might share the meaning of each child's name, bless each child, and then present the family with a gift symbolizing the moment of dedication. The pastor might then ask parents questions such as, Will you choose this day to live with the commands of God on your own hearts? Do you accept the responsibility as your child's primary faith-trainer to impress the truth and love of God on her as you live life together? Will you choose to love this child unconditionally as Christ loves you? Will you pray for your child to know Jesus Christ as her Lord and Savior?

The congregation might then respond to similar questions: Will you partner with these parents by praying for them as they lead their children spiritually? Will you partner with these families by investing actively in their children's spiritual development? Will you support what parents are teaching at home by modeling a Christlike lifestyle in this community? This first rite of passage sets the tone for subsequent passages and connects the church and home for the journey.[3]

---

3. Haynes, *Shift*, 54.

2. Salvation and Baptism

The second—and the most important—rite of passage includes salvation. Every Christian parent yearns for the day when his or her child receives Christ as Savior. The implications are enormous and eternity literally hangs in the balance. This is the most important decision anyone can lead children toward making. Often children are converted when they are between the ages of seven and eleven. Family-equipping churches help parents to look for the work of the Holy Spirit in their child's life. The church partners with families by preparing parents to lead their children to Christ at the right time.

Practical Equipping Methods

Potentially, seven to ten years pass between Parent/Baby Dedication and Salvation and Baptism. In that time period, parents equip their children with the truths and awareness necessary to make a sincere commitment to follow Christ. Offering a seminar or a class called "How to Lead Your Child to Christ" provides an excellent opportunity to equip parents for this crucial passage. The contents of the seminar should include a basic theology of salvation and baptism. Do not assume that parents already understand salvation!

The seminar should also teach parents how to lead faith talks to convey the core competencies that will be needed to understand salvation and baptism. Place resources in the hands of parents to help them as they lead their children toward salvation. A crucial aspect of parent equipping involves helping parents discern the work of the Holy Spirit in their child's life. Too many parents perceive that bringing a child to Christ involves simply having them repeat a preprepared prayer. Pastors and ministry leaders must equip parents by helping them to look for key indicators of the Holy Spirit's work. Does a child exhibit unsolicited conviction of sin? Is there evidence of true repentance? Is the child asking questions about salvation, heaven, and baptism? Does the child have a comprehension of sin, repentance, confession, and salvation through Christ? Does the child have an awareness of how an eternally holy God must punish sin in infinite and eternal ways? Does the child know that Jesus died as a sacrifice for sin and that he rose from the dead? Family-equipping churches teach parents to look for these phenomena in the lives of sons and daughters.

Important Core Competencies

Families focus their faith talks around key issues leading toward the Salvation and Baptism passage. Churches echo the voices of the parent by teaching the same biblical core competencies in children's Bible study classes. Prospective points of focus include Jesus, faith, belief, biblical truth, personal sin, repentance, salvation, and baptism.

Celebrating the Passage
Churches in the credobaptist tradition celebrate the second milestone when the entire congregation witnesses the new believer's baptism. If your congregation does not practice believers' baptism, you might develop some other means of celebrating a child's conversion with the gathered congregation.

The family celebrates afterwards by hosting a home celebration that commemorates the work of Christ in the life of the child. Key influencers—including extended family or church members—may join the family for table fellowship. Here some symbol might be presented to remind the child of his salvation. Influencers offer words of blessing over the child and praise to God for salvation.

> ✦ **What if a child doesn't become a Christian until later?** ✦
> Children who do not become believers during their childhood years continue along the path of legacy milestones. Theologically we cannot mandate an age range for salvation. This is determined individually according to the sovereignty of God. While it is generally true that many children come to Christ between the ages of seven and thirteen, not all do. Even if salvation and baptism has not yet been celebrated, we encourage parents to continue leading their children toward the future milestones. It is often in this leading that children become believers as teenagers, while pursuing the third or fourth milestones.

3. Preparation for Adolescence

The mere thought of adolescence causes anxiety for many parents! Family-equipping churches partner with parents to equip their children to live biblically in this potentially tumultuous phase of life. During this rite of passage, the church and the family together work together as guides for children ages ten through twelve.

Practical Equipping Methods

Seminars offered in advance of the Preparation for Adolescence passage strongly emphasize each parent's role as primary faith trainer. Parents should understand what physical and emotional changes are happening within their child, how the culture perceives teenagers, and how Scripture addresses the issues that they will face—all of this is invaluable information as parents shepherd their child in this season of life. Parents learn to lead faith talks and to capture God moments in ways that will make sense to tweenagers.

Important Core Competencies

The family faith talk and the Bible studies for preteens teach core competencies designed to bolster a biblical worldview in preparation for the teenage years. Locating one's identity in Christ—not only spiritually but also emotionally and physically—are important topics along with developing spiritual disciplines and actively seeking spiritual growth.

Celebrating the Passage

Parents celebrate the third milestone by taking their child on a road trip both for fun and for intentional conversations about potentially awkward topics. In two-parent homes, fathers take sons and mothers take daughters on a trip that's designed to celebrate God's work in the growing child and to address the biblical core competencies. The church might offer tools like *Passport2Purity* from FamilyLife or *Secret Keeper* by Dannah Gresh.[4]

4. Purity for Life

Biblical purity—abstaining from all sexual activity until marriage, then enjoying the gift of sexuality with one person until parted by death—is becoming an archaic concept even among Christian teenagers. The fourth milestone enables parents to lead their middle school student to make a lifelong commitment to purity.

---

4. Dennis Rainey and Barbara Rainey, *Passport2Purity: A Life-Changing Getaway with Your Preteen!* (Little Rock, AR: FamilyLife, 2008), kit available at http://www.shopfamilylife. com/passport-2-purity.html; Dannah Gresh, *Secret Keeper: The Delicate Power of Modesty* (Chicago: Moody, 2002), available at http://purefreedom.org/.

Practical Equipping Methods

Parents attend a seminar called "Purity for Life." The seminar covers topics like biblical standards for human sexuality, the roles of parents and the church in training teenagers, the importance of accountability, and maintaining a relational connection with your teenager. Parents learn about practical tools designed to help them lead faith talks that will lead toward the Purity for Life passage.

Important Core Competencies

Through family faith talks and church ministries, students learn crucial core competencies before celebrating Purity for Life: what it means to practice biblical purity, healthy relationships, identity in Christ, and biblical sex.

Celebrating the Passage

Families gather for Purity for Life weekend; here pastoral leaders and others lead parents and teenagers to open the lines of communication around subjects that could otherwise be awkward. Parents promise to keep holding their teenagers accountable to a biblical standard of purity. Parents and teenagers commit to keep the lines of communication open by pursuing relationship with each other. Teenagers pledge themselves to purity for life as defined in Scripture and enter into a covenant with their parents and with God as they receive a symbolic ring.

5. Passage to Adulthood

The fifth milestone is a rite of passage from childhood to adulthood. Parents are trained in a seminar to lead faith talks with their teenagers for two years—from the age of fourteen until sixteen—focused on several core competencies: biblical roles for men and women, spiritual gifts and services, and doctrinal knowledge. Using John Piper's *A Baptist Catechism*[5] or some other catechetical tool, parents lead faith talks around basic doctrines of the Christian faith. This provides a much needed foundation for these young men and women. The student ministry echoes these core competencies on campus by setting a high standard for biblical maturity as men and women.

---

5. John Piper, *A Baptist Catechism* (Minneapolis: Bethlehem Baptist Church, 1992), http://www.desiringgod.org/about/our-distinctives/our-beliefs/a-baptist-catechism.

Celebrating this rite of Passage of Adulthood is no less important than a Jewish bar mitzvah. Drawing from the model in Robert Lewis's *Raising a Modern Day Knight*,[6] fathers host a celebration for their son. Mothers use a creative approach for their daughters based on similar principles.

Powerful and moving, the ceremony begins with a sense of mystery. The child may not know the location, attenders, or details of the event. The parent invites persons of the same sex as the child who have been key spiritual influencers in the child's life. Letters of remembrance, encouragement, and future blessing are presented. The apex of the ceremony is a commitment to biblical manhood or womanhood. The parent may read a pledge and the young adult kneels and accepts his or her responsibility. Often a symbol is given in honor of the moment. For sons, a sword—engraved with the words of Deuteronomy 6:4–9—may be especially fitting as he leaves boyish ways behind to become a man and a warrior in God's kingdom.

6. High School Graduation

Graduation represents a launching pad into life away from home. Central to this season are the core competencies of skill in apologetics, a clear understanding courtship and marriage, and a consideration of God's plan for my life. Parents use *The Truth Project* material[7] to train their seniors in basic apologetics. Parents also learn about the importance of the biblical blessing to their son or daughter. The student ministry guides parents to write a parental blessing for the teenager who will be leaving home. The presentation of this blessing is a touching moment ensuring the young man or women of their blessing and place in the family. Through the first six milestones, the family, supported by the church, has been empowered and equipped to lead the spiritual formation of a child from infancy to high school graduation.

7. Life in Christ

The seventh milestone includes adults from their late teenage years all the way through their transition from this life to the next. Within this

---

6. Robert Lewis, *Raising a Modern Day Knight: A Father's Role in Guiding His Son to Authentic Manhood* (Carol Stream, IL: Tyndale House, 2007).

7. Del Tackett, *The Truth Project* (Colorado Springs: Focus on the Family, 2006), DVD, http://www.thetruthproject.org/.

age range, so many life-changing events occur. Some are young and single while others are married with two or three children. Many adults are empty nesters, widowers, divorcees, or parents of adult children. In the midst of this diversity, there is one commonality: we are all pursuing life in Christ.

A study of the Gospels reveals several core competencies that Jesus taught his followers: prayer, Scripture, authentic faith, obedience to God's Word, making of disciples, generosity, and living in community. The disciple-maker core competency is extremely important to the rites of passage strategy. Scripture calls all Christian adults to be disciple-makers (Titus 2:1–8). If they do not have children in their households, they might become leaders in an age-level ministry. Adults might become preschool teachers or student life group leaders and partner with other families to equip the generations. If they have children at home, though, their *primary* responsibility is to disciple their own children by leading faith talks, capturing God moments, and celebrating milestones.

USING RITES OF PASSAGE TO COORDINATE THE CONGREGATION IN COMPREHENSIVE WAYS

Once again, consider the foundational teachings of the Old Testament:

> Foundational to all theory on the biblical concept of family is the Jewish teaching that the home is more important than the synagogue. In the Jewish tradition, the center of religious life has always been the home. The church has yet to grapple seriously with this crucial concept. Unfortunately, many Christians believe it is God's purpose that the church functions as the main formative influence in the spiritual development of the family. For various reasons—ignorance, convenience or default of responsibility—the church has often taken the place of the family. But the church was never intended to be a substitute for the home. Nothing in God's plan has ever replaced the home as bearing the primary responsibility for imparting Christian values and insuring godly nourishment and growth for each family member.[8]

---

8. Marvin Wilson, *Our Father Abraham: Jewish Roots of the Christian Faith* (Grand Rapids: Eerdmans, 1989), 216.

The segmented-programmatic approach adopted by most twentieth-century churches allows individual ministries to thrive in compartments. These compartments, though possibly producing high numbers of attendees, result in strategic incongruence and disjointed spiritual formation processes. Worst of all, segmented-programmatic ministry works against the biblical expectation—an expectation that identifies parents as primary disciple-makers in their children's lives.

Any church considering the family-equipping model must grapple with the question, How can existing segmented-programmatic churches comprehensively reorient their ministries to coordinate church and home? Using rites of passage as the common strategic path for church and home can function as one component of this comprehensive reorientation. In coordinative models that align the ministries of the church and the family around milestones, each ministry within the church is working to equip parents as they lead their children along a common path of Christian formation.

The preschool and children's ministries partner with parents so that parents lead their children through the first three milestones. Pastoral leaders resource and equip families for the journey while supplementing parental instruction with core competencies that are needed to proceed. The student ministry equips parents as they lead their children through the next three milestones. Parents cannot—as is common in many segmented-programmatic youth ministries—simply plug their youth into a youth ministry and expect overhyped events to lead their child to Christian maturity. In a comprehensive-coordinative family-equipping congregation, the student pastor and other pastoral leaders function as equippers of parents. They train parents to lead faith talks with their teenagers, and they partner with parents to teach biblical truths.

→ What coordinated rites of passage could be implemented in your congregation in the upcoming year? What would be the primary challenges in this transition? ←

The adult ministry trains adults in the seventh milestone. Sunday morning Bible study equips adults—who are also parents—by teaching Scripture effectively. Special emphases in class or in small groups train all adults to embrace the rites of passage as a spiritual formation journey that coordinates church and home. Stories and testimonies are shared as parents experience both successes and failures in training their children in the fear of God. Adults who are not parents are encouraged to develop habits of discipleship by serving in children's ministry or student ministry, partnering with parents to equip the emerging generation. Together, leaders of these ministries gather around a common table weekly to discuss how best to equip families. All the ministries work together; a biannual event known as the "parent summit" helps parents to understand the milestones.

Such alignment becomes possible only when the church's mission and vision flow from a clear theology of spiritual formation that requires a partnership between the church and families. Using rites of passage as a strategic plan for accomplishing such a grand vision reflects the essence of the family-equipping model and can result in a congregation filled with families who are training their children in the fear of God.

13

WHY YOUR CHILD'S BRAIN NEEDS FAMILY MINISTRY

George Willard Cochran Jr. and Brian C. Richardson

I f the terms *children* or *adolescents* popped up in a word association game with fellow parents, what would come to mind?

For laughs, someone might blurt out "mature," "stable," or "predictable"—but parents know better. From the parent's perspective, training, guiding, and discipling children in each stage of life is hard work. As children grow older the processes seem to grow more difficult—or, at least, more mystifying. What we may not recognize is that, as children grow older they need both their families and their faith communities perhaps more than ever before.

WHY WE CAN'T BLAME IT ALL ON HORMONES

The father of a fifteen-year-old daughter feels his blood pressure rising as he waits for her to come home from her date, more than an hour past her curfew. She has always been his obedient little girl, but recently she has changed. They have always been able to communicate well, but lately she seems to put him off like an old coat. His emotions zigzag from anger at her defiance to worry about her well-being, then to the possibility that her date may be taking liberties with his daughter. When she finally floats in, she responds to his queries with a blank stare, and in a huff dashes to her room and slams the door. The father reacts in stunned anger. His wife says, "Don't you think it's just her hormones that cause her to behave this way?"

Attributing the irrational behavior of teens to hormones has long been our answer for conduct that we do not understand. Yet—viewed in light of the divine story of creation, fall, redemption, and consummation—hormones provide an inadequate answer to the teenager's behavior. In the first place, God designed the patterns of growth in his creation and designated these patterns as "good," even "very good" (Gen. 1:11–12, 27–28, 31). The hormonal patterns that bring teenagers to maturity are not the source of sinful behaviors; behaviors flow from the dispositions of the heart (Luke 6:45). As Jesus grew "in wisdom and in stature" (Luke 2:52), he endured all the hormonal urges and surges of puberty, yet he remained "without sin" (Heb. 4:15).

At the same time, the created order groans beneath the weight of the primeval fall (Rom. 8:22–23). Good aspects of God's creation have been perverted to perform in ungodly ways. Developmental patterns that were designed to drive us toward God-centered maturity serve instead to influence us toward actions that are unrighteous or unwise. At times, it can be difficult for an adolescent to sort out which actions are wise and which ones are foolish. During these particular periods of development, adolescents are still responsible for their actions, but they deeply need the influence of parents partnered with the church.

HOW THE BRAIN IMPACTS YOUR CHILD'S BEHAVIORS

It's more than hormones that are at work in these difficult transitions, however, even when viewed from a purely physical perspective. Patterns of development in the teenager's brain cause difficulties too. It's as if the gas pedal is to the floor in some areas of the brain but the brakes have not yet been fully installed.[1] One part of the teenager's brain is running forward at full speed while another portion of the brain is working to catch up.

Even with this struggle, however, this much is clear: well-being on the road to adulthood for both children and teens hinges on family relationships. Recent brain research underscores the importance of constant, close parental involvement in shaping a child's future. Parents who hope to bridge the gap between childhood and maturity through risk-management strategies that focus only on external behaviors will miss a divine

---

1. David Walsh, *Why Do They Act That Way? A Survival Guide to the Adolescent Brain for You and Your Teen* (New York: Free Press, 2004).

opportunity to invest in their child's long-term growth. Parents who disengage and surrender their children's development to peer groups will miss even more.

God commanded humanity's first parents to "subdue" and to "rule over" the earth (Gen. 1:28 NIV). For Adam this task included exercising godly leadership within the family. As parents we need to understand how God created our child's brain and its development so that we can exercise godly dominion within our families as our children grow toward adulthood.

Experts Change Their Minds

For years scientists and educational experts declared that the human brain was fully developed between ages four and seven. As late as 1996, a _Newsweek_ article reported that most brain growth occurred during the first two years of life and that brain development was virtually over by age four. A few years ago, however, Dr. Jay Giedd—chief of brain imaging at the National Institute of Mental Health—reported findings that challenged earlier assumptions.[2] Giedd and other scientists scanned teenagers' brains in a functional magnetic resonance imaging (fMRI) instrument. The fMRI is used to determine precisely which part of the brain is handling critical functions such as thought, speech, movement and sensation, which is called brain mapping; using real-time imagery, researchers could finally study the brain while teenagers were engaged in thought.

Brain mapping revealed that the adolescent brain is an intensely active work in progress. The areas of the brain reaching maturity first are the areas that mediate direct contact with the environment. These early maturity areas include the amygdala, which is associated with emotions, and the areas dealing with sensory functions such as hearing, speech, vision, and creativity. However, one of the _final_ areas of the brain to develop is the prefrontal cortex—and this is the section of the brain most responsible for rational thinking and decision making. As a result, important cognitive functions that relate to self-control, judgment, and emotional control are not yet fully developed in teenagers.[3]

---

2. Sharon Begley, "Getting Inside a Teen Brain," _Newsweek_, February 28, 2000, 58–59, http://www.newsweek.com/2000/02/27/getting-inside-a-teen-brain.html.
3. See Arthur W. Toga and John C. Mazziotta, eds., _Brain Mapping: The Methods_ (New York: Academic Press, 1997); National Institute of Mental Health, "Teenage Brain: A Work in Progress" (fact sheet), NIH publication, http://www.nimh.nih.gov/health/publications/teenage-brain-a-work-in-progress-fact-sheet/index.shtml; and Daniel R.

Why Do Teenagers Make Such Foolish Choices?

The fact that teenagers can be so intelligent in some situations often confuses parents and adult mentors. Some parts of the adolescent brain are fully developed and function as well as or even better than an adult brain. However, it takes longer than most people expect for teenagers to develop mature impulse control.

The most dramatic difference between the brains of teens and young adults is the development of the dorsolateral prefrontal cortex. The prefrontal cortex is responsible for planning, strategizing, assessing risks, and organizing actions. Even as emotion-related portions of the brain develop early, this portion of the brain does not reach adult dimensions until a person is in his or her twenties.[4]

Among teenagers, the result can be an increased likelihood of engaging in dangerous but emotionally stimulating behaviors—including alcohol abuse, viewing of pornography, and reckless driving habits. By late adolescence, it becomes statistically aberrant for teens to avoid risky behaviors. They tend to embrace risk whenever they have the opportunity, perceive the benefits, and find it stimulating.[5]

Alone, these facts could become excuses for a teenager's behavior—but such a response is inadequate because it views the teenager only in light of God's creation and humanity's fall. The fall is, however, not the endpoint of God's story. In the death and resurrection of Jesus, God redeemed his creation and promised a glorious consummation. God plants this truth in the human heart through the gospel. As they guide their teenagers to live in light of the gospel, parents face not only the challenge of humanity's fall but also a profound opportunity that is rooted in creation and redemption: the opportunity to train their children in ways that, literally, are building their teenagers' brains for adulthood.

Weinberger, Brita Elvevag, and Jay N. Giedd, *The Adolescent Brain: A Work in Progress* (Washington, DC: National Campaign to Prevent Teen Pregnancy, June 2005), http://www.thenationalcampaign.org/resources/pdf/BRAIN.pdf.

4. Dante Cicchetti and Donald J. Cohen, eds., *Developmental Psychopathology: Risk, Disorder, and Adaptation*, 2nd. ed., vol. 3 (Hoboken, NJ: John Wiley & Sons, 2006), chap. 18; and Jay N. Giedd, "Structural Magnetic Resonance Imaging of the Adolescent Brain," *Annals of the New York Academy of Science* 1021 (2004): 83. doi: 10.1196/annals.1308.009.

5. Ty W. Boyer and James P. Byrnes, "Adolescent Risk-Taking: Integrating Personal, Cognitive, and Social Aspects of Judgment," *Journal of Applied Developmental Psychology* 30 no. 1 (January–February 2009): 23–33. doi:10.1016/j.appdev.2008.10.009.

THE ADOLESCENT BRAIN: USE IT OR LOSE IT

During the teenage years, in a sweeping "use it or lose it" overhaul, the brain undergoes extensive pruning of unused connections. The least-used cells and pathways in the brain die out as white matter forms and firms up the most robust connections. The gray matter, or thinking part of the brain, thickens during the entire childhood years as the brain cells grow extra connections. These cells then begin to arrange themselves into patterns depending on which connections are reinforced by mental or physical activity on the part of the child. What teens do during their adolescent years affects how their brains grow—whether they're playing sports or studying a language, playing video games or learning to redirect emotions in constructive ways, memorizing Scripture, or any of a host of other activities. What all of this means is that the brain develops according to how it is used.

Persons who are not held accountable for their actions during the teenage years will have difficulty controlling their impulses as adults. The more we encourage teens to stop and think before they speak or act, the stronger and more permanent these positive connections become. The more we teach them to live their lives in light of the gospel, the more they are likely to pursue these patterns of grace, holiness, and forgiveness throughout their lives. Adolescents who exercise their brains by learning to order their thoughts, understand abstract concepts, and control their impulses are laying the neural foundations that will serve them for the rest of their lives.[6]

A young person's experiences in the home and at church help to shape the neural circuitry that will determine how and what that brain learns for life. "The chance to help shape this pruning makes parents more crucial, not less."[7] No wonder God declared to Israelite parents through Moses,

> You shall therefore lay up these words of mine in your heart and in your soul, and you shall bind them as a sign on your hand, and they shall be as frontlets between your eyes. You shall teach them to your children,

---

6. Jay Giedd, *Adolescent Brain Development, Research Facts and Findings* (Ithaca, NY: Cornell University Press, 2002); and Jay N. Giedd, "Structural Magnetic Resonance Imaging of the Adolescent Brain," *Annals of the New York Academy of Science*, vol. 1021, (2004), 83. doi: 10.1196/annals.1308.009.
7. Tim Wendel, "The Teen Brain," *USA Weekend*, May 16–18, 2003: 24, http://159.54.226.237/03_issues/030518/030518teenbrain.html.

talking of them when you are sitting in your house, and when you are walking by the way, and when you lie down, and when you rise. You shall write them on the doorposts of your house and on your gates, that your days and the days of your children may be multiplied in the land that the LORD swore to your fathers to give them, as long as the heavens are above the earth (Deut. 11:18–21).

Characteristics of Adolescents[9]
➸

1. Adolescents lack longing for wisdom or correction. Most teenagers think they are wiser than they are. They mistakenly believe their parents have little or no insight into their lives.
2. Adolescents tend to focus on external rules rather than deeper realities. "They tend to emphasize the letter of the law rather than the spirit. Teenagers tend to push at the fences while telling you that they are still in the yard."[10]
3. Adolescents tend to be unwise in their choices of companions, selecting friendships based on fleeting surface factors instead of wise long-term relationships.
4. Adolescents are susceptible to sexual temptation. Their bodies are developing desires for the opposite sex along with the capacity to reproduce, and the emotional growth of their brains is outpacing rationality and risk assessment.
5. Adolescents lack an eschatological perspective on life. They think more in terms of immediate stimulation than delayed gratification.
6. Adolescents exhibit a lack of heart awareness. They are aware of deep inner longings for something beyond their present experience, but they fail to see that temporal gratifications can never satisfy these longings.

WHY YOUR CHILD'S BRAIN NEEDS FAMILY MINISTRY

Why Are Families Necessary?

---

8. Developed from Paul David Tripp, *Age of Opportunity: A Biblical Guide to Parenting Teens* (Phillipsburg, NJ: P&R, 2001) 53–72
9. Ibid., 70.

Sadly, a significant number of parents disengage from their children's lives at precisely the time when the adolescent brain is most pliable. In the closing decades of the twentieth century, the typical American parent spent fewer than fifteen minutes each week in significant dialogue with his or her child. The percentage of parents highly or moderately involved in their children's lives declined from 75 percent in elementary school to 50 percent among middle schoolers.[10] Some 75 percent of teenagers reported that they had *never* experienced a meaningful conversation with their fathers.[11] "A clear picture of adolescents, of even our own children, eludes us," Patricia Hirsch observed, "not necessarily because they are rebelling, or avoiding or evading us. *It is because we aren't there.* Not just parents, but any adults."[12]

Many segmented-programmatic churches have responded to the dilemma of adult disengagement by calling youth ministers—in many cases, someone barely beyond adolescence himself, with skills to amuse the students but minimal interest in partnering with parents—to retain and to entertain adolescents. Mark Yaconelli referred to such programs as "ministries of distraction."[13] One young adult reflected on her years with such a youth leader in this way:

> Youth group was some of the worst times of my life. I felt incredibly lonely, isolated, depressed, worthless. The youth pastor was too busy working his own clique within the group and trying to be so cool and funny that he forgot to cultivate community among the teens.[14]

While such occurrences may be the exception rather than the rule, they do serve as reminders that no superstar youth pastor can fill the role of primary disciple-maker for an entire youth group.

The relationship between parents and children remains the central

---

10. Quoted in Mark DeVries, *Family-Based Youth Ministry*, 2nd ed. (Downers Grove, IL: InterVarsity Press, 2004), 34.
11. Josh McDowell and Norm Wakefield, *The Dad Difference: Creating an Environment for Your Child's Sexual Wholeness* (San Bernardino, CA: Here's Life Publishers, 1989), 13, quoted in DeVries, *Family-Based Youth Ministry*, 41, 70.
12. Patricia Hersch, *A Tribe Apart: A Journey into the Heart of American Adolescence* (New York: Fawcett Columbine, 1989), 19.
13. Mark Yaconelli, *Contemplative Youth Ministry: Practicing the Presence of Jesus* (Grand Rapids: Zondervan, 2006), 44–45.
14. Female young adult in Louisville, Kentucky, February 15, 2010.

powerhouse for animating God's blueprint for spiritual maturity. The family is God's primary learning community.[15]

> The evidence clearly shows that the most important social influence on the religious and spiritual lives of adolescents is their parents. Grandparents and other relatives, mentors, and youth workers can be very influential as well. But normally parents are most important in forming their children's religious and spiritual lives.[16]

Mentors, peers, and others may play supporting roles—but parents possess a primary influence in God's design. Helping children know that they matter to *God* may impact their well-being more than any other variable.[17] Parents are the persons best positioned to actualize this awareness in adolescents' lives.

> "Inspired by parachurch youth ministries from the 1950s, . . . ministries of distraction keep youth moving from one activity to the next. . . . It's a Nickelodeon approach to youth ministry that seeks to appeal to kids' propensity for fun and recreation. This is how churches respond to youth who cry, "Church is boring!" It's the ministry of excitement, discipleship through fun, culture-friendly, "Christian-lite" events. Like parents who pop in a video to entertain the kids when relatives arrive, the idea is to keep the young people from running out, to keep them in the general vicinity of the church, to keep them happy until they're mature enough to join the congregation."
>
> ✢✦
>
> Mark Yaconelli, *Contemplative Youth Ministry*

What Can Parents Do?

So what can parents do to develop their children's brains? Parents can partner with their congregations to guide their children through rites of passage, presenting maturity in Christ as a desirable goal. Parents can provide

---

15. Tripp, *Age of Opportunity*, 40.
16. Christian Smith with Melinda Lundquist Denton, *Soul Searching: The Religious and Spiritual Lives of American Teenagers* (New York: Oxford University Press, 2005), 56.
17. Charles H. Hackney and Glenn S. Sanders, "Religiosity and Mental Health: A Meta-Analysis of Recent Studies," *Journal for the Scientific Study of Religion* 42, no. 1 (March 2003): 43–55. doi: 10.1111/1468-5906.t01-1-00160.

opportunities for enriching experiences that include healthy risks. Such experiences might include mission trips, helping underprivileged persons, engaging in challenging studies or developing difficult skills, and taking leadership responsibilities where appropriate. Video games, televisions, and movies, as well as Internet usage, should be monitored and limited.

> Television, like all other forms of mass media, represents great potential for good and great potential for evil. . . .[18]

Generally speaking, television makes few demands of the viewer and stimulates the brain, providing the sensation of thinking without the discipline of actually using the mind's intellectual powers. . . . According to industry reports, as many as one third of all American children have a television in their bedroom. That probably says more about the state of America's families than we would like to know, but it represents a truly frightening statistic in itself. "The truth is there are lots of reasons for children not to watch television," Dr. Christakis argues. "Other studies have shown it to be associated with obesity and aggressiveness," as well as anger and intellectual passivity.[19]

Excessive playing of video games may also stunt brain development. One researcher compared the brain activity of teens playing video games with that of teens doing arithmetic. He found that the gaming group used only the parts of the brain associated with vision and movement, while the math group had activity not only in the vision and movement areas, but throughout the frontal lobe—including the areas associated with the development of memory and

> ✢✢
> Look carefully at the calendar of events from your church's youth or children's ministry. What sort of brains are these events developing? What is your congregation doing to equip parents to shape their adolescents' brains in ways that move their children toward Christ-centered maturity?
> ✢✢

---

18. R. Albert Mohler Jr., "The Tempter in the Child's Bedroom," *AlbertMohler.com* (blog), March 14, 2008, http://www.albertmohler.com/2008/03/14/the-tempter-in-the-childs-bedroom-television-2.

19. R. Albert Mohler Jr., "Television and Children—Rewiring the Brain," *AlbertMohler.com* (blog), May 6, 2004, http://www.albertmohler.com/2004/05/06/television-and-children-rewiring-the-brain/.

impulse control. His study shows that teens who play video games at the expense of other activities, not only math but also socializing or simply enjoying the outdoors, negatively affect the growth of their prefrontal cortices.[20]

God has provided parents with a vast responsibility to help their children to grow in ways that bring glory to Jesus Christ. Not only brain research but also Scripture and experience make it clear that this task is not easy. It requires time, patience, commitment, and work; most of all, it requires the Christian household to provide a place where habits of faith are practiced daily, in every part of life.

The family-equipping church partners with families to build awareness, provide training, and hold Christian parents accountable as shepherds of their children's souls. In such a context, parents can partner with the church to provide appropriate spiritual stimuli for their children's physical, cognitive, and spiritual development. Together, parents and communities of faith can work together to mold supple brains by helping the adolescents to internalize gospel-centered values, attitudes, and structures of regulated behavior.

---

20. Tracy McVeigh, "Computer Games Stunt Teen Brains," *The Observer, guardian.co.uk*, August 19, 2001, http://www.guardian.co.uk/world/2001/aug/19/games.schools, posted January 11, 2002.

14

FAMILY MINISTRY, *THE* PRIORITY OR *A* PRIORITY?

Lilly Park

I vividly recall driving across country to begin graduate school in California. Three *thousand* miles from home.

This cross-country trek separated me from parents, friends, church—everything that was familiar to me. The separation was far more difficult than I anticipated, but the time was fruitful as I learned the significance of a church family. I left a church family behind in Maryland, but I gained a church family in California.

Three years later, I found myself driving across the country again; same reason, different state, this time two thousand miles away, to earn another master's degree and to begin my doctoral studies. And so, three years after leaving my home area the first time, I found myself in yet another state, beginning the dreaded process again.

For me, one of the hardest aspects of moving to a different state has been the relationship factor—not dating or courtship but family and friendships. Developing close friendships takes time and effort. What I have discovered over and over is that most of my dearest friendships have formed while attending church together. As a single woman, joining a local church has been instrumental in developing a sense of belonging in places far from family.

FAMILY MINISTRY AS A PRIORITY

Do family-equipping churches disregard singles? It's a valid question and a very real concern. Church leaders—while recognizing how parents should function as primary disciple-makers in children's lives—may fear that emphasizing this truth will offend or exclude singles. One solution has been to establish separate programs for singles. Another solution might be to avoid topics related to marriage and parenthood altogether; some churches rarely or never discuss singleness or marriage. But, privately, singles are talking about both subjects, and guidance from church leaders is deeply needed.

A considerable part of that concern may understandably stem from the description "family-equipping," which could implicitly convey to singles that they don't belong. One of the aims of family-equipping churches is to partner with parents in discipling their children, but—in a healthy family-equipping context—this aim is never elevated above the church's mission in furthering God's kingdom.[1]

Family ministry is not *the* priority, but it is *a* priority. Timothy Paul Jones clarified this by putting it this way: "If 'family' becomes the center of any church's ministry, family has become an idol—and that false god is no less odious in God's sight than the golden calves and fertility poles that Israel served in ancient times."[2] Neither parents nor couples nor singles are *the* priority in the church; all of them are part of a church family in which Jesus Christ should be preeminent.

In family-equipping churches, family discipleship is emphasized, but this emphasis benefits not only parents and children but also the entire church family, including singles.

> Because of the close relation between family and church, godly family life stimulates appreciation of God as our heavenly Father, and appreciation of God stimulates godly family life. Both are enhanced by the example of mature, fatherly leaders within the church. Conversely, disintegration of household order within the church adversely affects both our consciousness of being in God's family and the quality of love within Christian families.[3]

1. Jay Strother, "Family-Equipping Ministry: Church and Home as Co-champions," *Perspectives on Family Ministry: 3 Views*, ed. Timothy Paul Jones (Nashville: B&H, 2009), 144.
2. Timothy Paul Jones, "Models for Family Ministry," in *A Theology for Family Ministry*, ed. Michael Anthongy and Michelle Anthony (Nashville: B&H, 2011, forthcoming).
3. Vern Sheridan Polythress, "The Church as Family: Why Male Leadership in the Family Requires Male Leadership in the Church," *Recovering Biblical Manhood and Womanhood*, ed. John Piper and Wayne Grudem (Wheaton, IL: Crossway, 1991), 245.

Furthermore, in the list of qualifications for elders, Paul required the elder to be "one who manages his own household competently, having his children under control with all dignity" along with other character qualities (1 Tim. 3:2 HCSB). Clearly, the presence of godly families glorifies God and strengthens the church, and they also provide singles with examples of biblical manhood and womanhood.

Churches can positively influence singles as they move toward marriage. Sociologist Robert Wuthnow has demonstrated that decisions about marriage are influenced by church attendance.

> Suppose a man or woman decides, for whatever reason, to be actively involved in a church. Chances are, that man or woman will be in a context where programs are geared toward families, where other young adults are married, and where there may even be sermons and classes about marriage. Any of these influences might encourage a person to think more seriously about getting married.[4]

Single persons benefit from exposure to family topics, and these topics guide singles toward healthy marriages.

Defining Singles

I suspect that many singles in the church can relate to my experience of moving to a new city, finding a local church, meeting new friends, and finding my place in a local church. Some singles may, however, be at a stage in life where they are starting anew but for reasons other than mine. Perhaps they were divorced from their spouse and now they find themselves single again. Maybe they are single and have the responsibility of caring for a son or daughter—and, they may or may not have been married before. Perhaps someone is a widow or widower who lost a spouse several years ago yet still thinks about their life partner every day. The status of being single has

> Carefully consider how your church ministers to singles. How might your church's singles ministry support a comprehensive-coordinate approach to family ministry?

4. Robert Wuthnow, _After the Baby Boomers: How Twenty- and Thirty-Somethings are Shaping the Future of American Religion_ (Princeton, NJ: Princeton University Press, 2007), 137.

long referred to never having been married, but now it extends to include persons who are divorced, separated, single parents, and widows. Simply put, it is crucial to see that the category "always single" no longer aptly describes singles in the church.

Prior to the twentieth century, people married at an earlier age, so there were not as many singles in society.[5] Until the 1960s, 2 to 3 percent of the adult population was single.[6] By 1977, one-third of the American population was single, including the never-married, divorced or separated, and widowed."[7] By the early twentieth century, 42 percent of American adults were unmarried.[8] Also, men and women are marrying at an older age: between 1950 and 2006, the median age of first marriage for women rose from 20.3 to 25.9. For men during that same time the median age rose from 22.8 to 27.5.[9]

The church faces a challenge in reaching out to singles and incorporating them in the church body. Differences in generation among singles also exist. Placing a forty-two-year-old single parent in a singles group with a twenty-eight-year-old single man incorrectly assumes that they share a common life experience simply because they are both single.

COORDINATING FAMILY-EQUIPPING MINISTRY TO INCLUDE SINGLES

The place of singles in churches becomes clearer when we understand the meaning of *the church family*. Family-equipping churches can and

5. As far back as the Jewish and Greco-Roman world, marriage has been an expected part of life. Craig Keener provides a detailed overview on marriage in Jewish and Greco-Roman households: "Some Gentiles advocated singleness, and a few advocated celibacy; some Jews also advocated celibate singleness. But the Roman world emphasized marriage and the bearing of children, and many Jewish teachers took this emphasis further." Craig Keener, "Marriage," in *Dictionary of New Testament Background*, ed. Craig A. Evans and Stanley E. Porter (Downers Grove, IL: InterVarsity Press, 2000), 691.

6. Carolyn A. Koons, "Today's Single Adult Phenomenon: The Realities, Myths, and Identity," *Baker Handbook of Single Adult Ministry*, ed. Douglas L. Fagerstrom (Grand Rapids: Baker, 1997), 18.

7. Carolyn A. Koons and Michael J. Anthony, *Single Adult Passages: Uncharted Territories* (Grand Rapids: Baker, 1991), 48.

8. US Census Bureau, America's Families and Living Arrangements, 2008, http://www.census.gov/population/www/socdemo/hh-fam/cps2008.html.

9. Christian Smith, *Souls in Transition: The Religious and Spiritual Lives of Emerging Adults* (New York: Oxford University Press, 2009), 5.

should develop attitudes within the congregation that enfold every church member into this local gathering of the family of God, a community that serves as a context for training us to live biblically as men and women.

1. The Body of Christ as a Family

The concept of God's family and—with that—a clear understanding of adoption are foundational in talking about how singles fit into the family-equipping church. Paul used the concept of adoption to describe the Christian's permanent status in God's family: "He predestined us to adoption as sons through Jesus Christ to Himself, according to the kind intention of His will" (Eph. 1:5 NASB). "And because you are sons, God has sent the Spirit of His Son into our hearts, crying, 'Abba, Father!' So you are no longer a slave, but a son; and if a son, then an heir through God" (Gal. 4:6–7).

> "All women except one—your wife—are in the category of mother, grandmother, sister, daughter. Your girlfriend or fiancée is a 'sister' first of all and should be treated as such. All men except one—your husband—are in the category of father, grandfather, brother, son. Your boyfriend or fiancé is a 'brother.'"[30]
>
> ✦ ✦
>
> David Powlison
> and John Yenchko

The adoption into God's family requires faith in Christ (Gal. 3:26) and results in becoming part of the body of Christ. Single and married persons alike have been adopted into the same family and are equal in their value and standing before God. God calls his people to unity within this one body (Eph. 4:4)

In 1 Timothy 5:1–2, Paul made it clear that church members were to interact with one another as family members: older men as fathers, younger men like brothers, older women as mothers, younger women like sisters. This passage explicates how all Christians, single or married, must treat one another as well as the broader scope of family relationships in the church.

---

10. David Powlison and John Yenchko, "Should We Get Married? Five 'Pre-Engagement' Questions to Ask Yourselves," *Journal of Biblical Counseling* 14, no. 3 (Spring 1996): 5. The relationships are written in the context of sexual purity for dating couples, but the authors present them in relation to the church being a family.

2. The Body of Christ as Community

The creation story is not only about the beginning of the world but also the beginning of human relationships. Until Eve was created, Adam had no human companionship; God created a spouse for him (Gen. 2:18–25) and declared that this was "very good" (1:31). In this passage, companionship for Adam is provided through a wife. The divinely spoken clause "It is not good for the man to be alone" points to the value of marriage; however, this text also applies to single persons.

> [Genesis 2:18] must not be interpreted as implying that only a married person can experience what it means to be truly and fully human. Marriage, to be sure, reveals and illustrates more fully than any other human institution the polarity and interdependence of the man-woman relationship. But it does not do so in an exclusive sense. . . . The man-woman relationship, therefore, implies the need for fellowship between human beings. But what is said in Genesis 1 and 2 about this relationship has implications also for our relationship to our fellowmen in general.[11]

Marriage is one form of companionship, and it is basic to God's design for his creation—but marriage is not the sole expression of companionship. "Community in the true family is the call to every Christian—those with the gift of celibacy for life, those who should seek marriage, and married people alike."[12] Singles are called to pursue companionship, community, and accountability in their relationships.

On the flip side of companionship is loneliness, which can be a common struggle for singles. But limiting prospective friendships based on age or marital status only deepens one's loneliness. God has created Christians to enter into fellowship with the *church*—not with a specific demographic within the church. It is not good for persons to be alone—but it is also not good for a person to practice fellowship only with others from a similar social demographic.[13] An example of fellowshipping only with one's "own

---

11. Anthony A. Hoekema, *Created in God's Image* (Grand Rapids: Eerdmans, 1986), 77. See pages 75–82 on how humans are to function in a threefold relationship: between humanity and God, between humanity and other human beings, and between humanity and nature.
12. Alex Chediak, "Conclusion: How This All Comes Together," in *5 Paths to the Love of Your Life: Defining Your Dating Style*, ed. Alex Chediak (Colorado Spring: NavPress, TH1NK, 2005), 195.
13. Hoekema, *Created in God's Image*, 78.

kind" may include singles exclusively spending time with other singles or married couples doing the same. Such habits of life miss opportunities for singles and married couples to submit to Titus 2:1–8 by teaching and serving one another.

3. The Body of Christ as Context for Training

God designed men and women with different roles not only in the household but also in the church. Some singles may view masculinity and femininity to be an issue for husbands and wives, but God desires these virtues in every male and female. Masculinity and femininity "are not simply reflexes of a marriage relationship. Man does not become man by getting married. Woman does not become woman by getting married."[14]

Whether single or married, Christian men are to cultivate biblical manhood and women cultivate biblical womanhood. The church provides a context to learn and to practice masculinity and femininity. Being surrounded by married couples enriches the learning experience and reminds singles of the relationship between Christ and his church.[15]

Indeed, young men and women are in need of godly examples. Many younger singles "want to spend a good chunk of their twenties enjoying their newfound freedom, having a good time, doing things they think they will never be able to do again—maybe traveling, maybe partying, having lots of different kinds of relationships, and so on."[16] These young men and women desperately need older, godly mentors to equip them and to help them to view their lives more biblically.

The church, along with the home, must be a safe environment where men and women can practice godly gender roles with the support and loving guidance of other godly examples. Moreover, a church that emphasizes the family will promote and exemplify biblical manhood and womanhood. Single men and women are in need of such examples in their lives and benefit greatly from the wisdom of older and godly Christians.

---

14. John Piper, "Foreword," in _Recovering Biblical Manhood and Womanhood_, ed. John Piper and Wayne Grudem (Wheaton: Crossway, 1991), xxvi.
15. Marriage reflects Christ and the church (Eph. 5:23). Marriage between a man and woman is more than a union between two persons; it is an image of the union between Christ and the church (v. 32).
16. Smith, _Souls in Transition_, 56.

DEVELOPING A BIBLICAL PERSPECTIVE ON SINGLENESS

In many churches, both singles ministry and the lack thereof have been established for purely pragmatic reasons. Without a theological understanding of singleness, perceptions and opinions about singles ministry replace thoughtful theological reflections on singleness in light of Scripture.[17]

Paul specifically addressed marriage and singleness in 1 Corinthians 7. According to the apostle, single persons can live with the privilege of undivided focus on pleasing the Lord: "The unmarried man is anxious about the things of the Lord, how to please the Lord. But the married man is anxious about worldly things, how to please his wife, and his interests are divided" (1 Cor. 7:32–34a). Such texts should call singles to ask themselves if they are responding redemptively to their opportunities as singles.

> While singleness was not in view at God's creation of humanity, and was somewhat uncommon and often undesirable in Old Testament times, in the New Testament both Jesus and Paul speak positively of the advantages for Christian ministry afforded by singleness, and according to Jesus' teaching there will be no marriage in heaven.[18]

The unchanging truth is that Christians, including Christian singles, are complete in Christ (Eph. 2:10; 2 Pet. 2:3). If congregations lack a healthy theology of singleness, they may inadvertently imply that one's identity is to be found in marriage or children rather than Jesus Christ.

What about a Singles Ministry?

Focused ministry to singles is relatively new. "As the 1970s began, you could have counted the single adult ministries in local churches across the country on the fingers of both hands," one veteran singles minister has pointed out. "By the mid-'70s, a few conferences and publications were available. But not until the early 1980s did a national network come into being."[19]

---

17. Stephen Clyborne, "A Biblical Theology of Singleness" (DMin diss., Erskine Theological Seminary, 1996), 5. TREN database (064-0019).
18. Andreas J. Köstenberger with David W. Jones, *God, Marriage, and Family: Rebuilding the Biblical Foundation* (Wheaton, IL: Crossway, 2004), 198 (stylistic italics in original removed).
19. Bill Flanagan and Bill Smoke, "Foreword," in Fagerstrom, *Baker Handbook of Single Adult Ministry*, 10.

Debates about the validity of age-organized ministries often revolve around ministries to children and youth—but the same issues apply to singles ministry. Some singles want a singles-only ministry while others prefer a fellowship group where ages and statuses are mixed. Any ministry model that excludes singles from ministry is a deficient model—but so is a model that fails to draw singles into fellowship with the whole congregation. Both the existence and function of ministry to singles must be driven by a biblical ecclesiology, not by perceived needs.

Many single adult resources emphasize the "community," but by "community," they mean fellowship within the singles group.

> Singles need to believe there is a safe place in the church for them to deal with the distinctive, substantive issues they face. However, they do not need to be so separated that they become isolated from and stigmatized by the rest of the body of Christ. Any singles ministry should provide built-in opportunities for singles and married to work, study, serve, pray, fellowship, and worship together.[20]

Isolating people by their status as singles makes it harder to interact with other church members—and it's not as if a church-based singles ministry is the only opportunity that singles have to spend time with other singles! It only takes one person to gather a group for activities.

The central issue should not be *whether a singles ministry exists* but *whether the church leaders are ministering to singles and connecting them to the church body*. How singles are connected within the larger fellowship may vary church by church. At one family-equipping church, singles attend adult Bible study classes with similar peers and likewise for the married couples while meeting midweek in integrated groups.[21] In another family-equipping church, the adult Bible study groups mingle singles and married couples, except for a few classes that focus very specifically on issues related to single adulthood.[22]

In every case, leaders should encourage singles to participate in

20. Clyborne, "Biblical Theology of Singleness," 29.
21. Aaron Bryant (Young Adult Discipleship, Brentwood Baptist Church), in telephone interview with the author, February 12, 2010.
22. The classes specifically for single adults focus on evangelism. Most of the new single adults tend to gravitate toward a class with mostly singles. Brian Frost (associate pastor for singles and young adults, Providence Baptist Church), in telephone interview with the author, February 12, 2010.

projects and learning experiences where singles interact with married couples from multiple generations. Author Lauren Winner shares why she intentionally searched for a church without a singles ministry:

> I didn't want to be part of a singles ministry because the majority of my needs don't have anything to do with being single. I need prayer. I need to serve others. I need to be held accountable for my sins. And I figure married people need those things, too. I don't want to be segregated with people who, superficially, are just like me. The eye cannot say to the hand, after all, "I don't need you."[23]

From my perspective, the most insightful point in Winner's comment is her realization that "the majority of my needs don't have anything to do with being single." Too many segmented-programmatic churches have assumed that people in a certain life category find meaningful fellowship only when they are placed with others in the same life category. The consistent testimony of the New Testament is, however, that the persons who rub shoulders in the shadow of the cross are people from a multitude of backgrounds—people that the world might never dream of mingling together (1 Cor. 1:23–29; 12:13; Gal. 3:28; Eph. 2:14; Col. 3:11; Rev. 7:9).

A recent social-scientific study has demonstrated the strengths of mixed-fellowship groups. Based on the premise that "singles often feel like outsiders," the researchers identified structures and practices that caused singles to feel this way.[24] Three recommendations emerged from the study to help singles feel part of the family of faith: (1) instead of placing singles in separate ministries, integrate them into the processes and structures of church life; (2) view singleness as an acceptable stage in life, not an incomplete stage; and (3) foster opportunities for singles and married persons to learn from one another.

---

23. Lauren F. Winner, "Solitary Refinement," *Christianity Today*, July 11, 2001, 32, http://www.christianitytoday.com/ct/2001/june11/1.30.html.

24. Elizabeth M. Goering and Andrea Krause, "Odd Wo/Man Out: The Systematic Marginalization of Mennonite Singles by the Church's Focus on the Family," *Mennonite Quarterly Review* 75, no. 2 (April 2001): 211, http://www.goshen.edu/mqr/pastissues/apr01goering.html. This study examined singleness in Mennonite churches but its findings provide relevant insights for our discussion on integrating singles in family-equipping churches.

How Singles Can Serve the Church

In a family-equipping congregation, singles should be known as a reliable group of men and women for service to the church. This might consist of babysitting for a conference, parking lot patrol, meeting with shut-ins, and a multitude of other church needs. The goal of singles in a church should not be their own internal fellowship; they—with every other member of the body of Christ—should seek to meet the needs of others.

Singles may not have the responsibility to support a spouse or children. Yet as part of the church body, a host of families are available for them to join and to support. As part of God's family, singles can become sons and daughters that support older members, older brothers and sisters for youth and children, aunts and uncles to the children of beloved married couples. Older widows and widowers can serve as the spiritual parents of younger singles and couples.

Parenting is a full-time responsibility and the burden may seem heavier for single parents who must attempt to fulfill dual roles in their children's lives. No one can replace the presence of a father or mother in a child's life. A single man or woman *can*, however, invest time in that child, sharing the gospel truths on a consistent basis.

> In a family-equipping congregation, ministry to singles is not a holding pattern for marriage but a training ground for spiritual maturity and service.

How the Church Can Equip Singles

Most singles do desire to marry. It is a good desire. Jesus values marriage (Matt 19:4–6). The moment of decision making is significant and calls for godly counsel. And such counsel requires more than discussions with other singles! When a single person is contemplating courtship, pastoral leaders and other mature Christians have a tremendous opportunity to counsel that person in biblical decision making. "We need the perspective and wisdom of fellow believers of all ages as we walk the path to marriage," Josh Harris has pointed out. "And it won't end there. After we get married, we'll need this community of support even more!"[25]

---

25. Joshua Harris, *Boy Meets Girl: Say Hello to Courtship* (Sisters, OR: Multnomah, 2000), 37. His book is filled with biblical wisdom and anecdotes on courtship. In chapter 8, he focuses on the role of the church community: "The couple you're accountable to should be a husband and wife you respect and who are willing to challenge and

The relevance of biblical teachings on marriage is obvious for married couples—but Christians need to hear these truths before they walk the aisle. Training for marriage begins long before anyone says, "I do." To be sure, no one is completely prepared at the time of marriage—but some *can be* more prepared than others! The family of faith has a crucial responsibility in this process of preparation.

Don't merely teach about marriage and family. Help singles in these areas. For singles who desire to marry, help them to balance the principles of divine sovereignty and human responsibility. Emphasizing God's sovereignty in bringing people together may translate into an unintended message: "Don't do anything; wait for God to provide a godly spouse." God's sovereign provision *is* crucial—but human responsibility is also very real. A church can equip men to initiate relationships in godly ways as well as help women to respond appropriately by clarifying intentions and motivations.[26]

A TRAINING GROUND FOR SPIRITUAL MATURITY

Church leaders and singles must view ministry to singles not as a holding pattern for marriage but as a training ground for spiritual maturity and service. Church leaders can equip parents to function as primary faith trainers in their children's lives while, at the same time, celebrating singleness and connecting singles with the congregation.

At the end of my three-thousand-mile journey away from my family, I reached Southern California. That first year in California was challenging—but the three years that I spent there also included some of my life's most precious memories so far. Many of the best memories occurred in the context of a church, a church where I formed deep and lasting friendships. Now, after a two-thousand-mile trek to Kentucky, I am forming new memories and new friendships.

In a way, those two moves tested whether I was willing to obey the words of Jesus: "If anyone comes to me and does not hate his own father and mother and wife and children and brothers and sisters, yes, and even

---

confront both of you when necessary. The person you're accountable to individually should be a godly [person] of your own gender with whom you can talk easily and frequently and who is strong in the areas where you're weak" (136).

26. Debbie Maken, *Getting Serious about Getting Married: Rethinking the Gift of Singleness* (Wheaton, IL: Crossway, 2006), 154. Maken embraces God's sovereignty but also warns against passivity and selfishness while waiting on the Lord.

his own life, he cannot be my disciple" (Luke 14:26). I grew up in a very close family; leaving my family behind was a step of faith. But those times when I felt like an orphan only served to deepen my understanding of the Christian's adoption into God's family. In both places that I moved, thousands of miles apart, I gained spiritual fathers and spiritual mothers in local churches. I am complete in Christ, and I have a family of faith that Christ purchased with his very life. His gospel and his kingdom remain the priority, but—even for singles—family ministry can and should be *a* priority.

15

THE FREEDOM OF CHRIST AND THE UNFORESEEN CONSEQUENCES OF FEMINISM[1]

Carolyn McCulley

There is a certain response from men that both feminist and Christian women desire to elicit: a masculine benevolence that knows how to live with women in an understanding way, being both considerate and respectful toward those who are co-heirs in the gracious gift of life. Secular feminists approach this desire stridently, from a position of anger. Christian women learn to approach it gently, from a position of trust, knowing that God's Word commands men to live up to this desired standard and calls women to cultivate a gentle spirit (1 Peter 3:4–7).

In my own generation, it has been quite evident that marginalizing men through anger has had disastrous cultural effects. We have told men that we cannot count on them, and we have provided a plethora of ways to duck responsibility for the relationships they initiate and the children they create.

Growing up in the 1970s, I did not foresee these consequences. Even as a child, my femininity was a source of confusion for me. The oldest of three daughters, I felt that I always had to prove something to the boys—that I could be faster, smarter, and more aggressive. I did not want any

1. Originally published as "My Liberation from Feminism" on the website http://www. CBMW.org. Used by permission.

limits, and I looked for every opportunity to show my independence. How I gloated and swaggered when Billie Jean King beat Bobby Riggs in the well-publicized tennis match that was billed as a "battle of the sexes"! As a teenager I did not respect my father's decisions, and I worked to wear him down through constant arguing. My mother faithfully took my sisters and me to Mass each week. Yet I lacked any personal spiritual compass, and I pursued whatever philosophies seemed popular.

I reached college filled to the brim with the "wisdom" of *Cosmopolitan* magazine, but I was to encounter something more insidious than any fashion magazine: Feminism and the Women's Studies Department. Class after class promoted perpetual victimhood, disrespect toward *all* men, an overt embrace of lesbianism, and broadly directed anger. I became a teaching assistant in that department for a semester before graduating with a bachelor's degree in journalism and a certificate in women's studies.

My twenties were more of the same and then some. By the time I turned twenty-nine, I was so confused and depressed that I entered into therapy to figure out why I was so angry—and for that matter, why I was still single. (Not that the two could possibly be related!) My therapist did not make much headway.

God, however, graciously intervened just as I turned thirty. I took a pleasure trip to South Africa to visit my sister who was living there at the time. While there, I heard the gospel; during the last week of my trip, I heard an American pastor, C. J. Mahaney, preach in a church in Cape Town. His relationship with Christ appealed to me, and I responded in faith to the regenerating work of the Holy Spirit in my life. When I returned home, I called C. J. Mahaney's congregation to obtain a recommendation for an evangelical church in my town.

THE CULTURE SHOCK OF CHRISTIANITY

I felt that God was calling me to this church—but I was certainly in for a culture shock! It was like being on another planet. The women and their viewpoints there were completely foreign to me. I remember meeting with my pastor and his wife shortly after I started attending and making a crack about submission. I did not think anyone still believed that part of the Bible. My pastor wisely asked me if I liked to read and recommended *Recovering Biblical Manhood and Womanhood* to me—not the type of reading typically recommended to a two-month-old convert!

Beginning with that conversation, God began retooling my concepts of femininity and sexuality, overhauling my lifelong views on abortion, sexual immorality, and even submission. From the book of Genesis, I came to understand that God is purposeful in his creation. From the Gospels, I came to understand that God is purposeful in his redemption. I saw that God was quite serious about preserving sex for marriage and remaining faithful to one's spouse within marriage. I became convicted that abortion was a terribly selfish attempt to avoid the consequences of sexual sin. Just as importantly, I saw that God had made me female and that he had specific tasks and roles for women that would glorify him in the eyes of an unbelieving world. Slowly, I was becoming more concerned with his glory, and not with my own.

As I studied the Bible I also watched the marriages of my new friends. I was eager to see what this Christian concept of benevolent masculine leadership and joyful feminine submission looked like in real life. Though not perfect, what I saw was attractive. I saw men who sacrificed their own preferences and pleasures to make certain that their wives and children were cultivated spiritually. These were men who took seriously their responsibilities to be servant leaders. They did not see marriage as a trap, and they refused to treat their children as impediments to the pursuit of their own leisure and weekend hobbies. They saw their families as gifts that were worthy of hard work.

Likewise, I saw how married women worked to respect and to build up their husbands. I was accustomed to a steady stream of cracks from women about the uselessness and unreliability of men—but that's not what I heard from the mature, married women in my church. Their submission seemed freeing; it was—dare I say it?—*liberating*. They were free from so much of the discord, sarcasm, and disappointment that I had seen in so many modern marriages.

Slowly, I also began to notice how the teamwork in these marriages mirrored the teamwork in the church. While married men had the responsibility of leading their families, these same men submitted to the spiritual leaders God had put over them. Before, when I was focused on the "limitations" that I perceived in a wife's submission to her husband,

> ➤➤ Do the marriages in your congregation model the love of Jesus for his church (Eph. 5:23)? If not, how can your church equip husbands and wives so that they exemplify Christ-honoring love and submission?

I failed to understand how submission undergirds the entire concept of Christianity. My greatest role model for submission is the Lord Jesus himself—the one whose obedient submission guaranteed my redemption. In the words of the author of Hebrews, "During the days of Jesus' life on earth, he offered up prayers and petitions with loud cries and tears to the one who could save him from death, and he was heard because of his reverent submission" (Heb. 5:7 NIV).

The independence that I had worked so hard to protect as an unbeliever had been a complete charade. As a helpless, finite creature I was completely dependent on God for my very life and breath. I had never been independent. Instead, I had been stiff-necked, stubborn, and rebellious. I came to realize that submission did not strip me of my dignity; it simply stripped me of my contentiousness.

THE SWEET FRUIT OF FEMININE SUBMISSION

Once I embraced the sweet fruit of feminine submission, I still had to figure out how to apply it to my everyday life. One area where I struggled was in discerning what femininity might look like for a single woman. God created the woman to be a helper; so, the contours of biblical femininity are usually sculpted through relationships with others—wife, mother, daughter, sister, aunt. Though I am definitely a daughter, a sister, and an aunt, I am not yet a wife or mother. Yet I know that God created me female in his own image, and that he has given me this gift of singleness in this season of my life. These are not mutually exclusive concepts, yet sometimes I still wrestle with how to express them both to the glory of God.

Through the teaching of Carolyn Mahaney, I realized that, of the seven qualities that Paul urged for more mature women in his letter to Titus, only two are explicitly directed at married women while one is written to mothers (Titus 2:3–5). That leaves four for all women, married or single. Regardless of my marital status, I was to be self-controlled, pure, busy at home, and kind. Those four alone are a tall order no matter how you look at them! This does not mean,

> "Older women . . . are to teach what is good, and so train the young women to love their husbands and children, to be self-controlled, pure, working at home, kind, and submissive to their own husbands, that the word of God may not be reviled."
>
> ✢✢
>
> Titus 2:3–5

however, that I can ignore the other three qualities. There are implications for single women in the commands to love husbands and children as well as the one for wives to be subject to their own husbands. Here are some ways in which God has given me the grace to apply these virtues in my life and genuinely enjoy my femininity.

To Love Their Husbands

Because of all the worldly ideas that I had imbibed on the topics of feminism and relationships, I read quite a few books on Christian marriage early in my Christian walk. I have continued to read widely on Christian marriage; where appropriate, I have even attended marriage seminars. I want to have a biblical view of marriage should the Lord bring that gift—but there is also practical application for my life now. Here and now, I can serve my married sisters best by working to strengthen their marriages.

In conversations and with my observations of their lives, I want to help my married friends to think biblically about their marriages and to think the best about their husbands. Among unbelievers, I want to be prepared to explain the mystery of Christ and the church in the institution of marriage. The world tells us we have no valid knowledge to share unless we have experienced a particular aspect of life; God's Word equips us for wise discernment regardless of our experiences—or perhaps, in spite of them!

If God does bring the gift of marriage into my life, I want to love my future husband now by developing biblical perspectives on love, marriage, and a wife's role well before our wedding. The "wife of noble character" described in Proverbs seeks the good of her husband "*all* the days of her life"—that includes the days before marriage *and* the days afterward (Prov. 31:12 NIV). What I am sowing now in these days of my life may be part of God's design in blessing my husband.

To Love Children

Whether or not a woman ever gives birth, God calls her to nurture the life around us. Before I became a Christian, I was not very interested in children. I assumed that I might have children one day. Yet I was oblivious to the children around me, and I certainly did not care to spend any time with them. This is one area where God made a tremendous change in my life. Over the years, I have developed rich relationships with many children. God has even given me evangelism opportunities with children in my neighborhood.

Even though I do not have children of my own, I do have three nieces and one nephew in whom to invest. It takes planning for me to be involved in their lives, but the cultivation of those relationships is well worth it. I have vicariously experienced the thrills and sacrifices of motherhood as I have helped my sisters over the years; in this, I have gained a window into that aspect of femininity. Just as importantly, through these times together, I have developed one-on-one friendships with these relatives of mine that I hope will flourish through the changing seasons of life ahead of us. I want to be a relevant relative, not a distant aunt. At times, that means declining vacation opportunities with friends to spend my vacation with my faraway nieces. That may mean declining social events on weekends to babysit my nearby niece and nephew. That may entail taking a day off during summer to plan a special day of adventure with them. But that also means I am the beneficiary of funny voice mail messages, elaborately drawn pictures, special "treasures" wrapped in thick layers of tissue and tape, and excited hugs when I arrive at front doors. Somehow, it does not seem one bit like sacrifice. Perhaps these things contributed to a recent decision by one of my sisters and her husband to name me as guardian for their two daughters should they die in a mutual accident. Despite my being single, they thought I would rear their girls as close as possible to their values. Words cannot express how much that act of trust encouraged me.

To Be Self-Controlled

As a single woman my greatest challenge in the area of self-control has been in the area of speculation about men and marriage. I do not think I am alone in this. I know I am called to wait and trust, but it is so easy for me to do the opposite—either attempting to manipulate circumstances in my favor or complaining when others are blessed in courtship or marriage. Over the years, the Lord has done much to kill the sin of self-pity in me regarding deferred hopes for marriage; one fruit of that is that I can now joyfully serve many couples as a wedding planner. But contentment can seem to come and go in my life like waves lapping the shore. Sometimes joy cascades over my soul like waves breaking on the beach. Other times joy seems to seep out of my life like the undertow of receding water. This is not the result of anything other than changing my focus: when the joy seems to be receding, I find myself critically regarding my circumstances instead of beholding the glory of God.

One specific way I do this is by "trying on" men in my mind. Judging from the conversations I have had with many single women, this is a common temptation. We tend to meet godly, attractive single men and immediately head down the path toward marriage, imagining what it would be like to court and wed this man. In my life, I have found that I head into trouble when I record at length in my journal every interaction I have with a single man or if I am discussing this man with a broad range of friends. Self-control includes limiting these detailed conversations to my accountability partners and to those over me in the Lord, such as my small group leader and his wife or my pastor and his wife. They know where I am weak, and they prayerfully encourage me to keep my focus where it belongs.

To Be Busy at Home

I must be intentional about scheduling time so that I can *be* at home at least one or two evenings a week. That can be difficult in a busy church, but this virtue described in Titus 2:5 gives me the vision to make it a priority.

In my twenties, I lived with piles of dirty clothes and newspapers. My house was the crash pad between outside engagements. I had no vision for domesticity. My family had a nickname for my cooking in this period: *fish wads and pudding lumps*. However, after I saw a love for the home arts modeled by the women of the church, I desired to change. I practiced cooking, began hosting dinner parties and started buying home décor, and even picked out my own china pattern. That was actually a big step for me because it was hard to visit china departments without being forced to admit you don't have a wedding date.

How might your congregation equip members to cultivate opportunities for evangelism through Christian hospitality?

Though single women may not be afforded the blessing of being busy with families at home, we *can* be busy with kingdom business at home. Our homes provide places where we can pray with others, counsel others, and serve through hospitality. Paul clearly commanded Christians to practice hospitality—and his command did not differentiate between married and single persons (Rom. 12:13)!

THE FREEDOM OF CHRIST

Paul urged the Galatians to remember that "it is for freedom that Christ has set us free" (Gal. 5:1 NIV). Prior to my conversion, I saw Christianity as a burden, a confining religion with many rules and regulations. I was not equipped to see that my own sin was the greatest slavery of all. As we have all done since Adam and Eve, I blamed others for the oppression of sin in my life. I thought I needed to be set free from men and from the "burden" of traditional sexual morals. I could not see that my own self-righteousness, pride, anger, and willfulness caused greater damage to real joy than any perceived curtailment to my freedom.

When Christ ushered in his kingdom, he surprised everyone—including his own disciples—with the "opposite world" that he introduced. Everything seemed backward to the natural thinking of human beings. The greatest among us were servants. Our enemies were to be prayed for and even loved. What makes us unclean comes from inside of us, in our hearts, not from what we put on or in us. To have life everlasting, we must be born again. And the truest liberation is gained through godly submission. It does not make sense on first reading, but the Bible promises that God's wisdom is foolishness to a perishing world (1 Cor. 1:18–21). I am most grateful that he liberated me from my futile thinking and the bondage of sin, and led me into the way everlasting.

16

BUILDING AND EQUIPPING MISSIONAL FAMILIES

Michael S. Wilder

W ith Genesis 1:1, of course!" she replied incredulously.

The conversation had started with a fatherly reminder regarding a younger boy who lived across the street. I wanted my three middle-school daughters to consider how they could make time for him—even when they might prefer to play their newest video game or to curl up in a chair with a favorite book. Then, I ventured another reminder: to consider how building relationships can lead to intentional proclamation of the gospel.

When I queried them about Zachary's relationship with God, all three unanimously agreed that he had never trusted Jesus. As we discussed how they might guide Zachary toward faith in Jesus, I asked a simple question that elicited quite an unexpected response.

"What Scripture would you begin with?"

My daughter's tone wasn't disrespectful but did suggest that I had asked an utterly ridiculous question: "With Genesis 1:1, of course!" The other two nodded in agreement. From there, they skipped along to the fall of humanity, the call of Abraham, the work of Jesus, and then to the Great Commission.

Then and now, what intrigued me was where their gospel presentation began. It began where it must: With God and with his plan. "The notion of mission is intimately bound up with [God's] saving plan which moves from creation to new creation, and has to do with his salvation reaching the ends of the earth,"[1] Peter O'Brien and Andreas Köstenberger declare

---

1. Andreas J. Köstenberger and Peter T. O'Brien, *Salvation to the Ends of the Earth: A Biblical Theology of Mission* (Downers Grove, IL: InterVarsity Press, 2001), 25.

in their biblical theology of mission. That's not exactly how my daughter would have put it, but it's clearly what she was trying to communicate.

THE GOSPEL CHANGES EVERYTHING

God's Plan in Creation

I do love the creation story for many reasons. The narrative begins with God's creation of the cosmos—a creation that culminates in the formation of the first family. God rests, and this reference to God's rest does not include the phrase "there was evening and there was morning"—a phrase that clearly demarcated the other days of creation (Gen. 2:3). This seems to suggest that this is not only a description of divine rest but also an invitation to humanity to join God in his rest.[2]

God's Plan in the Fall

But, of course, the story quickly takes a tragic turn. Humanity spurns God's invitation and falls into sin instead of divine rest. And so, to this very day, most of the world and many of our neighbors live consumed by the curse of sin, haunted by the question, Is there any real and lasting hope? Thankfully, the story does not end with the fall but moves on to redemption. Even in the garden, God hinted at the redemption, restoration, and rest that would be made available through the death and resurrection of Jesus (Gen. 3:15).[3] Through him, eternal rest is available to anyone who trusts in Jesus alone (Heb. 4:3).

God's Plan in Redemption

God's commitment to redeem a people for himself was unwavering, even as sin covered the face of the earth—the very earth that God created as a place where the dry lands would be covered with his glory. God gave Adam and Eve a new son who stood at "the head of a new line of people

---

2. Kenneth A. Matthews, *New American Commentary: Genesis 1–11: 26*, New American Commentary Old Testament, vol. 1B (Nashville: Broadman & Holman, 1996), 179–81.

3. Köstenberger and O'Brien, *Salvation to the Ends of the Earth*, 27. See also Walter C. Kaiser Jr., *Mission in the Old Testament: Israel as a Light to the Nations* (Grand Rapids: Baker, 2000), 7.

through which the blessings of God [would] come to the world."[4] The family of Noah, descended from Seth, filled the earth with children again, but the result was not the multiplication of God's manifest glory but the construction of the Tower of Babel. At Babel, disbelieving people sought their own glory once again; the result was a division of people into nations, tribes, and languages—a division that is a root of tensions and wars still today.

God's Plan in the Consummation

Such divisions would be utterly discouraging apart from the recognition that, one day, God will be glorified even in the differences between human beings. In the final book of the New Testament, a blood-bought multitude from "every nation and tribe and tongue and people" gives glory to the God who has brought them together (Rev. 14:6; 5:9). This reality represents the fulfillment of God's promise to Abraham, "in you all the families of the earth will be blessed" (Gen. 12:3).

It has been said before and remains true that *the gospel changes everything*. This story must sculpt how we live our lives and make our daily decisions. The telling of it must consume our waking hours and our prayerful sleep. Most important for the purposes of this text, this story must shape our understanding of our family's mission.

But how exactly should the redemptive message of God transform the functions of our families? Specific to this chapter, how should the gospel shape the ways that our families proclaim God's message to those who live not only within our homes but also beyond our driveways?

WHERE GOSPEL-CENTEREDNESS BEGINS

The family is a God-ordained launching pad for gospel ministry. The primary human relationship, second only to our relationship with God, is the covenantal union of a husband and wife. God gave Eve to Adam. In this act of grace, God revealed his covenant-keeping character and created an analogy of his relationship with his people. "The highest meaning and the most ultimate purpose of marriage," says John Piper, "is to put the covenant

---

4. Graeme Goldsworthy, *According to Plan: The Unfolding Revelation of God in the Bible* (Downers Grove, IL: InterVarsity Press, 1991), 113.

relationship of Christ and his church on display. That is why marriage exists."[5]

If this is the case, the question for the Christian husband and wife becomes, "How can our family rehearse and display the glory of Jesus in our relationship?" This display of divine glory happens as the husband demonstrates sacrificial love and becomes a means of sanctification in his wife's life (Eph. 5:25–26). It happens as wives respond to their husband's nurturing leadership in ways that honor him (Eph. 5:22–24).

The display also happens as husbands partner with their wives to train their children in the fear of God (Eph. 6:4). Gospel-centered family relationships provide necessary foundations for a gospel-centered family mission. If a family desires to develop a missional mind-set that displays to the world the glory of Jesus, the gospel must first mold relationships within our households.

> "Paul's conversion approach to urban missions was family-centered. The households mentioned in the New Testament (Acts 16:15; 1 Cor. 1:16; Gal. 6:10) were not unlike the extended families and kinship ties found in Southern (frequently called 'Third') World cities today, and Paul used these households to establish the faith in each area he evangelized."
>
> ✢
>
> Roger S. Greenway
> and Timothy M. Monsma
> *Cities: Missions' New Frontier*

WHERE GOSPEL-CENTEREDNESS LEADS

In our family, the Great Commission from Jesus to his followers has been central in providing a framework for developing a missional mind-set (Matt. 28:18–20).[6] In this text, Jesus declared, "All authority in heaven and on earth has been given to me. Go therefore and make disciples of all

---

5. John Piper, *This Momentary Marriage: A Parable of Permanence* (Wheaton, IL: Crossway, 2009), 4, http://cdn.desiringgod.org/pdf/books_bmm/bmm.pdf.
6. Robert Plummer offers an understanding of the theme of the Great Commission that includes several elements: (1) the command to make disciples (Matt. 28:19); (2) "the role of God's Spirit in empowering and directing the Gospel's spread" (Acts 5:32); and (3) Paul's epistles, for example, which focus on "the Gospel as God's dynamic word that inevitably accomplishes his purpose" (Col. 1:6). Robert L. Plummer, "The Great Commission in the New Testament," *Southern Baptist Journal of Theology* 9, no. 4 (Winter 2005), http://www.sbts.edu/resources/files/2010/01/02sbjt_094_win05-plummer.pdf.

nations, baptizing them in the name of the Father and of the Son and of the Holy Spirit, teaching them to observe all that I have commanded you. And behold, I am with you always, to the end of the age."

Let's look together at what these words mean for our mission as a family. The Great Commission calls us to *intentionality*: "Go therefore and make disciples of all nations." Making disciples requires the proclamation of gospel truths, but it also includes intentionally investing our lives in the persons who need this truth. The Great Commission also calls us to *biblical community*: "baptizing them in the name of the Father and the Son and the Holy Spirit." When we receive baptism, we commit ourselves to the accountability, discipline, care, and nurture of biblical community.[7] *Passion for teaching truth* is also essential to missional living: "teaching them to observe all that I commanded you."[8] Every believer has a responsibility to teach the words of God to others (Heb. 5:11–6:2). In missional households, parents must embrace their calling to teach their children (Deut. 6:4–9; Ps. 78:1–8), functioning as missionaries and ministers first in their own household and then beyond their household.

Of course, parents cannot do this in their own power; they embrace this task with *joyous abandonment*, recognizing that their Savior is "with [them] always." This awareness of God's empowering presence with them is expressed and rehearsed week by week in faith talks and family worship times.

DEVELOPING A FAMILY MISSION STATEMENT

When I think of establishing a gospel-centered purpose for my family, I am drawn to the words that Joshua spoke to the nation of Israel at Shechem. The occasion of the public gathering was a covenant renewal before the Lord. Israel was reminded of God's faithfulness to his chosen people through the generations and his expectation of their faithfulness in serving

---

7. The phrase "baptizing them in the name of the Father, the Son, and the Holy Spirit" points toward a trinitarian perspective. This trinitarian perspective should rightly be seen as the foundation for biblical community. The relationships within the context of the Trinity highlight the relational nature of God and subsequently humanity. For more on the meaning and significance of the Trinity for life and ministry, see chap. 3.

8. See John D. Harvey, "Mission in Matthew," *Mission in the New Testament: An Evangelical Approach*, ed. William J. Larkin Jr. and Joel F. Williams (Maryknoll, NY: Orbis Books, 1998), 131–32. See also Lucian Legrand, *Unity and Plurality: Mission in the Bible*, trans. Robert R. Barr (Maryknoll, NY: Orbis Books, 1990), 78.

Yahweh and rejecting the false gods of the land. It is in this context that Joshua declares "as for me and my house, we will serve the LORD" (Josh 24:15). Here, Joshua leaves no room for his family to acquiesce to the gods of the people around them.

Neither should we leave any room in our family life for chasing after the idols of this world. Our earthly sojourn is a limited one, and every moment must be redeemed for the cause of Christ. It is said of Joshua, after his death, that he was "the servant of the LORD" (Josh. 24:29).

This leader of Israel knew that serving the Lord entailed more than individual faithfulness; to serve the Lord is to serve together. One of the primary places that believers practice serving together is in the context of the Christian family. Such service has a lasting effect on children. Strong relationships exist between the Christian commitment of parents—particularly fathers' service in the church—and their children's continued participation in church after high school. Not surprisingly, family meals and family discussions about faith during teenage years also impact whether young adults continue in church.[9]

But how, at a practical level, can families develop a clear vision for how they will be used in God's service and mission? Here is one simple possibility: *develop a family mission statement*. The precise process of developing such a statement may vary from family to family. The parents in the household, and particularly the father, are ultimately responsible for the content and implementation of this statement. At the same time, this is a process that your family can undertake together.

As you consider the process, do recall that God has already made his central mission clear in the ministry of Jesus: his mission is his own glory (John 17:1–5, 22–24). Rightly understood, any Christian family's mission statement could begin with "Our family exists to glorify God by . . ." With that in mind, here's one way to begin the process of developing a clear mission statement for your family:

- Discuss your values. Ask your family what is most important to each of them and record the answers.

9. Wesley Black, "Stopping the Dropouts: Guiding Adolescents toward a Lasting Faith Following High School Graduation," *Christian Education Journal*, 3rd ser., 5, no. 1 (Spring 2008): 34, http://apps.biola.edu/cej/. See also Wesley Black, "Youth Ministry That Lasts: The Faith Journey of Young Adults," *Journal of Youth Ministry* 4, no. 2 (Spring 2006): 19–48, http://www.aymeducators.org/.

- Evaluate your values. Ask your family to evaluate each response in light of Scripture. Rework or eliminate responses that are not in agreement with Scripture. Together, perhaps over a few weeks, pray and reflect on what will become your family's core values.
- Compose your family mission statement. As a husband and wife, allow the Scriptures to shape the direction and language of your family's mission statement (see, e.g., Gen. 12:1–3, 18:19; Josh. 24:15; 1 Kings 2:1–4; 1 Cor. 16:15). If you have children, discuss the statement with them; clarify your family's expectations based on this scripturally shaped statement. How your family will engage in outreach and evangelism should be essential to this statement.
- Make a family commitment. Work with the entire family to memorize the family mission statement.
- Establish a game plan. Parents—and especially fathers—must take the initiative in planning and setting goals to implement the mission statement in specific ways in daily living.

Few Christians are clear about their personal place in God's plan; even fewer families can clearly articulate how they plan to proclaim God's glory to the ends of the earth. Family mission statements can provide direction in decision making and stir a missional passion for the expansion of God's kingdom.

→ Consider leading a family-equipping class in your congregation that helps every family to develop a family mission statement. ←

FINDING YOUR FAMILY'S MISSION

But simply developing a family mission statement is not enough! The desire of every gospel-centered family must be to participate in God's plan in real and mighty ways. In segmented-programmatic churches, the tendency has been to sponsor mission trips and service opportunities that isolate family members from one another. Coordinative-comprehensive churches seek ways for families to engage in service and mission together.

So what should your church do first to move families toward serving together in God's mission? Any congregation can commit to a family service project once each month. Such a commitment might include serving food, cleaning, or sorting donations in a local homeless shelter. Or how about a family volunteer relationship with a crisis pregnancy center? Families might also assist senior adults in the church or in the community by providing home repairs or yard work. In preparation for such endeavors, train parents to model missional attitudes with the people that they serve, investing in people's lives and initiating spiritual conversations.

For many of us in the Western world, the world has come to us—and this has brought vast possibilities for service and mission. In the United States alone, sixty thousand immigrants are admitted each year.[10] Families could minister to refugees in their communities in ways that fulfill their responsibility to extend Christian hospitality to strangers (Heb. 13:2; 1 Peter 4:9; James 1:27) and guide our children to appreciate other cultures.[11] Many of these immigrants are in dire need of help simply to navigate the systems and to find housing and jobs. Sponsoring a child through a reputable international organization is another way that families can connect with people from other cultures. Another effective way for families to serve together is through family mission trips. Many churches already provide these opportunities. If your church does not sponsor family mission trips, look for opportunities to guide your congregation toward that possibility.

My last suggestion is perhaps the most powerful for developing a missional mind-set within your family: It is the habit of hospitality with your neighbors. Set a goal to invite one unbelieving family each month to eat dinner with you. There is something powerful about families witnessing to families. "The family table is a beautiful picture of gathering and blessing. . . . There is nothing more warming, more inclusive, than the sharing of a meal. What a joy to sit at [the] table and make room for the world to join us."[12]

10. There are over 15.2 million refugees worldwide and in 2007, 65,722 were admitted to the United States. "Report to Congress on the Refugee Resettlement Program" (Washington, DC: US Department of Health and Human Services, 2007) (Annual Rep.), i, www.acf. hhs.gov/programs/orr/data/ORR_2007_report.pdf (accessed February 16, 2010). Also see a refugee locator map at http://maps.servicelocator.org/refugeemap.
11. Jennifer Bradbury, "Backyard Mission: Refugees—Welcoming the Strangers," *Youth-Worker Journal* (October 2009): 47, http://www.youthworker.com/youth-camps-missions /11610391/.
12. Lila W. Balisky, "An Ordinary Family in Mission," *Evangelical Missions Quarterly* 44, no. 4 (2008): 444, http://www.mfest.ab.ca/An%20Ordinary%20Family%20in%20Mission. pdf.

FRINGE BENEFITS OF LIVING
AS A GOSPEL-CENTERED FAMILY

God could have revealed himself to the world without using people—but he chose instead to work through humanity.[13] So if God could have communicated the message of redemption without us, why were we included? One possible response to this question is that as we participate in making disciples, *we* are transformed. God gave the Great Commission both so that his glory would be proclaimed to the nations and so that his people would be transformed through their service. As families participate in serving and making disciples, this participation can transform not only the persons who *hear* the gospel but also the families who *proclaim* the gospel.

Numerous studies have demonstrated the transformative effects of involvement in service and missions. Persons who participate in service projects as children or adolescents tend to grow into adults who are more mature in their faith.[14] The more adolescents participate in service in a church, the more they remain committed to their church, even into their adult years.[15] Participants in mission projects are more open to serving as vocational missionaries, and they develop helpful leadership skills for life.[16] God's

> Numerous studies point toward the idea that service-type project involvement increases one's commitment to the church and matures one's faith. In a national study of 561 congregations in six denominations, adults were asked to recall their church experiences in childhood and adolescence. The findings indicate that those who rated higher in faith maturity were more likely to have been involved in service projects as a child or as an adolescent. The findings also indicate that involvement in service opportunities was a better predictor for faith maturity than one's experiences in Sunday school, Bible studies, or worship services.
> ✦
> Peter L. Benson and Carolyn H. Eklin
> *Effective Christian Education*

---

13. Some portions of the following section have been drawn from Michael S. Wilder and Shane W. Parker, *TransforMission: Making Disciples through Short-Term Missions* (Nashville: B&H, 2010), 55–56; 60–61.

14. Peter L. Benson and Carolyn H. Eklin, *Effective Christian Education: A National Study of Protestant Congregations; A Summary Report on Faith, Life, Loyalty, and Congregational Life* (Minneapolis: Search Institute, 1990), 26–29, http://www.search-institute.org/system/files/ece_summary_report.pdf.

15. Ibid.

16. See Wilder and Parker, *TransforMission*, 61–83 for a review of more than two dozen studies.

glory is the goal of a missional mind-set. At the same time, as your family serves together and seeks opportunities to proclaim the gospel, your family is likely to experience transformation in ways that you may not have expected.

When families participate in missions together, another potential point of transformation has to do with confronting our materialism. North American parents in particular tend to idolize their children. We want our children "to have, do, and be more than anyone else. . . . We've created a culture of childhood royalty by treating our children like princes and princesses, a step that creates a lifelong sense of entitlement that's very hard to break."[17] Missional attitudes, service, and exposure to other cultures can help Christian families to see their unhealthy tendencies toward child-centered materialism. These experiences can foster a theological understanding that we serve a God who has a heart for the poor and who desires justice to be accomplished in this world (Deut. 10:17–19; Ps. 146:7–9; Isa. 56:1, 61:8). One of the greatest ways to do this is by placing our families in situations that cause us to minister to the desperate and the despondent in our own communities and around the world. Our many resources call us to much responsibility.

> "If we are raising our kids to worship the holy trinity of me, myself, and I, their eyes never will see beyond themselves to the world's needs."
> → Walt Mueller, *"Why I Am Rich"*

WHY GOD HAS BLESSED YOUR FAMILY

Developing globally minded missional families—it's a goal that every church and every Christian family should share. This will not happen by accident, and it is unlikely to happen unless churches and families work in partnership with one another. God designed families to be missional. He created Adam and Eve to multiply and to fill the earth (Gen. 1:26–28) so that the dry lands would be covered with God's glory (Isa. 11:9; Hab. 2:14). He blessed the family of Abraham so that, one day, the nations would be able to sing his praises (Gen. 12:1–3). And God has blessed your family so that children yet unborn and nations yet unknown would ascribe glory to their Redeemer and King.

---

17. Walt Mueller, "Why I Am Rich," *YouthWorker Journal* (October 2009): 13, http://www. youthworker.com/youth-ministry-resources-ideas/youth-culture-news/11610193/.

17

MAKING THE TRANSITION TO FAMILY-EQUIPPING MINISTRY

Jay Strother

oral therapeutic deists.

In 2005, University of North Carolina sociologist Christian Smith coined that phrase to describe the primary religious values held by the emerging generation in the United States of America. Summing up four years of research for the National Study of Youth and Religion, Smith demonstrated that—despite deep interest in matters of religion and active participation in churches—millions of students were unable to articulate even the most basic beliefs about God and salvation.

Young people were emerging from dazzling children's ministries and youth programs with the belief that religion is all about feeling happier and doing better. God was, in their minds, a distant and benign Creator whose purpose was to help them feel better about themselves. Of 267 teens interviewed about their faith, only 12 mentioned "repentance," 7 talked about the "resurrection," and 4 had something to say about "discipleship"—but 112 mentioned "personally . . . feeling happy."[1] For most of them, church was little more than spiritualized, emotionalized personal

---

1. Christian Smith with Melinda Lundquist Denton, *Soul Searching: The Religious and Spiritual Lives of American Teenagers* (New York: Oxford University Press, 2005). For a shorter summary, see Andy Crouch, "Compliant but Confused," *Christianity Today*, April 2005, http://www.christianitytoday.com/ct/2005/april/25.98.html.

therapy. "Much of the ministry to teenagers in America needs an overhaul," Dave Kinnaman has noted, "not because churches fail to attract significant numbers of young people, but because so much of those efforts are not creating a sustainable faith beyond high school."[2]

It turns out that the apple doesn't fall far from the tree. A 2009 Lifeway Research survey of parents revealed that having children who become "happy adults" tied for first place as the most common goal for parenting. By comparison, only 9 percent of parents mentioned godliness or faith in God.[3] What this suggests is that, even with all the time and energy that we have devoted to influencing children and students in the context of the church, the home retains the greatest influence on a young person's spiritual formation. And parents, while aware of their responsibility for their child's spiritual development, have failed to make discipleship a priority in their own homes.[4] Many churches are still trying to ignore these warning signs. Yet a growing movement in the evangelical world is rallying around the conviction that the best path to affect future generations is found in recovering a model of spiritual formation that recognizes parents as primary faith trainers in their children's lives.

Convicted by this truth, our church began a new journey in 2005 that reenvisioned our entire approach to discipleship and spiritual formation. The Generations team was formed with the purpose of synchronizing and aligning all of our age-graded ministries, cradle through college.[5] Church leaders charged our team with two key goals.

---

2. Dave Kinnaman, quoted in the Barna Group, "Most Twentysomethings Put Christianity on the Shelf Following Spiritually Active Teen Years," Barna Update, September 11, 2006, http://www.barna.org/barna-update/article/16-teensnext-gen/147-most-twentysomethings-put-christianity-on-the-shelf-following-spiritually-active-teen-years.

3. Mark Kelly, "LifeWay Research Looks at Role of Faith in Parenting," LifeWay Research, http://www.lifeway.com/article/168964/. The research surveys of parents across the United States were conducted in September 2007. This research was conducted for and is discussed in Rodney Wilson, and Selma Wilson, and Scott McConnell, *The Parent Adventure: Preparing Your Children for a Lifetime with God* (Nashville: B&H, 2008), xi–xii, 117, 224n4.

4. While 83 percent of parents believe they should be most responsible for a child's spiritual development, only 35 percent say their religious faith is one of the most important influences on their parenting. Kelly, "LifeWay Research Looks at Role of Faith in Parenting."

5. We originally titled our team "Emerging Generations" (a dynamic term used often in books such as John Burke, *No Perfect People Allowed: Creating a Come-as-You-Are Culture in the Church* [Grand Rapids: Zondervan 2005]) in order to capture the idea that this generation was not just "next" but that they were "emerging" now with the potential to shape

The first key goal was to develop a comprehensive vision for the spiritual formation of young people that was biblical, intentional, and consistent. It was not enough to have excellent individual preschool, children, student, and college ministries. Those ministries had to coordinate with each other, agreeing on key philosophies and serving side by side on a weekly basis. The second major goal was to reengage parents in discipling their own children and to equip parents to turn their homes into centers for ministry.[6]

The team quickly came to the realization that both of these initial goals were in reality one goal. God designed church and household to serve as the two faces of one intentional process of proclaiming and practicing the gospel. The church and the household function as two sides of a single coin. Our segmented-programmatic model had drastically overemphasized one side of the coin while almost completely ignoring the other—and a one-sided coin isn't worth much.

COMPREHENDING THE FAMILY-EQUIPPING CHURCH

Our team quickly discovered that "family ministry" can be a confusing label. For some persons, ministry to families meant having a separate ministry for every member of the family. For others, family ministry meant providing resources to help families. But there are more than seventy-five thousand books presently in publication that are aimed at parents![7] And, when it came to coordinating a partnership between families and the church, none of them seemed to address the core issues in any comprehensive way. They were like placing an adhesive bandage on a broken arm.

Partly because of confusion about the nature and purpose of family ministry, there was a great deal of confusion early in the journey. It was necessary to clarify that family ministry, in our congregation, was not simply hosting a parenting seminar, offering a small group for parents, or

the church's present and future. However, the close association of the term "emerging" to "emergent" led to confusion for those outside our church. We are now placing our emphasis on the term "generations" for greater clarity.

6. The *church-wide* goal ratified by our church leaders and congregation in 2005 states: "A key seven-year goal of Brentwood Baptist Church is to equip and support parents as the primary disciple-makers of their children and to train them to see their homes as centers of ministry."

7. George Barna, *Revolutionary Parenting: What the Research Shows Really Works* (Carol Stream, IL: Tyndale House, 2007), xi.

relabeling the gym a "Family Life Center." It was not simply creating some family-based activities or adding "family" to someone's job title. It was not even talking the senior pastor into preaching an annual sermon series on family-related issues.

Family ministry of the sort that we were seeking—an approach that has now become known as "family-equipping ministry"—coordinates the entire congregation's culture to connect church and home as co-champions in the disciple-making process.[8] Every practice at every level of ministry is reworked completely to champion the place of parents as primary disciple-makers in children's lives. Family equipping is not a program that you can *do*; it is a key part of who you *are*. It is central to the culture, ethos, and DNA of your congregation.

MARKS OF A FAMILY-EQUIPPING CONGREGATION

The goal of equipping families is a church-wide emphasis, owned by all church ministries and leaders. Even though the emphasis is quite visible in the events and activities, family-equipping ministry must move beyond events and activities to become an integral part of a church's culture.

Imagine an iceberg floating in the ocean. Two-thirds of the mass of an iceberg rests below the water, unseen from the surface. For a family-equipping congregation, the critical mass beneath the surface includes the teachings of Scripture about the role of the church and home as well as an intentional spiritual formation strategy.

Marks of a Family-Equipping Congregation
>←

1. Coordination around a strategic question
2. Parenting with an eternal goal
3. Parenting with a lifelong plan
4. Appreciation for the generations
5. Faith-training in the home
6. High expectations for husbands and fathers
7. Compassion for orphans and widows

---

8. For the term "co-champion," see Steve Wright with Chris Graves, *reThink: Decide for Yourself, Is Student Ministry Working?* (Raleigh, NC: InQuest Publishing, 2007).

Above the surface of the water, it is possible to see some distinctive marks of a family-equipping church. These marks are what you might notice first if you visited one of these churches—but these marks are not the essence of family-equipping ministry. They are the effects of deeper biblical assumptions and practices. The essence of family-equipping ministry is biblical foundation and intentional strategy that remains unseen, beneath the surface.

In dialogue with key family-equipping leaders around the nation, Timothy Paul Jones developed and refined a list of seven key "marks" of a family-equipping church.[9]

1. The Strategic Question

Family-equipping leaders have guided their churches to develop a strategic question as a filter for all events or activities, How will this element of our ministry equip families to function as a foundational unit of discipleship? Follow-up questions might include: Does this activity bring families together or pull them apart? How can we intentionally connect this program or event back to what could be taking place in the home? How will this program or event resource, train, or involve parents to disciple their children?[10] Such questions lead to transformation in some areas of ministry as well as the elimination of many others. This "strategic question" is supported by church leaders and embraced at all levels of church life.

2. Parenting with an Eternal Goal

The purpose of parenting is seen to be _not_ cultural favor or economic success. Instead, parenting guides the child toward conformity to the character of Christ. "All young people should be raised with the conviction that they are to be missionaries and that their primary goal is to use their gifts and resources to advance God's kingdom."[11]

---

9. This list was first generated by Timothy Paul Jones and then refined through discussions with Brian Haynes (Kingsland Baptist Church, Katy, Texas), Steve Wright (Providence Baptist Church, Raleigh, North Carolina), and myself. Ryan Rush (Bannockburn Baptist Church, Austin, Texas) also contributed to the discussion.
10. For the principle of resourcing, training, or involving, see Wright with Graves, _reThink_.
11. Ken Hemphill and Richard Ross, _Parenting with Kingdom Purpose_ (Nashville: Broadman & Holman, 2005).

3. Parenting with a Plan

Parents are equipped, through pastoral proclamation and church practices, with a plan for their child's discipleship. The church and its leaders may serve as a catalyst for this process, but parents take responsibility for the Christian formation of their children. This may take the form of an individualized plan that develops out of meetings between parents and leaders; this may also take the form of "milestones" or "rites of passage" that provide parents with goals for their children in each phase of the child's development.[12] In each plan, the parent is recognized as the primary faith trainer in the child's life. Throughout church programs and activities, leaders seek ways to uphold fathers and mothers as spiritual leaders.

4. Intergenerational Interaction and Appreciation

In most family-equipping contexts the generations worship together—but their interaction doesn't end there. Consistent, intentional opportunities are developed for intergenerational mentoring, service, and recreation.

5. Faith Is Taught in Homes

Families are trained to engage in consistent times of family worship—"faith talks"—within their homes. Through proclamation, practices, and provided resources, the congregation equips parents for regular faith training in their homes and consistently challenges parents to maintain this practice. Expectations such as this are often built into every level of the church's life, including new members' classes. This is a key metric for almost every family-equipping church: How many families are intentionally training their children in their homes on a regular basis? Are we hearing stories about decisions for Christ that are being made at home? Are our young people reflecting biblical teaching and values that they have received from their parents?

---

12. For a comprehensive and biblical model of using spiritual milestones as a catalyst for family ministry, see Brian Haynes, *Shift: What It Takes to Finally Reach Families Today* (Loveland, CO: Group, 2009). Brian also invites ministers to his campus twice a year to experience their Parent Summits firsthand; this is one of the most practical and powerful examples of a family-equipping model I have seen at work in the life of a church. Visit www.legacymilestones.com for more information.

6. High Expectations for Husbands and Fathers

Beginning even before they even reach adulthood, young men are trained and held accountable to become spiritual leaders in their homes. This training includes guiding men toward embracing responsibility, praying with their wives and children, and functioning as spiritual shepherds in their homes. Family-equipping churches recognize that many fathers were not discipled by their fathers, and so many congregations offer specific training for fathers to embrace and understand their role biblically.

7. Compassion for the Orphan and the Widow

Family-equipping churches refuse to elevate the concept of an "ideal" family above the gospel. They grapple with the difficult reality of calling parents to their biblical role in a world that groans under the weight of the fall. The congregation develops a compassionate heart and a conscientious plan for incorporating and discipling persons who lack spiritually involved spouses or parents. In addition, they see family ministry through an evangelistic lens, recognizing that—as the church serves and unconditionally extends love to children in the community—the Holy Spirit may work through that ministry to draw unbelieving parents into a relationship with Jesus. As a natural expression and outcome of this calling, family-equipping churches have a strong missional ethos that extends beyond their own communities as well. It is not uncommon to find these churches partnering with national and international ministries to reach out to children in need across the world. Many have also established strong adoption ministries that support families in making their homes centers of mission to the very "ends of the earth."

MOTIVATIONS FOR PURSUING FAMILY-EQUIPPING MINISTRY

Moving a church to embrace the family-equipping model seems like an enormous challenge. Most parents in your church come from a generation that was raised on the segmented-programmatic model. Many will express confusion and even disappointment when they see your church shifting from the familiar models and strategies that are all they know. Many evangelical parents are dangerously codependent on church leaders and programs to raise their children. What's more, many key stakeholders in the church—elders, deacons, even staff members—have been trained in ways that view each age-organized church ministry as a separate "silo." The family-equipping transition may threaten their roles as well as their thirst for the short-term tangible results of the segmented-programmatic approach—events and programs that generate much hype but leave little lasting spiritual impact.

Family-equipping ministers do not see the other two comprehensive-coordinative models—family-based ministry and family-integrated ministry—as competitors but as allies with a common objective. That said, we do believe that family-equipping ministry is the most effective means for moving congregations to a place where ministries are comprehensively realigned to equip parents as primary disciple-makers in their children's lives.

The shift to family-equipping ministry is based on biblical principles that can be adapted and applied in a wide range of settings. Family-equipping ministry does not rest on specific methodologies but on a shared mission. Family-equipping churches enable their ministers to live out their God-ordained calling to equip the local church. Segmented-programmatic churches tend to place the burden of discipleship on what happens in the church building for a few hours a week. This inevitably leads to frustration for pastoral leaders who can never do enough. But God didn't intend for a few very committed ministers to bear the burden of discipling a generation alone, even with programs that have been designed to help them! Jesus discipled a group of twelve for three years. Why would any of us imagine that we can effectively shape dozens or even hundreds of children or students in only a few hours each week?

As Reggie Joiner has noted, it's a sobering reality for ministries that invest so many resources into on-campus programs to realize that active young people still receive only about forty hours of instruction each year. Parents, however, can spend more than three thousand hours a year with their child![13]

Many churches have embraced a business model that makes pastors the equivalent of CEOs and ministers the "middle managers," and leaves members to be nothing more than consumers. Family-equipping churches

---

13. Reggie Joiner, *Think Orange: Imagine the Impact When Church and Home Collide* (Colorado Springs: David C. Cook, 2009). A counter to this statistic from parents is often, "But with hobbies, sports, entertainment, and extracurricular activities, we don't have three thousand hours a year." Gently but firmly remind parents that you do have a choice about how to spend those three thousand hours; if you choose not to be together, you are "teaching" your children what you truly value.

are convinced that the role of vocational ministers is to call God's people to pursue their purpose in God's plan and to equip godly leaders to serve.

Relatively few parents ever experienced discipleship in their households with their parents. In a family-equipping congregation, ministers will pour much effort and energy into equipping parents. What is stunning to me is that so few churches have attempted to put into practice what clearly makes sense biblically and practically: less than one in five churches has even attempted on any level to equip parents for any sort of intentional church-home partnership.[14]

A 2005 survey in our own congregation revealed that more than one-third of our parents had never even personally shared with their children how they had come to faith in Christ! The default approach to parenthood in our culture outsources nearly every component of a child's life. Teachers in public schools take care of education, the youth league take care of teamwork, and—in the hours between the time when children arrive home and parents leave work—the children take care of themselves. In such a culture, parents tend to see the church as the place that takes care of moral and religious formation. Parents outsource their children's discipleship to trained religious professionals and expect church programs to make their child spiritually mature—or, at least, sufficiently happy that maturity doesn't matter.

Family-equipping churches refuse to allow parents to abdicate their roles as primary faith trainers. Students will graduate from our programs and may lose their connections with pastoral leaders—but they never graduate from their relationship with the parents that God has placed in their lives. Family-equipping churches create a culture that honors the central role of the parents in the spiritual formation of their sons and daughters.

MAKING THE TRANSITION TO FAMILY-EQUIPPING MINISTRY

Leading change in the church is no easy task. It's even more difficult when there isn't a guide or blueprint to follow. When working toward family equipping, you will find no paint-by-numbers approach. I like to think in terms of *foundational platforms* and *frameworks* to address as you make the

---

14. The Barna Group, "Parents Accept Responsibility for Their Child's Spiritual Development but Struggle with Effectiveness," Barna Update, May 6, 2003, http://www.barna.org/barna-update/article/5-barna-update/120-parents-accept-responsibility-for-their-childs-spiritual-development-but-struggle-with-effectiveness.

transition. Walk with me, then, through five foundational platforms, followed by five frameworks that may be helpful as you develop a family-equipping culture in your congregation.

Five Foundational Platforms for Family-Equipping Ministry

The first platform, and the most foundational, is to *rediscover the richness of biblical theology on connecting the church and home.* There is "soul work" that must be done in our own hearts before we are ready to teach others. As a leader in your church, ground yourself first in the biblical truths that drive this approach to discipleship. While you may need surveys and statistics to help as you make your case, there is no substitute for the proclamation of the Word of God on any subject, including the family's role in discipleship. While most churches have a natural inclination toward helping the family, few have mined the rich depths of Scripture on this subject. Study the Word more than you read the latest books. Then take your team and your church on the journey and joy of discovery with you.

The second platform is to *listen.* Surveys and stories are two of the best ways to "listen" and to document the personal accounts of the families around you. Listen for the threads of how God is at work. Listen to the questions that the Spirit is prompting people to ask. Listen for the stories already embedded in your church's culture. Listen to other family pastoral leaders as they share valuable lessons from their experience, saving you time and heartache. Listen for the genuine concerns of staff, church leaders, and parents who may not understand. As you listen, journal and document those conversations so that you can look back and see the consistent issues that keep popping up—good ideas that the Spirit prompts you to consider as well as the threads that tell you what God has already been doing long before you started this process. "Many are the plans in a man's heart, but it is God's purpose that prevails" (Prov. 19:21 NIV).

The third platform is *repentance.* "Repentance" might seem like a strong word to use for adopting a family ministry strategy; the term means to turn away from the direction we were headed and to return to God's plan. That image is powerful for our leaders and our churches: we must turn our backs on the false gods of popularity, numeric success, and spiritual pride. The New Testament word that is translated "repentance" means a new mind, a redeemed imagination and a rethinking of everything based on the gospel. A move to family equipping will require us to repent of hidden agendas that drive our ministries. It will require us to turn away from models of church that set up professional ministers instead of parents as the spiritual champions for children and youth.

The fourth platform is *the test of authenticity*. The question is as simple and direct as this: Are you practicing discipleship in your own home? If the answer is no, then the home you need to begin with is your own. Timothy Paul Jones has put it this way: "What you do for God beyond your home will typically never be greater than what you are practicing with God within your home."[15] If you are not at least attempting to disciple your own children with an intentional plan and on a consistent basis, then your church will not hear the message you are speaking because your life is shouting a louder message. You don't have to feel a pressure to be perfect; in fact, the more human and transparent you are with your people about your own struggles, the more trust and credibility you will earn. Many family pastoral leaders are convinced that the single reason we haven't seen an even greater movement to embrace teaching faith at home is because so many pastors are ashamed that they aren't practicing it themselves. Too many pastoral leaders are in more love with their churches and careers than they are their own marriages and children. Family ministry must begin in our very own homes.

The fifth platform is *teamwork*. If you are reading this book, there's a good chance that God is already stirring a passion for families within you. But keep this truth in mind: God can use you as a catalytic force within your church culture, but he does not want you to take this journey alone. Even if you are the senior pastor, shifting a church's culture requires far more than a series of top-down commands. Our church cultures

---

Foundational Platforms for Family-Equipping Ministry
⇥⇤
1. Rediscover the richness of a biblical perspective on the roles of church and family
2. Look for the threads, listen for the questions
3. Repent of previous idolatries
4. Be authentic
5. Develop a team

---

have drifted so far from the biblical picture that you will need prayer warriors and strategic thinkers to partner with you. You need peers to come alongside you and to speak into the process as you grow and refine how

---

15. See the introduction in this book.

family ministry looks in your setting. And you need to engage your senior pastor and church leaders with biblical vision and well-considered strategy.

Framework for a Family-Equipping Culture

The next five steps move you and your church toward practicing family-equipping ministry. Now that you've laid the foundation, you build the framework. Please recognize: this movement is not formulaic; you are the missiologist in your culture. Your goal is not to implement a pragmatically driven program; your goal is to create a biblically rooted culture. This will take time and patience; you will measure your progress in years, not months. Your real impact will be measured by what happens generations from now, not by average attendance numbers today. As leadership expert John Maxwell says, "We overestimate what we can do in one year, but underestimate what we can do in ten."[16]

The first framework step is to *agree on a model and to cast a vision*. While emphasizing family-equipping ministry, this book has presented three comprehensive-coordinative models for family ministry—family-based, family-integrated, and family-equipping. A wide array of variations exists within each of these models. Whatever model God leads you toward, remember that almost everyone in your congregation will support "family ministry" with their words; it will be necessary to communicate clearly what you intend and to cast a unified vision for what this means for the church's future. Don't rush the process but do urgently communicate that the home is too vital to the mission of the church to be marginalized any longer.

Second, *develop your strategies*. As you look at every key purpose of the New Testament church, how can you intentionally connect each to the home? What elements of your on-campus discipleship would better take place in the home? What can you still do at church, and yet drive the discussion back to the home in order to create "baby steps" and "easy wins" for parents who are learning for the first time to discuss faith at home? Do you need all your existing programs and events? Or could you eliminate many programs to provide parents with time to disciple their children? Are worship services age-segregated? How might your church move toward

---

16. John Maxwell, *Developing the Leader Within You* (Nashville: Thomas Nelson, 2005), 79.

intergenerational worship? In missions, are you splitting families in their service to the community and world when you could be bringing families together? According to Dr. Richard Ross, the activity that leaves the greatest lasting positive impression on Christian young people is serving in ministry or on mission alongside of their parents.[17] Every department and every key leader must understand and champion partnership between the church and home.

Third, *overcommunicate your family-equipping approach* at every level of church life. From the pulpit all the way down to the precamp parent meeting, use every opportunity and venue you have available to you promote the coordination of church and family. Develop statements that clarify your goal. Many churches even weave the family message into their mission statements: "Changing our world for Christ, one home at a time" or "Where faith meets home."[18] Be creative with your approaches, remembering that people need to hear or see something several times before it sinks in. Be intentional about clarifying your language. Many churches use the term "family devotions" or even "family worship" to designate the formal moments of spiritual instruction that take place in the home. I once had a parent who told me that he really felt called to lead his children in "family worship" at home, but he was frustrated because he felt like he couldn't play guitar or sing well enough! I assured him that he didn't need a church music degree to lead his family at home, sharing with him several ideas for nonmusical "worship." We laugh about it now, but I came away from that experience wondering how many other parents—especially those who grew up outside the church—are intimidated by such phrases. Many leaders are very careful about the language they use to communicate. If "faith talk" or "primary faith trainer" brings greater clarity to your congregation than "family worship" and "primary discipler," then adjust accordingly for impact.

Fourth, *implement your strategies.* Instead of overhauling every program and activity in the church at once, most churches discover that wise leadership requires incremental changes. With your staff, list your strategies for change. Then, draw a triangle. On one point of the triangle, list "must do" priorities—these may be items that must be done immediately because obedience to Scripture compels them. On another point, place "should do"

---

17. Richard Ross, interviewed by the author, Turning Hearts Tour, February 2006.
18. Kingsland Baptist Church, Katy, Texas, and Bannockburn Baptist Church, Austin, Texas, respectively.

priorities; on the final point, write "nice to do" priorities?[19] Use this "priority triangle" to consider how many "should do" and "nice to do" priorities we can pursue before we are diverting time and energy away from our "must do" priorities.

Finally, *evaluate your progress continually and never stop learning.* Evaluating the impact of a family ministry is much more difficult than evaluating programs and events. Family ministry doesn't fit nicely into the typical three-fold formula that evangelical churches use to evaluate success: buildings, budgets, and

> ## Fivefold Framework for Building a Family-Equipping Culture
> ⊁⊰
> 1. Agree on a model and cast the vision
> 2. Develop strategies
> 3. Overcommunicate the vision
> 4. Implement strategies
> 5. Learn by continually evaluating progress

bottoms in the seats. The goal of family-equipping ministry is training our children to love God and love others; our greatest measures of success may not be seen for twenty or more years down the road. There is no foolproof metric for measuring this sort of success.

It is possible, however, to gain some awareness of what's happening through *surveys* and *stories.* Timothy Paul Jones has developed a survey that can measure the level of spiritual engagement in the households in your congregation, asking questions about prayer with children, family devotional times, and perceived support in the congregation for these practices.[20] Many churches that think of themselves as family-friendly are shocked by the lack of intentional spiritual development that takes place in households in their congregation. Such metrics can also become tools to motivate church leadership and parents alike.

Numbers, however, can't tell the whole story. As a leader, create environments where stories can be captured and shared. You will know a significant shift is underway in your culture when you hear stories of what is happening at home not just at church, what is happening when families are serving together instead of just stories of what happened on the student mission trip. As you learn from your setting, share what you're learning

---

19. The "Priority Triangle" is a management model developed by Main Event Management Corporation, Houston, Texas, and is utilized in their Model-Netics course, http://www.maineventmanagement.com/.
20. For more information on this survey, go to the Family Ministry Today Web site, http://www.sbts.edu/family/.

with other churches and like-minded leaders. Always be open to refining and improving your model.

NEEDED: A WAVE OF LEADERS

While focusing ministry on the home has always had a strong undercurrent in the evangelical church, its rediscovery in the past several years is without a doubt a movement of the Holy Spirit. A decade ago, the focus was on programs and events. Now, there is strong shift underway to understand the principles of family ministry and to deploy them effectively in households and congregations.

As the conversation continues and expands, the family-equipping movement needs a wave of leaders who are willing to implement, to innovate, and to bring their creativity and passion for ministry to connecting the church and home. This generation, with a faith foundation from home that is surrounded by Spirit-fueled community in the church, has the potential to change churches throughout the world. What if every parent in our churches answered the call in the psalm? "We . . . must tell a future generation the praises of the LORD, his might, and the wonderful works he has performed" (Psalm 78:4 HCSB)?

Our great hope is to see a generation emerge from our homes and churches that lives out their faith and understands the call to develop faith in *their* sons and daughters, voicing their beliefs as clearly as the psalmist: "God, you have taught me from my youth and I still proclaim your wonderful works. Even when I am old and gray, God, do not abandon me. Then I will proclaim your power to another generation, your strength to all who are to come" (Psalm 71:17–18 HCSB).

AFTERWORD

One of God's greatest gifts this side of heaven is the family. It was the first institution that God ordained. It is a good gift from a great God. The contributors of this book have presented a vision that is in harmony with the psalmist's words, "Behold, children are a gift of the LORD, the fruit of the womb is a reward. Like arrows in the hand of a warrior, so are the children of one's youth. How blessed is the man whose quiver is full of them" (Psalm 127:3–5 NASB).

Tragically, many in our fallen world are not experiencing what God designed for marriage and family. Sin and confusion have robbed them of the delights and joys God intended in this sacred covenant relationship. Divorce, marital disharmony, and broken lives surround us, and the heartache and disappointment we see day after day causes us to weep and cry out to our Lord for help and healing.

Placing marriage within the great redemptive story line of the Bible is instructive in seeing what God planned, what went wrong, and how we can regain something of "Paradise Lost" in our homes:

CREATION	FALL	REDEMPTION
Genesis 1–2	Genesis 3	Ephesians 5
Equal image bearers	"Battle of the sexes" begins	"Redeemed and restored marriage"

The New Testament grounds both the assignment of the redeemed husband and a redeemed wife in the atoning work of the Lord Jesus. In Ephesians 5:25–33, Paul draws on the themes of sacrifice and substitution (v. 25 in particular) in addressing the responsibility of a saved husband. In 1 Peter 3:1–6, Peter calls upon a saved wives to submit to an unsaved husbands that they "may be won [to Jesus] without a word by the behavior of their wives, as they observe your chaste and respectful behavior"

(vv. 1–2). The grounding or basis for this charge is found in verses 21–25 where Peter highlights the redemptive emphasis of Christ's example (esp. vv. 21–23).

Family ministry must be biblical and theological in both its theory and its practice—but it must also pursue with a laser-beam focus the risen Savior who is to be the Lord of the home. It must be saturated in the gospel that saves, redeems, and restores what was lost when sin made its ugly entrance into the garden. Marriage and family are good gifts from a great God. Our Lord has provided a blueprint for us to follow. When we do, we will find the joys and blessings he intended from the beginning when he put a man and woman together in this holy covenant, a covenant that allows us to produce and raise a godly generation of children and grandchildren who will bring praise and glory to his Name forever.

DANIEL L. AKIN, PRESIDENT,
Southeastern Baptist Theological Seminary

CONTRIBUTORS

George Willard Cochran Jr. (JD, Case Western Reserve University; PhD cand., The Southern Baptist Theological Seminary) is a practicing attorney and director of Mobile Justice. George has managed in-house legal matters for a Fortune 500 computer division, led a negotiation team to the People's Republic of China, formed numerous nonprofit organizations, and created a legal advocacy group concentrating on consumer class actions. Noted for changing the landscape of mobile home park law in the Midwest, he was recently awarded the Gold Medallion by the Alliance Defense Fund for championing the rights of marginalized and disenfranchised people. George attends the Midtown Campus of Sojourn Community Church; his hobbies include hiking, tennis, photography, and traveling. He is married to Wanda. Their children reside in the District of Columbia, Chicago, Berkeley, and Soc Trang, Vietnam.

James M. Hamilton Jr. (PhD, The Southern Baptist Theological Seminary) serves as associate professor of biblical theology at Southern Seminary and as preaching pastor at Kenwood Baptist Church. He previously taught at Southwestern Seminary's Houston campus and was the founding pastor of Baptist Church of the Redeemer in Houston. He blogs at http://jimhamilton.wordpress.com and is the author of *God's Indwelling Presence* (B&H) and *God's Glory in Salvation through Judgment* (Crossway). He is blessed to be married to the woman of his dreams, and their four children are like olive shoots around his table.

Brian Haynes (DMin, Liberty Baptist Theological Seminary) serves as senior pastor of Bay Area First Baptist church in League City, Texas, where he oversees spiritual formation. Brian is the pioneer of the Legacy Milestones strategy designed to link church and home to equip the generations. He is the author of *Shift: What It Takes to Finally Reach Families Today* (Group). He has also contributed to the book *Collaborate: Family + Church* (Ministers Label). Brian is married to his high school sweetheart, Angela, and they have three daughters, Hailey, Madelyn, and Eden. Brian is a graduate of Baylor University, Southwestern Seminary, and Liberty Baptist Theological Seminary. If you are looking for him you might find him riding bikes with his family, at Starbucks pounding out an article, or leading hiking tours of Israel. For more information on Brian visit www.legacyblog.org.

Timothy Paul Jones (PhD, The Southern Baptist Theological Seminary) is a CBA-bestselling author and associate professor of leadership and family ministry at The Southern Baptist Theological Seminary, where he coordinates family ministry programs and edits the *Journal of Family Ministry*. Previously, he spent sixteen years as a pastor, youth minister, and children's minister. Timothy has taught Greek for Midwestern Baptist Theological Seminary and in Oklahoma Baptist University's Ministry Training Institute. A recipient of the Baker Book House Award for Theological Studies and the NAPCE Scholastic Recognition Award, Timothy has authored or contributed to more than a dozen previous books. Timothy lives in Louisville with his wife, Rayann, and daughters Hannah and Skylar. He enjoys hiking, playing games with his family, and drinking French-pressed coffee. The Jones family is involved in SojournKids children's ministry at the East Campus of Sojourn Community Church.

Carolyn McCulley (BS, University of Maryland) is the author of *Radical Womanhood: Feminine Faith in a Feminist World* (Moody) and *Did I Kiss Marriage Goodbye? Trusting God with a Hope Deferred* (Crossway). Carolyn is also a contributor to *Sex and the Supremacy of Christ*, edited by John Piper and Justin Taylor (Crossway) and to Focus on the Family's Boundless webzine. For ten years, Carolyn served as media specialist for Sovereign Grace Ministries; now, she is the founder of CityGate Films. After eleven years at Covenant Life Church, she became part of a new congregation, Redeemer Church of Arlington, in 2009.

R. Albert Mohler Jr. (PhD, The Southern Baptist Theological Seminary) serves as the ninth president of The Southern Baptist Theological Seminary—the flagship school of the Southern Baptist Convention and one of the largest seminaries in the world. He holds a master of divinity degree and the doctor of philosophy degree from Southern Seminary. He has pursued additional study at the St. Meinrad School of Theology and has done research at Oxford University. In addition to contributing to a number of collected volumes, he is the author of several books, including *Culture Shift:*

Engaging Current Issues with Timeless Truth (Multnomah), *Desire and Deceit: The Real Cost of the New Sexual Tolerance* (Multnomah), *Atheism Remix: A Christian Confronts the New Atheists* (Crossway), *He Is Not Silent: Preaching in a Postmodern World* (Moody), and *The Disappearance of God: Dangerous Beliefs in the New Spiritual Openness* (Multnomah). Dr. Mohler teaches an adult Bible fellowship class at Highview Baptist Church. He is married to Mary, and they have two children, Katie and Christopher.

Bryan Nelson (PhD cand., The Southern Baptist Theological Seminary) is the pastor of student discipleship at Providence Baptist Church, where he serves alongside one of the pioneers of the family-equipping movement, Steve Wright. Previously, Bryan served as a student pastor in Kentucky and as the director of financial aid at Union University in Jackson, Tennessee. Bryan has earned undergraduate and graduate degrees in business from Union University, as well as a master's degree from Southern Seminary. Bryan lives in North Carolina with his wife Ellie, two daughters and a son. Bryan loves spending time with his family; when he is not chasing his children around the house or neighborhood, he can be found chasing turkeys and deer around the southeastern United States.

Lilly Park (PhD cand., The Southern Baptist Theological Seminary) has earned the bachelor's degree in business from the University of Maryland as well as master's degrees from The Master's College and from The Southern Baptist Theological Seminary. She is a doctoral candidate in family ministry at Southern Seminary and serves as book review editor for the *Journal of Family Ministry*. Lilly also works with the Center for Biblical Counseling and is a certified member of the National Association of Nouthetic Counselors (NANC). She leads a women's accountability group at Kenwood Baptist Church and enjoys running and spending time with family and friends.

Robert L. Plummer (PhD, The Southern Baptist Theological Seminary) is associate professor of New Testament interpretation at The Southern Baptist Theological Seminary. Rob is the author of *40 Questions about Interpreting the Bible* (Kregel), *Paul's Understanding of the Church's Mission* (Paternoster), and numerous articles and essays. Rob is also an elder at Sojourn Community Church. He has served on mission assignments in China, Malaysia, Ghana, Israel, Turkey, and Trinidad. He and his wife, Chandi, have three daughters, Sarah Beth, Chloe, and Anabelle. During his spare time, Rob enjoys running minimarathons and drinking hot tea.

David Prince (PhD cand., The Southern Baptist Theological Seminary) is pastor of preaching and vision at Ashland Avenue Baptist Church in Lexington, Kentucky. He also serves as adjunct professor of Christian preaching at Southern Seminary. The central labor and passion of David's life and ministry is preaching Christ. He is committed to Christ-centered, kingdom-focused, expository preaching. The second greatest day of David's life was when he married Judi—the first was when he trusted Jesus. God has blessed David and Judi with a gloriously full quiver of eight children.

Brian C. Richardson (PhD, Southwestern Baptist Theological Seminary) is the Basil Manly Jr. Professor of Leadership and Church Ministry at The Southern Baptist Theological Seminary. For twenty-four years, Brian was professor of Bible, Christian education, and youth at Bryan College, where he also chaired the Ancient Languages, Biblical Studies, and Philosophy Division. He has been president of the North American Professors of Christian Education and currently serves on the board of the Youth Ministry Educators' Foundation. He has contributed to several previous books, including *Christian Education: Foundations for the Future* (Moody), *Transforming Student Ministry* (LifeWay), *Evangelical Dictionary of Christian Education* (Baker), and *How to Have Real Conversation with Your Teen* (Standard). Brian and his wife, Sharon, are members of LaGrange Baptist Church; they have three grown children, Rebecca, Deborah, and John.

C. Jeffrey Robinson Sr. (PhD, The Southern Baptist Theological Seminary) is pastor of Philadelphia Baptist Church in Birmingham, Alabama. A longtime newspaper journalist before surrendering to the gospel ministry, Jeff has earned the bachelor's degree in journalism from the University of Georgia in addition to his master's and doctoral degrees from Southern Seminary. Jeff and his wife, Lisa, have been married for sixteen years and have four children: Jeffrey, Hannah, Lydia, and Jacob. Jeff is coauthor with Michael A. G. Haykin of *The Great Commission Vision of John Calvin* (Crossway). He has published numerous articles on theology, church history, fatherhood, and gender.

Peter R. Schemm Jr. (PhD, Southeastern Baptist Theological Seminary) is is pastor of Cave Spring Baptist Church in Roanoke, Virginia. He is the former editor of the *Journal for Biblical Manhood and Womanhood* and an associate editor of *A Theology for the Church* (B&H). Pete and his wife Vicki have eight children.

Kevin L. Smith (PhD cand., The Southern Baptist Theological Seminary) is assistant professor of church history at The Southern Baptist Theological Seminary and pastor of Watson Memorial Baptist Church. Before being appointed to the faculty of Southern Seminary, Kevin served as the Martin Luther King Jr. Fellow at Southern Seminary. He has been a church planter in Tennessee and a pastor in Tennessee and Kentucky. He is a frequent conference speaker and has served in short-term missions in the Caribbean and Africa. In 2006, Kevin became the first African American to be elected first vice president of the Kentucky Baptist Convention. A visiting professor at Midwestern Baptist Theological Seminary and an instructor at Lee University, Kevin is also a member of the Organization of American Historians and of the American Society of Church History. He is married to the Patricia; three children and two great-nephews complete their family of seven.

W. Ryan Steenburg (PhD, The Southern Baptist Theological Seminary) is the associate editor of the *Journal of Family Ministry* and the director of administration and development for the Council on Biblical Manhood and Womanhood. Ryan has contributed to such projects as the multimedia curriculum for *Christian History Made Easy* (Rose) as well as editing the *Doulos Discipleship* curriculum and coauthoring leader guides for the book *Four Views of the End Times* by Timothy Paul Jones (Rose). Currently, Ryan is researching the role of fathers in family discipleship and the function of the church in equipping parents for home-based discipleship. Ryan lives in Louisville with his wife Kristen, daughters Caitlyn and Anabelle, son Wes, and another daughter on the way. The Steenburg family attends First Baptist Church of Prospect, Kentucky; they enjoy reading books together, playing games, and spending time outdoors. In addition to having a black belt in judo, Ryan lettered in NCAA Track and Field while at Calvin College, where he also earned his bachelor's degree.

Randy Stinson (PhD, The Southern Baptist Theological Seminary) is dean of the School of Church Ministries and vice president of Student Services and Institutional Improvement at The Southern Baptist Theological Seminary. He also serves as the president of the Council on Biblical Manhood and Womanhood. A recognized authority on the subject of biblical manhood and womanhood, Stinson is a regular conference speaker on the subjects of raising masculine sons and feminine daughters, parenting, marriage, and men's leadership. In his spare time, he enjoys hunting, fishing, and encourages his children in their pursuits of baseball, football, tennis, soccer, and gymnastics. Stinson and his family are members of Highview Baptist Church where he teaches a Bible study for young couples. He and his wife, Danna, have seven children: Gunnar and Georgia, Fisher, Eden, Payton, Spencer, and Willa.

Jay Strother (MDiv, New Orleans Baptist Theological Seminary) is the campus and teaching pastor of The Church at Station Hill, a regional campus of Brentwood Baptist Church. He previously served as the emerging generations minister at Brentwood, partnering with more than three thousand parents in the discipleship of their children. Jay grew up in southern Illinois and graduated from Greenville College. He has written several small group resources for Serendipity House, coauthored *Perspectives on Family Ministry* (B&H), and contributed to *Living with Teenagers* magazine. He has been a featured speaker at conferences such as D6 and Connecting Church and Home. His favorite stories come from the adventures of life with his wife, Tanya, their three lively little girls Eliza, Lexi, and Ella as well as their newly adopted son from Nepal. Jay enjoys good books, strong coffee, and St. Louis Cardinals baseball.

Bruce A. Ware (PhD, Fuller Theological Seminary) has served as professor of Christian theology at The Southern Baptist Theological Seminary since 1998. Previously, he taught theology, philosophy, and ethics at Trinity Evangelical Divinity School, Western Seminary, and Bethel Theological Seminary. He has served the broader evangelical community as president of the Council on Biblical Manhood and Womanhood and as president of the Evangelical Theological Society, where he continues on the executive committee. His scholarly writings are wide-ranging, with several books focusing on the attributes of God, divine providence, and the doctrine of the Trinity. He has also authored *Big Truths for Young Hearts* (Crossway), a systematic theology for parents, homeschoolers, and Christian schools to use with children and young teens. He is a member of Clifton Baptist Church. He has been married to his lovely wife, Jodi, since 1978; they have two grown daughters and one granddaughter. His favorite activities have involved his family—reading, hiking, singing, and traveling together.

Michael S. Wilder (PhD, The Southern Baptist Theological Seminary) is assistant professor and associate dean of doctoral studies in the School of Church Ministries at The Southern Baptist Theological Seminary. Michael is the coauthor of *TransforMission* (B&H) and *Perspectives on Your Child's Education* (B&H). He has served the church as a pastor and youth pastor for more than fifteen years. Michael and his wife, Ginger, reside in Jeffersonville, Indiana, with their three daughters, Daly, Ashton, and McKenzie. The Wilder family worships at the Midtown Campus of Sojourn Community Church in Louisville.

C. Michael Wren Jr. (PhD, The Southern Baptist Theological Seminary) is the senior pastor of New Life Baptist Church in Greencastle, Indiana. He has taught church history at the North Georgia campus of New Orleans Baptist Theological Seminary and Christian studies at Truett-McConnell College. He is the author of articles in the field of church history for *Tennessee Baptist History* and *Theology for Ministry*. Michael lives in Greencastle with his wife, Angela, and his children, William and Anna. He enjoys hiking, drinking Coca-Cola, and watching University of Georgia athletics.

SCRIPTURE INDEX

PERSON AND SUBJECT INDEX